When **Terror** Comes To Main Street

A CITIZEN'S GUIDE

to Terror Awareness, Preparedness and Prevention.

By Lieutenant Colonel Joseph A. Ruffini
United States Army (Retired)

Published by Archangel Group Inc.

First Edition 2006

The Library of Congress has cataloged this edition as follows:
ISBN: 0-9767753-1-X

LCCN: 2006903487

For information about special discounts for bulk purchases, or to purchase additional copies, send an email to jprallc@jpr-online.com with your name and contact number or order copies through www.antiterrorconsultants.org or write to info@circon.org.

Designed by Michel Hogan
Manufactured in the United States of America

*The first is freedom of speech and expression –
everywhere in the world. Second is freedom of every
person to worship God in his own way – everywhere
in the world. The third is freedom from want –
everywhere in the world. The fourth is freedom
from fear - anywhere in the world.*

Franklin Delano Roosevelt,
The Four Freedoms Address, 1941

Dedicated to the treasures of my life
My Wife, Patricia
My Daughter, Christina
My Son, Joey
Who together fill my world with more love, pride,
and support than I will ever deserve.

TABLE OF CONTENTS

Acknowledgments

Foreword 11

From the Author 19

Introduction 23

Briefing One:

Understanding the Hatred 29

Briefing Two:

A Run Down on the Bad Guys 53

Briefing Three:

Know the Enemy & Think as He Does 79

Briefing Four:

Know Ourselves 99

Briefing Five:

Terrorists Always Welcomed Here 117

Briefing Six:

Our Leaders Have Some Issues 131

Briefing Seven:

Our Own Kids Can Be Terrorists Too 159

Briefing Eight:

Anti-Terror Awareness & Planning in Our Schools 173

Briefing Nine:

We Are All Citizen Soldiers 183

Briefing Ten:

Keeping the Wolves at Bay 201

Briefing Eleven:

Sustaining Our National Economic Power 217

Briefing Twelve:

Communities Taking Charge 237

Briefing Thirteen:

Prepare for the Worst, Pray & Hope for the Best 245

Conclusion 263

Bibliography 267

About the Author 281

In Memoriam.

Anthony J. Ruffini
1923 -1992

First Generation Italian American
Who began a lifetime of selfless service to our nation
by enlisting in the U.S. Navy during War II and serving
as a machinist's mate aboard the USS Blackhawk and
who retired from the Navy's Senior Executive Service
as the Principal Deputy Commander for Logistics
Ships Systems Command Washington, D.C.

So singularly outstanding were his contributions to the
Navy that he was awarded the honor of commanding
active duty Naval officers as a civilian. He was the
only civilian during his time to ever be assigned to
an Admiral's command billet.

He was truly a great father and American patriot.

ACKNOWLEDGEMENTS

I begin by honoring the memory of my father. He is the finest man I ever knew. Anthony J. Ruffini was the consummate husband, father, and public servant. He taught me from a very young age the meaning of honesty, integrity, perseverance, and selfless service to my country. Dad left a great legacy. He is the father of the United States Navy's Preventive Maintenance System. He created, designed, and fielded this program for the fleet in 1962. It remains the standard for Navy and Marine operational readiness even today – more than four decades later. I miss him. I wish so very much that I could share this book with him.

Were it not for the love, patience, guidance, and perseverance of my life partner, Patricia, I could have never completed this book. She is a woman of extraordinary wisdom and foresight, and the most intelligent and well-read person I have ever known. Her council has always proved invaluable. Pat is brilliant with the English language. She managed to transform the disorganized ramblings of an old soldier into a readable, written work. The truth be known, most of the credit for anything that I have accomplished in my adult life goes more to her than me. After 35 years, and through some very tough times, we remain best friends. We must be in love.

I can't say enough about my children, Christina and Joey. I cannot recall how many times this past year I have apologized for not being able to spend as much time with them as I wanted due to the demands of simultaneously consulting and writing. Both kids know how much I wanted to get my message out in this book, and their support was unwavering. I love them so much. I'm so proud of them. They are both honor students, and perform hundreds of hours of humanitarian service each year. They love and care for each other, their mom and dad, and their fellow man. They may just be the most terror-aware twenty and sixteen year-olds in America.

I am honored and proud to know and work with true American heroes such as John Giduck. He is a valued friend, comrade in arms, and consummate patriot. John is an eclectic, larger-than-life American, who has accomplished more in his life to date than a dozen men combined: lawyer, warrior, weapons expert, Olympic weight lifting champion, member of the Russian Martial Arts Hall of Fame, diver, parachutist, author – his list of accomplishments seems endless. John and I share a passion as anti-terror educators and consultants. He inspired and encouraged me to commit to finishing this book. Here's to many more years together, fighting to protect and defend, and teaching others how to do so.

I cannot publish this book without thanking a truly outstanding civil servant to whom our country owes a great debt. Elena, I have enjoyed working both with and for you these past years. You are a true professional and a dear friend. Your service to our nation is characterized by patriotism, selfless service, and perseverance in the face of adversity. You remain a sterling role model for the new ones just beginning their careers. I wish that I could say more. Perhaps someday.

I have had the honor of working with and for so many outstanding fellow GIs. I would like to mention them here. Their guidance, camaraderie, friendship and support have meant so much to me these many years. I name them by the ranks that either they held at the time I worked with them or the rank they held at retirement. I fear I cannot remember all to whom I owe a debt of gratitude. For any lapses in my memory, I sincerely apologize:

Major Kerry Grigsby, Desert Storm veteran and Bronze Star awardee, is my first and longest-standing comrade-in-arms, whom I met at Fort Knox, Kentucky, in 1974. We were new second lieutenants, tank platoon leaders, and served as company executive and battalion motor officers together in Germany in the late 1970s. We commanded tank companies simultaneously in the 2nd Battalion, 63rd Armor, 1st Infantry Division (Mechanized). Thank you, brother, for your friendship, wisdom, and so many good times these past thirty years.

Lieutenant Colonel Ken King is my second adopted brother-in-arms. I met Ken in 1980. Ken was also a company commander in 2-63 Armor at the same time Grigsby and I were. Ken's quick wit, love of music and singing, and need to come to my Army quarters regularly to watch movies on cable TV led to our bonding early on. Thank you, brother, for the years of friendship, and so many hours of song and merriment.

To Lieutenant Colonel John T. Hoza; Lieutenant Colonel Gary D. Turner; Major Terry Bullington; First Sergeant Tito Bernal; Sergeant First Class Fenner; Captain James C. Bennett; General Chuck Horner; Rear Admiral Bruce Bremmer; Colonel Jeff Jones; Colonel John Kalb; Colonel "Ragin Cagin" Beau Bergeron; Colonel Mike Ingelido; Specialist Rodney Williams, Privates Gary Shumaker and "Hamhock" Hammerly, thank you one and all.

To the mentors who taught this retired soldier the ropes of the civilian business world – Bob Ben, Russ Huffman, Tim Emrick, Rich Roderigez, and Mark "Skip" Raimer – I thank you for your endless patience and all of the knowledge and wisdom that you imparted.

Since beginning my civilian career, I have had the privilege of working with many outstanding bosses, employees, co-workers and business associates. I learned much from them. Their professionalism, advice, camaraderie, and senses of humor contributed so very much to my life's positive and memorable experiences. I thank Steve Argubright, Tom Mauriello, Lynn Clarke, Ray "The DICEMAN" Semko, Patrice Rappelus, Richard Power, Steve Glennan, Dusty Rhodes, Marc Haggerty, and Ron Bliss.

And finally, my gratitude to two gentlemen for whom I have the utmost respect, and in whom I place so much trust and confidence.

I have known Mike Cimafonte for almost ten years, and have worked with and for him as a defense consultant since 1997. If there is a more honest, competent, dedicated, hardworking and amiable program manager within the defense industrial base, I have not met him. Thank you, Mike, for all of the opportunities and challenges you have afforded me, for your friendship, trust, and encouragement.

I began working with Bob Rusnak in 1993. We served side-by-side as strategic communicators and senior information operations warriors supporting the war efforts. We both share a common vision for the future and maturation of strategic communications and information operations throughout our government and military. We keep up each others' spirits during periods of intense frustration and aggravation, when we strive to break new ground and do innovative things, only to be slowed or stopped by the large and bureaucratic military organizations and commands that we support. Bob is totally dedicated and tireless. He, like me, refuses to be beaten down by the system. Thanks, Bob, for being a fantastic associate and friend.

I would be extremely remiss if I did not express my gratitude to those men and women who put their lives and loves on the line each and everyday so that I may live safe and free.

FOREWORD

America must wake up, lest it perish in its sleep. This book serves as that wake-up call. It is a harsh and shrill alarm clock shocking the American consciousness into a sober awareness of the threat that is poised outside its doors. Many do not want to hear this alarm, this call to arms, preferring to pull the fluffy, white blanket of denial over their heads. They would rather pretend that terror is not at our shores, does not threatened our homes and loved ones, and has not already killed almost 3,000 people on a single day in September 2001. They hit the snooze button of reality again and again.

The threat of Islamist terrorism in America has arrived and it is here to stay, until America rises up and with a single resounding voice declaring that it will not go quietly into the night, and will not perish without a fight; never quitting until the enemy has been completely vanquished.

So many Americans wish to delude themselves into believing that the luxury-ridden lives they have enjoyed since the end of World War II will simply go on forever. They somehow believe that it is their God-given rights as Americans to squander their lives on vapid and vacuous pursuits, filling their time with obsessions over golf, expensive cars, fantasy football, vacations, and lottery awards of money they have not earned. They worry more about jewelry, 401K plans, and pathetic and pointless television shows - caring more about Ben and Jen, and Jen and Brad, and who got thrown off the island - than they do about accepting the responsibility of taking part in the defense of not only their own nation, but their own families and homes.

So many of us have too quickly forgotten that the single greatest international terrorist attack in the history of the world that killed 2,986 people on September 11, 2001, occurred in America! We overlook the countless other terror attempts in America thwarted by the brave men and women of our law enforcement and government agencies. Memories of the single greatest domestic terror attack in Oklahoma City only a scant few years ago fade. We try to forget that the most deadly juvenile-on-juvenile mass murder in human history took place in America – at Columbine High School in Littleton, Colorado.

All of these horrific attacks have happened in recent years, on our watch. We are, indeed, a nation at war. But extending beyond the war on terrorism, we are a nation and culture under siege, under attack from forces both without and within. America is under attack. The valiant battle in which the brave men and women of our armed forces, law enforcement and government agencies are engaged cannot possibly be won without the support and direct involvement of America's single greatest resource: the American people. This is a nation forged out of a dark and violent wilderness by the People.

Today, the People of America are under attack once again. Some of us – terror's next victims - are living on borrowed time as our enemies prepare their next deadly assault. In a very real way, we are all passengers on United Flight 93, soaring unerringly over the lonely fields of western Pennsylvania, sitting in our comfortable seats and grappling with the question of whether we should take a stand and fight, assume the responsibility for our own survival and that of our countrymen, or sit acquiescent in the pathetic hope that if we do nothing – as we have done for decades – everything will be just fine. I fear that if we do not collectively take a stand and fight, we may not survive this struggle.

Make no mistake, the duty of preparing ourselves, defending our country, and protecting our homes and loved ones, falls upon the shoulders of each and every one of us. That is what this book is about. Lieutenant Colonel Joseph Ruffini dedicated an entire lifetime to doing that very thing: defending America, and protecting every American man, woman and child. For more than twenty years he served in the United States Army, commanding combat troops throughout the world. He served with and commanded not only American forces, but elite British units. Moreover, he is one of the rare individuals who spent decades serving America by developing both tactical and strategic defense plans to ensure our survival in a hostile world. He is a years-long top contributor for such critical Department of Defense commands as the United States Space Command, United States Strategic Command, North American Aerospace Defense Command in Cheyenne Mountain, and United States Northern Command. During Operation Iraqi Freedom, Joe Ruffini served as an information warrior, providing operational psychological warfare concepts to the White House National Security Council. During his twenty years of service in the Army, and ten years assisting the Defense Department and other front line U.S. government agencies in the War on Terror, Colonel Ruffini developed a peerless knowledge and experiential base. He is one of the very few experts who not only possesses the requisite diverse background, but the capability to apply that background, in first understanding, and second creating, tactics and strategic plans to confront the deadly threats our nation faces.

In addition to a lifetime spent learning about our enemies and working to defeat them by any means possible for the preservation of our way of life, Colonel Ruffini has come to recognize that nothing can be done without the education and involvement and support of the American people. This is one of the problems the United States currently faces. Our current administration is, in a way, a victim of its own success. After 9-11 the president told all of America not to panic, to go about their lives continuing to work and shop. This had the affect of preventing the spread of panic, as well as continuing to generate the tax base that would be needed to fight a costly global war. But this advice was heeded too well, for the American people did go happily about their lives, and the nation demanded nothing more of its government leaders. Now, more than four years later, they have forgotten, and argue endlessly about the uselessness of spending money to prosecute the engagements we are in, preferring to believe that the threat has gone away and can be forgotten.

Resultantly, the public – our greatest resource, largest defense force, omnipresent early warning system, and most expansive intelligence-gathering network – has abandoned its critical mission. Each and every American is needed in this war to preserve and protect our way of life. In the military, as well law enforcement and government service, no one is put "on the line" until they have been trained, prepared and educated about the task they will be asked to perform and complete to the best of their ability. That, too, is what this book is about. First, this critical, much needed and long-overdue work educates you, the American people, about what is really going on in the War on Terror, and our own, sometimes inadequate, efforts to fight it. Second, from that base of information, it prepares every American to take part, explaining exactly what each and every person's role can and should be. It teaches you to have the strength of your convictions, to stand up and make a difference, no matter how small that difference may seem. Finally, it encourages you to use your own experiences, knowledge and common sense to actually make sense of the news media and political doublespeak that we are all subjected to, and which serves little purpose beyond obfuscating our understanding and clouding the issues.

Perhaps no one else in America has the background, credentials and ability to impart this critical message. Colonel Ruffini most often delivers this message as a keynote speaker at public awareness, homeland security and counter-terrorism conferences and seminars. One of the most dynamic presenters in the country, his message to the average citizen resounds off the walls of the hall, compelling everyone to "take arms," whether literally or figuratively, and recognize that the price of freedom truly is not free and we all must pay some price. In person, his message is inspiring, compelling and all-too-necessary. There is never a drooping eyelid or restless listener when Colonel Ruffini's dynamism harkens to us all to wake up and realize that which we have all along known, but chose to ignore.

Colonel Ruffini offers this same message on the pages that follow. Read his decades of dedication and the wisdom that comes from them, feel them resounding off the pages of this book. Feel the compelling allure of a nation that, once again, must turn to its citizens to defeat an enemy intent on its destruction. Islamist terrorist groups, not the least of which is al Qaeda, have promised us that what they are doing in Russia, in Afghanistan, in Iraq, Indonesia, Spain, England, Turkey, and many other places, will be visited on America many times over. Osama bin Laden has promised us the deaths of four million American citizens, including one million children. He has never lied to us.

After returning from the Beslan School siege near Chechnya in Russia in September 2004 – and two subsequent trips there – I penned a book about that atrocity, committed by al Qaeda trained and commanded terrorists attacking innocent women and children. But my book, Terror at Beslan: A Russian Tragedy With Lessons For America's Schools, was not a story of Beslan or Russia, but of America. It was a story of a threat that every expert in America knows will come to our shores sooner or later. It was a call to arms for the American people and American government to begin preparing now for a battle we will surely fight in the future.

In the pages that follow, Colonel Ruffini has gone even further, providing a primer, a basic training manual of citizen knowledge, awareness and action. In the closing pages of *Terror at Beslan*, recognizing the lethargy of inertia that must be overcome for our nation and the people to be ready, I wrote:

So to an America tucked comfortably into beds at night: sleep well. Close your eyes and go quietly into each gentle night, refusing to acknowledge the danger that lurks outside your doors. But before you do, get down on your knees and pray for protection by those who have already heeded the call, who stand ready to do violence against those who would do you harm. For the day is coming when they, even with their tremendous courage, will not be enough. Then, the battle will fall onto the shoulders of each and every one of us.

Just as he has lived his life, Lt. Col. Joseph Ruffini has once again heeded the call and produced the manual for American citizen readiness. Read his words, learn his lessons. Study this work and then apply it to your every day lives and the lives of all those you know. For the survival of America does, indeed, depend on you.

John Giduck

JOHN GIDUCK

John Giduck has a Bachelor's Degree from Penn State and a law degree from the University of Denver. He also earned a Master's Degree in International Affairs, specializing in Russian studies, from the University of Colorado, which included completion of the Russian Culture and Language Program at St. Petersburg State University in Russia. He has traveled extensively throughout Russia and the former Soviet Union, training with Russia's elite special forces units for more than 10 years. He is certified through the VITYAZ Special Forces Anti-Terror School to conduct anti-terror training and operations, and is a certified instructor in Russian special forces hand to hand combat.

He has trained state and federal law enforcement officers and agents, including DEA, FBI, US Marshal's Service, and SWAT teams throughout the US. He has served as a consultant on various international and terrorism subjects, as well as a defensive tactics and Russian Organized Crime instructor, for numerous federal agencies, and in the FBI National Academy continued training programs. He currently devotes his professional time to the Archangel Group, a non-profit agency providing anti-terrorism consulting and training to U.S. law enforcement, government and military, part of which includes John serving as a U.S. Army Special Forces hand-to-hand combat and firearms instructor. As well, he holds several black belts, has been inducted into several international martial arts halls of fame, and is a former U.S. national weightlifting champion.

John is a lifetime member of the Special Operations Association and Rocky Mountain Tactical Teams Association, and a lifetime executive member of the British SAS Professional Bodyguard Association. He is a graduate of the FBI Citizen's Academy and holds the highest level expert certification in Homeland Security through the American College of Forensic Examiners International, and is a former member of the Executive Advisory Board of the American College of Homeland Security and a current member of the executive advisory board of Police Marksman magazine. In addition to other published materials and articles on terrorism, Russian organized crime and close quarters tactics, he has recently finished his book, Terror at Beslan: A Russian Tragedy With Lessons for America's Schools. Currently, John is traveling the United States speaking and training America's law enforcement and military on the Beslan School siege.

As part of his work with Archangel, John Giduck is also a scuba, tactical diving and CQB instructor, and teaches terrorist-hostage negotiations, narco-terrorism, terrorism and global organized crime, and Russian organized crime courses. He is now working on his next two books. One addresses the increasing joint efforts by international organized crime and terror groups, and the other, with co-author Special Forces Sergeant Major John Anderson, is entitled Living the Green Beret Lifestyle: Total Commitment to Work, Family and Life.

To order a copy of his book, Terror at Beslan, go to www.antiterrorconsultants.org or write to info@circon.org

FROM THE AUTHOR

I am convinced that the truth about just how bad terror attacks will get in America, and what we should collectively be doing now to prepare and prevent them, is being suppressed at the federal and many state levels of government. Perhaps our elected and appointed officials don't want to alarm us. Maybe they sincerely believe that the American public cannot handle the realities of this War on Terror and the worst that is yet to come. I think they are wrong. I believe that they are doing us a great disservice.

The horrific events of 9-11 should never have hit us like a wicked bolt out of the blue. Our government officials knew as early as 1995 that Al Qaeda was plotting to use airliners in attacks against us. It failed to institute proper terror preventive measures within the Immigration and Naturalization Service, the Federal Aviation Administration, and among the major airlines themselves. It did nothing to prepare us mentally. Our government fell short of providing for the common defense. It is regrettably guilty of the same today. Our borders remain porous, luggage and cargo loaded into the bellies of passenger aircraft are not one hundred percent inspected, and our Department of Homeland Security is a bureaucratic, ineffective nightmare. It is time for Americans at the grassroots level to assume ownership and responsibility in this War on Terror.

Citizens and their communities must become more aware, concerned, and involved in their own anti-terror preparedness and prevention. This is not a simple task. Americans' jobs, personal responsibilities, and hectic lifestyles do not always afford them the obligatory time required to sort fact from fiction, government and media propaganda from reality, and perception from truth on a consistent basis. I consolidated much of what I believe we all need to know within this one, quick and easy read, especially designed for those who have the desire but not the time to keep up with it all.

The War on Terror has all but consumed me these past several years - studying it, helping to fight it, and helping others to understand it. As a senior defense consultant, national presenter, analyst and academic, I am privileged to interact with a variety of experts from all walks of life. I learn much from their experiences, opinions, perspectives, and professional contributions. I hope that, from time to time, I am able to reciprocate.

Much of the support I rendered as a senior consultant to U.S. Space Command, U.S. Strategic Command, U.S. Central Command, the Interagency,[1] and the National Security Council during Operations Enduring Freedom and Iraqi Freedom revolved around counter terror and counter insurgency intelligence, plans, and operations. I wanted to translate this operational awareness into a sound and realistic guide for my readers.

Maintaining a high level of knowledge and expertise about terror and its imminent threats to America requires countless of hours of professional reading, scrutinizing of Internet web sites, and monitoring of national and international news media. I devote thousands of hours to this end, and am confident of the opinions and recommendations I offer.

Many of our key civilian and military leaders simply do not act as if they realize our nation is at war. They are either lacking in leadership and management skills, operationally ignorant, or just plain derelict in their duties. I observed and worked with those who fit nicely into one or more of these categories. Someone must properly focus our elected and appointed officials. That someone is the average American like you and me.

---

[1] Interagency is a collective term that encompasses representatives from all facets of the U.S. Government that support DOD intelligence, plans and operations. The Interagency includes action officers from Office of the Secretary of Defense (OSD), Department of Defense (DOD), Department of State (DOS), Central Intelligence Agency (CIA), National Security Agency (NSA) Defense Intelligence Agency (DIA), Department of Justice (DOJ), Law Enforcement Activities (LEA) , and a host of others as necessary.

Our homeland is threatened. Our leaders appear content to incessantly study issues and endlessly debate solutions. The word "action" appears to be all-too-often absent from their vocabulary. We can ill afford to wait until the next 9-11 before making a quantum leap in anti-terror consciousness and vigilance.

All Americans remain at risk from terror attack anywhere and at any time. This is not a time in our history for complacency and partisan politics. Our government officials at all levels are moving far too slowly in educating and training the American public for the worst that is to come and what they can do now to prepare, and even prevent, the inevitable terror attacks upon our communities. I wanted to consolidate need-to-know information and recommendations into one comprehensive, quick and easy read. I sought to write a book that could be easily read and understood by anyone, regardless of background, age or experience.

My statements of fact in this book are, as I believe them to be, based upon a lifetime of work and study. I spoke at and attended more than 60 national, regional, and local security conferences and seminars in the last ten years. These professional security venues focus on diverse topics, from cyber terror, corporate and information security, and information operations, to terror tactics, techniques, procedures and counter-terror operations. I supported both Operations Enduring Freedom and Iraqi Freedom at highly classified levels in my role as an information operations and strategic communications consultant. My work keeps me immersed in counter-terror and anti-terror intelligence, plans, and operations.

I firmly believe that some of the most useful knowledge and intelligence available comes from open sources. Open source intelligence, or OSINT, includes any and all unclassified information available to the public from a myriad of sources such as the World Wide Web, international media, and writings of subject matter experts. The information presented in this book is derived entirely from open sources.

I am not a Democrat. I am not a Republican. This book is non-partisan. I try my best to maintain an open mind. I strive to tackle each new event, issue and challenge in the War on Terror without bias or pre-existing prejudices. I "call 'em like I see 'em" based upon my twenty years as a combat arms officer, ten years as a commercial businessman and defense consultant, and my more than thirty years of service to my country.

Someone has to deliver the straight scoop about terrorism and what it is going to take to fight and win the war against it. Many fine authors have contributed positively to the fight since 9-11. I wanted to do so as well. It is my goal to provide citizens with what they need to know to establish a solid information base, make more informed decisions, and take action themselves.

If this book causes all who read it to be more mentally and physically prepared to ride out this storm of terror, then I accomplished what I set out to do. If my book enables Americans to make informed choices when electing public officials, work more effectively within their schools, churches, civic organizations and communities at large, then I met my objectives.

We can debate ad nauseam the primary motives behind terrorism and the terror attacks. But let us never forget the bottom line: We need to deal effectively and conclusively with those who seek to harm us, our children, our nation, and the freedom that so many men and women have fought and died to preserve.

To all who open this book's cover, I extend my sincere appreciation. I wish you a long, happy, and prosperous life, and pray that our children will one day come to know a world at peace.

Joe Ruffini

INTRODUCTION

It is time for all of us to individually and collectively toughen-up. Our American lifestyles have become so cushy and indulgent that we all too often forget preserving our American liberties today demands a mental and physical toughness this nation has not been called upon to muster since World War II.

It is not the college educations, six-figure salaries, SUVs, discount warehouses, or $300,000 homes that keep America the land of the free and the home of the brave. It is and will always be sacrifice, courage in the face of adversity, blood, guts, and the casualties of war, including the American soldiers, sailors, airmen, marines, and civilians laid to rest across the globe. It is solely our ability to face the cold, hard realities of a planet in continuous conflict and deal with them in stride that will preserve us and enable future generations of Americans to remain the envy of both the free and the not-so-free world.

Anyone who does not believe that our American republic remains the envy of the world should read the polls and think again. A June 24, 2005 survey conducted by the reputable Pew Research Center for the People and the Press yields some very encouraging facts.[2] The citizens within two of the most vocally, anti-American Muslim counties in the world, Jordan and Morocco, say that democracy could work in their countries. Eighty percent of the Jordanians and eighty-three percent of those Moroccans polled stated so. Forty-three percent of Pakistanis, eighty-three percent of Lebanese, and a hearty seventy-seven percent of Indonesians also agreed that democracy could work in their nations. This tells us that even though numerous Muslim populations disagree with America's foreign policies and its military actions in the Middle East, they whole-heartedly desire representative forms of government such as ours. They crave what all people, regardless of race,

---

[2] www.findfacts.com/irelandbusinesnews/publisher/printer10002364.shtml.

religion, color, or creed, yearn for: freedom of choice, freedom of expression, freedom of speech, freedom of the press, and the freedom and opportunity to create a better life for their children than they inherited from their parents.

The Pew Global Attitudes Project presents encouraging figures clearly demonstrating that, slowly but surely, support for global terror may be waning. When asked if violence against civilian targets was justified, the percentage of people agreeing with "often/sometimes" declined markedly within countries such as Lebanon, Pakistan, Indonesia, and Morocco. In Lebanon, seventy-three percent of citizens polled in the summer of 2003 thought it permissible. The 2005 survey shows that the number declined to thirty-nine percent, a drop of thirty-four percent in just three years. In March of 2004, forty-one percent of Pakistanis surveyed felt that violence against civilian targets was often or sometimes justified. But in 2005, that number fell to twenty-five percent, showing an encouraging one-year drop in support of violence against civilians of sixteen percent. In Morocco, support for terror acts against civilians declined from forty percent in 2004 to just thirteen percent in 2005. Anti-American sentiment in Indonesia, the most heavily populated Muslim nation on Earth, noticeably declined, resulting in part from the post-Indian Ocean Tsunami aid provided by the United States.

There has been a plethora of finger pointing since the 9-11 tragedy, and much of it is well deserved. Despite all of the investigations and studies and presidential commissions and millions upon millions of dollars spent to lay blame, I know of no public or private sector executives who lost their jobs as a result of negligence or incompetence surrounding the failure to thwart the 9-11 attacks; not one. This tells me that no one in our government will lay blame or accept responsibility. No one is accountable, and no one is really in charge. There remains a gross lack of accountability, and an overabundance of incompetence and denial among our elected and appointed officials at all levels of government. Our war against terror is a war by committee, generating lots of debate, opinions, and criticisms, but very little action where it counts, such as border control, port container inspections, and serious enforcement of immigration laws.

We all share the responsibility to fight and win this war against global terror. It is equally shared from the President of the United States right on down to individual citizens like you and me. There is so much we could and should be doing to prepare for, and possibly even prevent, the terrorists' next mass murder attacks.

This responsibility to be aware, prepared, and engaged begins at the local level. Every emergency situation, from fires, hurricanes and floods to 9-11 scenarios, begins and ends as the responsibility of the local governments and their first responders. If a situation is beyond the local municipality's expertise or resources to control and resolve, the municipality will request assistance from its state authorities. The state then responds. When the state responds, it asks the local authorities "What do you need and where do you need it?" The cities and counties must have requisite plans in place to answer these questions. If the state requires support, it turns to the federal government. When the federal government responds to a state's request for assistance, it asks the same questions and rightfully expects a prompt and accurate response. The Federal Emergency Management Agency (FEMA) may be able to deliver twenty million bags of ice and ten million Meals Ready to Eat (MREs) to a hurricane-stricken city such as New Orleans, but it will ask the state officials, "Where do you want us to drop the stuff and who will be picking it up and delivering it to the people who need the relief?" If the state has no plan of action, then the federal authorities will be at a loss to provide the necessary relief in an accurate and timely manner.

The State of Louisiana's, and the City of New Orleans', apparent lack of a workable disaster relief plan was painfully and pathetically obvious in the aftermath of Hurricane Katrina. While citizens suffered, the city, state, and federal officials pointed fingers at one another. All of the officials involved, from the city to the federal government, appeared inept and uncaring. We watched on TV as Americans suffered and died in their own hometown, and it was inexcusable and internationally embarrassing. The terror plotters most probably watched the Katrina debacle on satellite TV along with the rest of the world. They no doubt learned much about America's disaster response shortfalls related to water events. How they might exploit these weaknesses in future attack scenarios is most certainly being discussed.

Our elected and appointed officials often appear to remain detached and clueless when bad things happen. In the case of Hurricane Katrina, our top leaders showed themselves to be mournfully unaware, uninformed, and disengaged.

"I don't think anybody anticipated the breach of the levees." – President George Bush on Good Morning America September 1, 2005, six days after repeated warnings from experts about the scope of the expected damage from Hurricane Katrina, to include the fact that the levees would not hold against a category 4 or 5 hurricane.

"Considering the circumstances that we have in New Orleans, virtually a city that has been destroyed, things are going relatively well." – FEMA Director Michael Brown, September 1, 2005. (Katrina breached the New Orleans levees causing mass evacuations and panic on August 29, 2005.)

"I have not heard a report of thousands of people in the convention center who don't have food and water." – Homeland Security Secretary Michael Chertoff, on National Public Radio's All Things Considered, September 1, 2005, when for days every major network and cable news organization reported the dismal facts.

"We just learned of the convention center – we being the federal government—today." – FEMA Director Michael Brown to ABC's Ted Koppel, to which Koppel responded, *"Don't you guys watch television? Our reporters have been reporting on it for more than just today."* (September 3, 2005 – more than 48 hours after the situations within the superdome and convention center became untenable.)

If our Department of Homeland Security (DHS), FEMA, and state and local officials cannot work together to effectively respond to a disaster such as Hurricane Katrina, of which they were amply forewarned, how can we expect them to do what needs to be done when the next no-notice, 9-11-type attack is perpetrated on American soil?

Every American has a dog in this fight. Homeland security is an individual as well as a collective responsibility. Citizens and their communities must act now to ensure that their elected and appointed public officials at all levels are capable, accountable, effective, and responsive. It is often an uphill and extremely frustrating battle. And we must fight every step of the way. Someone has to effect positive change. That someone is you and me.

Every American from this moment forward must possess what military professionals refer to as an "operational awareness." This book provides that operational awareness. Senior military field officers must maintain an operational awareness of many diverse subjects from finances and logistics to troop readiness and vehicle maintenance. Commanders' staffs keep them up-to-date with a series of briefings. These briefings are "down and dirty." They give the commander all of the most important facts needed to make sound and accurate decisions. I view my readers as the new commander. I am the staff officer providing the facts via this book. Ergo, this book is arrayed as a series of critical briefings in lieu of chapters.

Eight and one half years transpired between the first World Trade Center bombing in New York City in 1993, and the 9-11 airplane attacks of 2001. Our enemies are patient. They are bound by no specific timeline. They tell us that they will strike again and again. We have no reason to doubt them. They pledge that subsequent attacks will be far more devastating than the previous ones. We have no reason to question their resolve. Suicide bombers will enter our restaurants and stores. Terrorists will take our school children hostage. Planes will be used to kill again. It is not a matter of if, but a matter of when. We must prepare ourselves, because **Terror is Coming to Main Street**.

BRIEFING # 1

Understanding the Hatred

The Attack "Out of Nowhere"

Many Americans viewing the horrific events of 9-11, as they unfolded on live television, asked themselves, "What did we do to deserve this?" We are a good and generous people. We fought for the freedom of Arabs and Muslims during Desert Storm. American blood, sweat, tears and dollars liberated Kuwait from Iraqi aggression and prevented Saudi Arabia from being invaded by Saddam Hussein. It was the American-led United Nations (UN) effort in Kosovo that saved thousands of Muslims from the atrocities of the Serbs. Why this horrific attack out of the blue?

Let's get one point crystal clear from the onset: 9-11 was not a "strike out of the blue." It was the result of decades of inbred hatred, resentment, deprivation, religious education, fanaticism, and political subjugation. It was the kickoff to an Islamist[3] game of terror in America's stadium with a continuous time clock,

---

[3] There is a key distinction between the terms "Islamic" and "Islamist." Westerners often make the inadvertent mistake of referring to the terrorists as "Islamic," which is incorrect. To Muslims, the expression "Islamic terrorists" accuses Muslims in general of being terrorists. The term "Islamist terrorist" is acceptable, as it denotes a terrorist who happens to also be a Muslim (follower of the religion Islam).

no rulebook, and an inexhaustible bench of players eager to hit the gridiron.

Though Americans have been victims of global terror attacks for decades, America refused to "get its head into the game" until September 11, 2001. Sadly, it took attacks on our home field to move us to don uniforms and step onto the playing field with our game faces on. September 11 marked the United States' great awakening and formal acknowledgement of a new age of global terror and the uphill battle against it.

In an effort to understand Middle Eastern resentment toward America and its foreign policy in that region, I begin by recapping the comments of Secretary of State Condoleezza Rice, during her visit to Egypt on June 20, 2005. Speaking at the American University in Cairo, Dr. Rice accurately and eloquently stated that: "For 60 years, my country, the United States, pursued stability at the expense of democracy in this region here in the Middle East – and we achieved neither. Now, we are taking a different course. We are supporting the democratic aspirations of all people."[4] Secretary Rice applauded the ongoing struggles for freedom throughout the Middle East, rising from the grassroots levels in nations such as Egypt, Jordan, Saudi Arabia, Kuwait, Iraq, Iran, Syria, Lebanon, and Iraq. She quoted George Bush from his Second Inaugural Address: "America will not impose our style of government on the unwilling. Our goal instead is to help others find their own voice, to attain their own freedom, and to make their own way."[5]

Doctor Rice's comments constitute an official admission that America has traditionally and mistakenly supported Middle Eastern monarchies and pseudo-democracies that exhibited less than stellar track records with respect to human rights and individual freedoms. America acknowledges it was wrong in that its Middle East foreign policy was flawed and misguided for much

---

[4] http://www.state.gov/secretary/rm/2005/48328.htm.
[5] Ibid.

of the last century. It must work hard to make things right in that region, and this will take time. The Muslim world is watching and waiting for our words to be followed up with appropriate actions.

Religion Is Truly the Opiate of the Masses

I know of no religion that does not possess its moderate, fundamentalist, and extremist followers. Christianity, Judaism, and Islam are no exceptions. Moderate Christians, Jews, and Muslims rarely draw attention to themselves or attract the global media, by virtue of their low profile temperance. Fundamentalists often make headlines when they attempt to regulate the lifestyles of the moderates, such as those Christians who seek to outlaw Halloween parties in schools or ban "unchristian" books from school libraries. Extremists regularly make the front pages; for example, the Christian terrorists who murder doctors, staff members, and patients at abortion clinics. Radical Jews, such as right-wing activist Yigal Amir who assassinated his own Israeli Prime Minister, Yitschak Rabin, enrage the vast majority of moderate, peace-loving Jews. Then there are the Islamist extremist terrorists such as Osama bin Laden who kill thousands, and in doing so, misrepresent and mischaracterize those whom I believe compose the vast majority of peaceable, moderate Muslims.

Be they Christian, Jewish, or Islamic murders, their deeds are performed in the name of their God. And in the name of their God, they draw others to their causes.

The Roots of Extremist Islam

Islam began with the Prophet Muhammad Ibn Abdillah, born in Mecca around the year 569 BC. He was a trader by profession and became known to his people as "al-amin," or "the trustworthy one." When Muhammad reached the age of 40, it is written that the angel Gabriel appeared before him with revelations that established him as a prophet of God. The angel commanded Muhammad to instruct his immediate family on Islam. It was later revealed to him that he should instruct all of mankind. For two decades, Muhammad communicated the message of Allah to his people, and set an example for how every person should live his or her life. Much of Muhammad's life was spent in a cruel and almost genocidal decimation of cites and regions and their inhabitants, in his endless search for revenge over their treatment of him as a young man. This expansion of Islam saw the beheadings, torture and rape of thousands upon thousands. This was Muhammad's legacy. He died in the year 632.[6]

Extremist Islam finds its roots in a sect founded by Muhammad Ibn Abdul Wahhab in the early 1700s known as "Wahhabism." It is a fundamentalist, right wing version of Islam based upon the Islamic extremist teachings and writings of Ibn Taymiyya in the early 14th century. These writing are still quoted regularly by Islamic extremists today. Wahhabism was rejected by most Islamic religious leaders of Wahhab's time. Around the mid-1700s, Wahhab joined forces with a local tribal leader named Muhammed ibn Saud. Together they established the first Saudi state. Saud became the leader, and Wahhab, the ultimate authority on morality and the behavior of the people. So radically strict was Wahhab's version of Islam, that he resurrected the 7th century Muhammedian practice of stoning women to death for adultery.

Wahhab's daughter married Saud's son. This began a period of influence by Saudi Arabian rulers immersed in ancient and extremist traditions that the world continues to encounter today.

Wahhabism is the foundation of the current Islamic extremist movement. It has spread seemingly without control, from Saudi Arabia to the rest of the world, especially during the last forty years. John Giduck, in his book, Terror at Beslan, makes the historical point that:

---

[6] The tutorial on Muhammad was paraphrased from an excellent summary found at http://www.usc.edu/dept/MSA/fundamentals/prophet.

Extremist, militant Islamic fundamentalism has so far succeeded where Communism failed. It has been exported from the Middle East to, first, the Soviet war in Afghanistan; once again with U.S. assistance in military training, weaponry, organization, and logistics. After that victory, it redeployed quickly to the first war in Chechnya. Though primarily, at the time, a war of the Chechen people for independence – much as the war in Afghanistan started – it has, since 1999, become completely perverted and conscripted into the greater jihad against infidels, against all non-Muslim oppressors. In the midst of this, the war in the Balkans saw another clash of religions. Though Serb atrocities against the Croat and Bosnian Muslims were real, often these were provoked - and nearly always retaliated against – by Mujahedeen Muslim fanatics intent on instigating another jihad in places like Kosovo and Bosnia. . . Assault by Islamic terrorists, working in concert through an elaborate and growing worldwide network, has now appeared in Indonesia, Australia, Malaysia, the Philippines, Japan, Spain, Turkey, Iraq, Lebanon, Saudi Arabia, Mexico, Central and South America, and the U.S., among others. [7]

How the Global Reach of Al Qaeda Began

The roots of Islamist extremism anchored to the soil of terrorism in the late 1970s. Terrorism expert Rohan Gunaratna notes: "Two momentous events in 1979 – the Islamic revolution in Iran and the Soviet invasion of Afghanistan – marked the rise of a new wave of Islamist movements." [8] The global impact of the Iranian Revolution that deposed the ruling shah, and the Muslim defeat of the Soviet Union after nine years of bloody conflict in Afghanistan, were the seeds from which more than a hundred Islamist movements grew. They sprang up across the globe, in the Middle East, Asia, Africa, the Caucasus, the Balkans, and in Western Europe. [9]

---

[7] Giduck, John. *Terror at Beslan – A Russian Tragedy With Lessons for American Schools* (Denver, Colorado: Archangel Group, 2005), p. 44.
[8] Gunaratna, Rohan. *Inside Al Qaeda: Global Network of Terror* (New York, New York: Berkley Books, 2002-2003), p. 4.
[9] Ibid.

Among these Islamist movements one calling itself Al Qaeda al-Sulbah (Al Qaeda meaning "solid base" or "foundation") advanced as their standard bearer around 1987. Al Qaeda existed to foster societies based upon the very strictest of Islamic principles. It was formed and led by a Palestinian-Jordanian named Abdullah Azzam. It was Azzam who defined its composition, goals, and purpose for existence. He envisioned Al Qaeda as the front line, advance guard, and global flag bearer for Islam. Azzam served as mentor to Osama bin Laden.

Azzam and bin Laden worked together to recruit mujahedeen, or "warriors of God," for the Afghan war against the Soviets. They did this through a worldwide network of offices in more than 30 countries, including recruiting stations in many of the United States' larger cities. When the Soviets pulled out, Azzam sought to re-direct the focus and fervor of these victorious Muslim fighters to other noble causes. Azzam feared that without leadership, discipline, and a reason to remain together as a fighting force, many of his warriors might be drawn towards a life of crime.

As soon as the Soviet Union pulled out of Afghanistan, Al Qaeda diverted mujahedeen and military resources to other places around the world where Islamists were also involved in conflicts with hostile governments, even before the final defeat of the Soviet Union in Afghanistan. These regions included Kashmir, Chechnya, Tajikistan and Uzbekistan in Central Asia, Algeria, Somalia and Egypt in Africa, and the Southeast Asian countries of Malaysia and Indonesia. Al Qaeda successfully intruded into ongoing conflicts in these countries by taking control of the Islamist terror groups already fighting there. It did so through its strong and alluring ideological, political, fiscal and military influence.

The spiritual leader of these global jihadists, or "holy warriors," Azzam, prescribed the training guidelines for his Al Qaeda. This guiding doctrine stressed prayer, devotion, loyalty, and an acute awareness of the many worldwide, anti-Islam movements as defined by Azzam. These attributes are still very visible in Al Qaeda loyalists today.

A steadfast principle espoused under Osama bin Laden's leadership made Al Qaeda different and distinct from the other Islamist organizations. Bin Laden's dogmatic belief argued that it was appropriate for people to be forcibly conscripted into Islam, and that targeting innocent civilians was an acceptable tactic in establishing a Pam Islamic caliphate across the globe. To him, violence must always be a part of the process. His philosophy was, and is today, that behind every pen must be a gun; bullets must accompany words.

A power struggle ensued between Azzam and bin Laden towards the late 1980s. Their relationship became strained over these philosophical differences as Azzam did not embrace forcible coercion of persons into the religion of Islam and viewed innocent civilians to be "off limits." The chasm between the two widened to such an extreme that in November 1999, Azzam and his two sons were killed when the car in which they were riding to Friday evening prayers was torn apart by a remotely-detonated bomb. It is widely suspected that Osama bin Laden sanctioned these murders to become the new Al Qaeda leader.

Osama bin Laden became the Islamists' poster boy and most commonly recognized symbol within the global, anti-American terrorist movement. It is important to understand the sources of bin Laden's hatred and aggression. He harbors specific grievances with the United States, the Saudi royal family, U.S. coalition partners, and selected Arab leaders who openly ally with the United States.

Osama bin Laden publicly declared war on the United States on more than one occasion. He did so most vocally on September 2, 1996 and February 23, 1998. Since 1996, bin Laden repeatedly warned Americans in public statements that he would incrementally increase the lethality of his attacks upon the United States' interests until the U.S. stopped supporting Israel, withdrew military forces from Saudi Arabia, and ended the embargo against Iraq. He made these claims before Operation Iraqi Freedom began in March 2003.

Osama bin Laden, and the thousands who seek to carry out his fatwa,[10] view Islamic governments that cooperate with or support U.S. foreign policy in the Middle East as "morally depraved hypocrites," which "champion falsehood, support the butcher against the victim, the oppressor against the innocent child."[11]

Saddam Hussein's 1990 invasion of Kuwait threatened the security of Saudi Arabia and its precious oil fields. Osama bin Laden offered to raise an Islamic army to defend his homeland from Iraqi aggression. He told the Saudi royal family that there was no need to permit the infidels (U.S.-led coalition) onto Saudi Arabia's Islamic holy ground. Rather than have non-Muslims set foot near the holy Islamic cities of Mecca and Medina, bin Laden pledged to rally thousands of the same freedom fighters, the mujahedeen, who had defeated the great army of the Soviet Union in Afghanistan in 1989. The Saudi royals rejected his offer and permitted the U.S.– led coalition to establish a presence on the holiest of lands of Islam. Bin Laden saw this as a blatant offense against Allah and all true followers of Islam. He dismissed the Saudi rulers as having sinned against Allah. He considered them to be sellouts that were just as guilty of blaspheming Islam as the armed U.S.-led coalition.

The Osama bin Laden followers of the world see the United States and its coalition partners as Crusaders, invaders, imperialists,

---

[10] Fatwa is a legal opinion or ruling issued by an Islamic scholar. A fatwa has no weight unless accepted by the community of scholars; their consensus is recognized as legal opinion to be followed. Islam has no central authority, which allows diversity of opinion, though major scholars agree on core issues.
[11] Scheuer, Michael. *Through Our Enemies Eyes* (Washington, D.C.: Brassey's Inc., 2003), p. 48.

aggressors, and a threat to the very existence of Muslims. They want the Americans out of their homelands, out of their politics, and out of their personal affairs. They want an America that is unable to influence and corrupt their youth with sex, drugs, alcohol, music and television. They do not want their women tempted with visions of equality, participation in government, education and job opportunities. They want everyone to convert to fundamentalist Islam. They see the future world as a global Islamist nation-state, or as experts refer to it, a "Pan-Islamic Caliphate."

Someone Has to Take the Blame

The U.S. aligned itself with too many absolute monarchies and dictatorships while looking out for its own national security and economic needs during the twentieth century. These Middle Eastern rulers, with whom the U.S. sought favor, denied their citizens rights to free speech, free press, and majority rule. Monarchs placated their citizens with guaranteed government jobs, freedom from menial labor, steady respectable incomes, and creature comforts such as: housing, air conditioning, and automobiles. This tactic of "buying off" the indigenous masses through placation worked well for many decades until globalization opened the eyes of millions of Muslims around the world.

Cable and satellite mass media, or the "CNN effect," brought a new awareness and awakening to millions of people in the Eastern Hemisphere. Muslims who were previously sheltered and protected from the influence and "evils" of the West were suddenly exposed to it streaming into their homes and businesses every day, and in real time. Satellite TV is so widespread throughout the Middle East that Western and Arab companies compete fiercely for market share. A recent survey by the Arab Advisors Group, for example, reveals that approximately eighty-nine percent of households in Saudi Arabia have satellite television.[12] A 2004-2005 survey conducted in Jordan's three major cities, Amman, Irbid, and Zarqa, documented that satellite TV is received in ninety-one percent of homes.[13]

Satellite news, shows, and movies display Americans and Europeans who are free to embrace higher education and new technologies, secure high paying jobs, live lavish and exciting life-styles, wear blue jeans and makeup, and listen to popular music. Women vote and hold public office. They swell the ranks of government, police and fire departments, the militaries and Fortune 500 companies. Human rights prevail among the major-ity of Western nations. Freedom of speech and the press remain the order of the day. Individual freedoms and human rights reign. More and more Muslims are asking themselves and each other, "Why not here? Why not now?"

There remains little hope at present for real freedom or advance-ment for many millions of underprivileged Muslims throughout the Middle East, Africa, Central and South Asian, and Pacific Rim countries. Children from poor and destitute Muslim fami-lies often grow up with little hope for productive lives. Many must avail themselves of the free education, room, and board at strict Islamic schools known as "madrasas." Thousands of unfortunate Muslim families have no alternatives but to send their children away to these schools, many of which are Islamist extremist breeding grounds. The vast majority of these madrasas focus their curriculum around the study of Islam and the Koran. Some of the strictest madrassas teach their students to memorize the Koran and to recite it verbatim. Stringent religious training yields steadfast followers of Islam, but does not provide the knowledge or skills needed to successfully compete within today's international business and technical arenas.

---

[12] http://www.ameinfo.com/56546.html.
[13] http://www.menfn.com/qn_news_story_s.asp?StoryId=78473.

Tens of thousands of madrasa-educated young Muslim men, in their late teens through their twenties, graduate with degrees in Islamic studies. The luckier graduates find work in the mosques or madrasas as teachers or staff members. Too many never secure adequate, paying jobs. They cannot afford to marry and raise a family without employment income. As a result, many never marry and sex outside of marriage is strictly forbidden under Islamic law. Possessing no genuine, competitive education or technical skills, no careers, no opportunities for advancement, and no wives and families, these men have no sanctioned sexual relations either. Their lives remain unfulfilled and riddled with feelings of frustration, despair and hopelessness.

Combine the simultaneous envy and loathing of Western life-styles, economic depravation, despair, sexual frustration, and anti-Semitic/Western indoctrination, and it is not difficult to understand why so many Muslim youths harbor such unwavering resentment towards American Christians and Jews.

These unfortunate Muslims desperately seek explanations for their plight. They are taught from a very young age that the Americans and Jews are to blame. They are told that the devious foreign policies of the immoral Westerners and the Israelis keep the Muslim populations suppressed and left behind in the dust of global economic advancement. They hear it for years in the madrasas, from the pulpits in the mosques, and yet again from the terror recruiters. Hence, resentment and despair fester, anger grows, and is fanned into hatred. Infuriated Muslims seek outlets for their rage. Leaders like Osama bin Laden offer them that outlet, as well as a noble Islamist cause behind which they can rally and exact their revenge.

Terror leaders are very smart men who know how to recruit. They are adept at deception, psychological operations, com-munications, the Internet, exploitation, and public information campaigns. Terror organizations and their leaders such as bin

Laden provide meaning to, and a purpose for, the lives of many Muslims. Joining a terror organization is often the one and only ticket out of their hometown. It brings a job, room and board, travel, adventure, respect, and opportunity for advancement. An AK-47 rifle becomes the first possession of value for many terror recruits. Opportunities denied them by their U.S.-supported, self-indulgent governments are presented to them by the likes of Al Qaeda. The first to offer a light at the end of the tunnel to these hopeless masses is all-too-often the terrorists. It could and should have been the open market democracies.

It is not difficult to understand how poor, destitute young Muslims are easily manipulated and indoctrinated to the extremist Islamist causes of Al Qaeda and other such terror organizations. Yet, it is not just the poor who are swayed. The anti-Western, violent ideology of Osama bin laden and his Al Qaeda also lures the middle-class and affluent Muslims. Many of the 9-11 Saudi Arabian homicide pilots came from wealthy families. Let us not forget that bin Laden himself is worth millions of dollars.

Prior to the explosion of the Information Age, ruling classes could, to a greater extent, keep their lavish lifestyles and selfish indulgences out of view if the general public. Average Middle Easterners either did not know of, or did not publicly question, the rulings and actions of their royal families and government heads. Late 20th century changed all of that. A voracious global media, coupled with an immediate information environment (tabloids, Internet, email, Web sites, and satellite television and radio) heightened awareness and fueled the thoughts and opinions of ordinary men and women. Knowledge of inequities, injustices, and double standards became widespread. Even many well-to-do Muslims appear to be growing tired of their rulers' lavish and wasteful lifestyles (paid for by the national wealth), religious hypocrisies, alliances with the West, and social double standards. They observe Westerners taking their public officials to task for offenses that pale in comparison.

Middle Eastern royal families may be digging their own graves. They have clandestinely fueled anti-Americanism and anti-Semitism for decades, while openly allying with the West. Their subjects view them more and more as dealers with the devil (the West). Middle Eastern monarchs may have trapped themselves in a "no win" situation; unable to take back their past while powerless to move their monarchies forward. This creates an ideal opportunity for the likes of Al Qaeda to sew seeds of dissent and rebellion, promoting fundamental Islam as the global cure all.

Osama bin Laden supports the ousting of the Middle Eastern ruling classes. He supports the overthrow of the Saudi royal family and replacement of the monarchy with a fundamentalist, Islamic theocracy. Some argue that if the bin Laden followers of the world were to eventually overthrow and control the oil-rich nations of the Middle East that the flow of crude would be cut off to the United States. I do not agree; all oil-rich nations need international trade to generate revenues. Osama bin Laden would certainly do business with the United States. He would, however, strive to reverse what he views as a decades-old trend of raping and robbing the Muslim world of its wealth by selling oil to Western nations at far too low a price. Osama bin laden would sell Saudi oil to us, but the price per barrel would make us wish we were buying at the "bargain price" of between fifty and sixty dollars per barrel, which we paid in 2005 and 2006.

There is a worldwide sector of conservative, fundamentalist followers of Islam from all socio-economic backgrounds who fear that the decadent ways of the West – force fed to them globally by way of American television, news, movies, music, and video games – pose a clear and present danger to Islamic teachings, culture and traditional Muslim family values. These Muslims remain convinced that the United States seeks to dominate, corrupt, and subjugate the Muslim world.

The U.S. is clearly the enemy in the eyes of too many Muslims from all walks of life. Their convictions have been "justified" by recent, aggressive U.S.-led military actions in Afghanistan and Iraq, preceded by its presence on sacred Saudi soil during Operations Desert Shield/Desert Storm. They blame Americans for: (1) promulgating the decadence of their immoral lifestyles abroad in an attempt to corrupt the innocent Muslim youth; (2) supporting the shady governments that squander national wealth and prevent Muslims from reaping the benefits of globalization; and (3) invading Muslim countries to dominate and control them. This presents a "no win" situation for an America that must somehow discover a way to win the hearts and minds of the Muslim world as a means to ending terror. Let us never forget that the events of 9-11 were the first huge taste of revenge for anti-American Muslims worldwide. They savored it. They reveled in it, and now they hunger for more.

Don't Blame The Innocent

Radical and extremist Islamists do not include all Muslims. The almost 1.5 billion Muslims in the world make up a fifth of all humanity. Countless Muslims are peaceful, devout followers of Allah who abhor terror, as much as any respectable Christian or Jew. A lot of Muslims can be labeled as "moderates." Our collective Western challenge over the next several decades is to do our best to ensure that growing numbers of followers of Islam remain moderate and tolerant, content to live side-by-side with non-Muslims in peace.

Muslim Generations Conditioned to Hate and Kill

Most Americans would be stunned to discover the depth and breadth of anti-Semitic and anti-American hatred in the Middle

East today. Kenneth R. Timmerman in his book *Preachers of Hate: Islam and the War on America*, points out with countless, disturbing examples that Arab leaders from Egypt to Saudi Arabia not only encouraged the hatred, but spent a great deal of time and money from the 1960s through present day to spread the kinds of lies, deceit, and hatred that fuel anti-Semitic and anti-Western sentiments and spur violent jihads.

According to Timmerman, these governments actively pursue methods to encourage hatred of non-Muslims. They include false reports, biased radio and TV interviews, and damning sermons in the mosques. The following examples from Timmerman's book illustrate the problem:[14]

• Speaking in Tehran, Iran, in the fall of 2001, Syria's ambassador to Iran, Turky Muhammad Saqr, stated "Syria has documented proof of the Zionist regime's involvement in the September 11 terror attacks on the U.S. . . ."

• Egyptian cleric Sheikh Mohammed Gamei – one of the Muslim world's most respected authorities on questions of ethics and religion – summed up what he categorized as an Israeli conspiracy in an October 5, 2001 interview. Referring to 9-11, he accused the Jews of being the "only ones capable of planning such acts."

• On September 25, 2002, Dr. Gamal Ali Zahran, head of the political science faculty at Suez Canal University in Cairo, Egypt, wrote in the Egyptian government daily Al Ahram, "At the WTC, thousands of Jews worked in finance and the stock market, but none of them were there on the day of the incident."

[14] Timmerman, Kenneth R.. Preachers of Hate: Islam and the War on America (New York, New York: Crown Forum, 2003), pp. 15-22.

- Doctor Saud Shawa, a prominent political leader associated with terrorist group Hamas and a member of the board of trustees for the Islamic University in Gaza, told Timmerman that "Just as the Israelis today control the national economy, so they want to control us." Shawa also emphatically denied that six million Jews were killed in the Nazi holocaust, stating that the Jews produced films of the exterminations because, "there were not any actual photographs from that period of history, which did not have film yet."

- A Saudi Arabian telethon was conducted to raise money for the families of Palestinian suicide bombers. One hundred nine million dollars were donated to the cause. Saudi Prince al-Waleed bin Talal contributed $27 million to the government-organized telethon. The show was hosted by a prominent religious cleric of the Saudi government – Sheikh Saad al-Buraik— who said during the broadcast, "I am against America until this life ends . . . my hatred for America, if part of it was contained in the universe, it (the universe) would collapse . . . she (America) is the root of all evils and wickedness on Earth . . . Muslim Brothers in Palestine, do not have any mercy on the Jews . . . their women are yours to take legitimately. God made them yours. Why don't you enslave their women? Why don't you pillage them?"

This nationally televised rhetoric is widely heard by all ages. It is not difficult to understand why thousands of Muslim children grow up desiring to kill American Christians and Jews for Allah and reap societal praise, glory, and financial compensation for their families following their acts of martyrdom.

Prime Time Propaganda

One of the most shocking and blatant examples of the brain-washing to which thousands of Muslim children are subjected is vividly and disturbingly illustrated in *Preachers of Hate*.[15] In it, Timmerman relates an example of anti-Jewish hatred promulgated on a popular Saudi television talk show – similar in format and celebrity to our Oprah Winfrey Show. This show, entitled *Women's Muslim Magazine*, was broadcast on location from Egypt on May 7, 2002. The show's very popular host, Ms. Doaa Amer, announced to her audience that she had a special guest: "a little girl, a Muslim girl but a true Muslim." "Allah willing," she told the mothers in the studio audience, "may our God give us the strength to educate our children in the same way, so that the next generation will turn out to be true Muslims who understand that they are Muslims and know who their enemies are."

With that introduction, Ms. 'Amer brought out onto the TV stage a three and a half year-old girl named Basmallah. Timmerman quotes excerpts from this TV interview:

'Amer: "Are you a Muslim?"
Child: "Yes."
Amer: "Basmallah, are you familiar with Jews?"
Child: "Yes."
'Amer: "Do you like them?"
Child: "No."
'Amer: "Why don't you like them?"
Child: "Because they are apes and pigs."
'Amer: "Because they are apes and pigs? Who said they are so?"
Child: "Our God."
'Amer: "Where did he say this?"
Child: "In the Koran."[16]

[15] Ibid, pp. 117-119.
[16] Koran—also spelled Qu-ran or Quran –is the Muslim holy book. It is the equivalent of the Christian Bible or Jewish Torah.

It is hard for Americans to imagine such words of denigration and hatred pontificated by a famous talk show host, let alone wholly and heartily embraced by the studio audience and hundreds of thousands of viewers. Unfortunately, this kind of indoctrination of children has occurred for more than 40 years of mass media dissemination throughout the Muslim world, especially within Saudi Arabia, Pakistan, the Palestinian territories, and the Southeast Asian island states.

Wahabbism

As discussed, the unique and widely exported Saudi brand of Islam is called "Wahhabism." One of the most strict and right wing forms of Islam, it evolved when the houses of Saud and Wahhab united in the 1700s. It is, by Western and even moderate Muslim standards, a harsh and restraining brand of Islam sent abroad exponentially by the Saudis beginning in 1962. Wahhabi Muslims live under numerous religious rules and restrictions in Saudi Arabia. Compliance is enforced by religious or "morality" police who are known to abuse their virtually unchecked powers, especially when dealing with non-Muslims and Westerners.

The Saudi government sponsored an international Islamic conference in the holy city of Mecca in May of 1962. Neighboring Egypt, led by Gamal Abdel Nasser, was trying to expand its influence over the Arab world. Nasser was marketing a brand of Arab socialism unacceptable to the Saudi king yet disturbingly supported by some of the Saudi princes. Saudi Arabia's King Faisal used Wahhabism as a counterweight to Nasser's socialism. It became the primary weapon in the fight for power and influence in the region. Religious dignitaries established the Muslim World League, an international organization dedicated to the global spread of Wahhabism. This marked the Saudi government's official movement to export its harsh brand of Islam to the world – and the anti-Jewish, anti-Christian, anti-American rhetoric that accompanied it.[17]

A few of the more notable Saudi efforts that markedly expanded Wahhabism include:

• Saudi religious oversight of that country's educational system, emphasizing Wahhabi Islam among many generations of Saudi students. The number of students in Saudi universities skyrocketed from 3,625 in 1965 to 113,529 in 1986,[18] during the quarter century from the mid-1960s (the beginning of the modern Wahabbi expansion) through the end off the 1980s.

• The Saudi government built 1,500 mosques, 210 Islamic centers, and 2,000 schools in non-Muslim countries alone between 1982 and 2002. Huge sums of money were distributed globally – all tied to the promulgation of Wahhabi Islam. Within a two-year period in the 1980s, the Saudi spent $10 million on the construction of mosques within the United States.[19]

• The Saudis provided an estimated $4 billion in aid to Afghan guerilla groups from 1980 through 1990.[20] (The United States also provided untold hundreds of millions of dollars in aid and arms to these same groups, but with geo-political, not religious, objectives.)

• As many as 25,000 Saudis received training abroad beginning in 1979, to include those who fought in the Afghan war against the Soviet Union. The Saudis invested heavily in the Peshawar region of Pakistan,

---

[17] For a more detailed analysis, see Dore Gold's *Hatred's Kingdom – How Saudi Arabia Supports the New Global Terrorism* (Washington, D.C.: Regnery, 2003), pp. 75-76.
[18] Ibid, p. 79.
[19] Ibid, pp. 73-88.
[20] Ibid.

where Al Qaeda members often hide out today. In 1988, the Muslim World League (created by the Saudis) opened 150 Koran study centers and 85 madrassas for Afghan students.[21]

Osama bin Laden used his personal wealth to spread Wahhabism among the Afghans. A great many of the volunteers who fought alongside the Afghans against the Soviets were Saudi Arabian Wahhabites. Wahhabism was ingrained within the Mujahedeen freedom fighters by the time Al Qaeda evolved and bin Laden took command of it in 1989.

Wahhabi extremism is preached globally today – even within Saudi-built and backed mosques and madrasas located in most major U.S. cities – to include our nation's capital.

We Refused to See the Writing on the Wall

The violent, open hatred of America by many Muslims permeated the global scene for more than twenty years prior to 9-11. America's leaders simply refused to acknowledge the inevitable escalation of global terror, and did not endeavor to preempt it.

Hindsight is always 20/20. The warning signs flashed ever so brightly throughout the 80s and 90s, but our leaders kept the blinders over their eyes and ours:

> **October 1983**: Two-hundred and twenty U.S. Marines were killed in their barracks by a suicide/homicide truck bomber in Beirut, Lebanon.

> **December 1988**: Five years later, Pan American Airline's Flight 103 was blown out of the sky over Lockerbie, Scotland, by Muslim extremists. There were no survivors.

---

[21] Ibid.

February 1993: Four years later, Al Qaeda's chief bomb maker, Ramzi Yousef, and his team set off a bomb in the underground parking garage of the New York World Trade Center. This first attempt failed to bring the building down.

December 1994: Ten years later, Ramzi Yousef planted a nitroglycerin bomb on Philippine Airlines Flight 434. The bomb blew a hole in the side of the 747-200 aircraft. The pilot managed to land safely at Naha Airport, in Okinawa.

April 1995: Five months later, Filipino police raided an Al Qaeda apartment and seized Ramzi Yousef's computer. Documents on the laptop laid out attacks against eleven American commercial aircraft flying in the Southeast Asian corridor. The plan – called Operation Bojinka ("Big Bang") – was supposed to cause 48 hours of terror in the skies over the Pacific Ocean.[22]

April 1995: That same month, Timothy McVeigh and Terry Nichols exploded a truck bomb, destroying the Murrah Federal Building in Oklahoma City, killing 168 men, women, and children. Abdul Hakim Murad, one of Yousef's cohorts in the Operation Bojinka planning, was taken into custody and transferred to the Metropolitan Correctional Center in New York City shortly before the incident. Soon after the bombing, radios reported that the federal building was destroyed by a very powerful bomb concealed in a rented truck. As soon as he heard the report, Abdul Murad told authorities that Yousef's "Liberation Army" was responsible for the bombing. Though he confirmed the statement in writing, the judge never allowed it into evidence at the trial

---

[22] Ressa, Maria A. *Seeds of Terror* (New York, New York: Free Press, 2003) , p. 35.

of Timothy McVeigh.[23] To this day, the U.S. government refuses to officially acknowledge that Al Qaeda had its hand in the Oklahoma City bombing.

June 1996: The next year, nineteen U.S. Air Force personnel were killed in the bombing of a dormitory at the Khobar Towers in Saudi Arabia.

August 1999: American embassies in Dar es Salaam, Tanzania, and Nairobi, Kenya became victims of terrorist bomb attacks, killing and injuring more than 5,000. There were many more global terror attacks between 1995 and 1999.

October 2000: The USS Cole, docked at a port in Yemen, was attacked by suicide/homicide bombers, resulting in the death of 17 sailors and crippling the U.S. warship.

America's leadership refused to prepare for, or prevent, attacks on American soil between 1983 and September 11, 2001. The terrorists understood this and exploited it to their advantage. Approaching five years since the greatest terror attack in world history, our borders remain porous and the vast majority of cargo loaded into the bellies of our passenger aircrafts is never subjected to rigorous inspection. The terrorists know these vulnerabilities, and will exploit them to our extreme detriment.

Conclusion

The many occurrences of death and destruction leading up to 9-11 never resulted in an all-embracing American call to arms. The terror events always upset us, but not as much as necessary, and only for a few hours or days, and then it was back to business as usual. Perhaps these attacks against Americans did

---

[23] Ibid, p. 41.

not cut deeply enough because they happened outside of the continental United States. Maybe we did not mobilize because a few hundred dead Americans here and there have always been an accepted cost of doing business abroad. Most likely, it was a combination of both that kept Americans and their leaders in denial and complacency until September 11, 2001.

The 9-11 murders demonstrated that in order to rally Americans to fight a determined terrorist enemy such as Al Qaeda, thousands must die on American soil. The question today remains, "How many more Americans will die before citizens and their leaders truly get serious and focused about protecting our homeland?" How many of us must perish before partisan politics, cheap labor requirements, and the corporate bottom line give way to a national commitment to fight and win this War on Terror? **Though it disturbs me greatly to say this, my answer is a five-digit body count: 10,000 or more killed on U.S. soil in a single or several related terrorist attacks.**

I anxiously await America's long-range, strategic plan to combat the preaching of hatred within mosques and madrasas in our own country. Eradicating the hatred from future Muslim generations will take decades. If we cannot find a way to exterminate the hatred, we will never end the terror. The sooner we start, the sooner we can finish it.

I believe that the attacks of September 11 fueled new bureaucracies, fostered patriotic rhetoric from the floors of Congress, and moved us as a nation off dead center. Patriotism abounded for many months after the attacks. Old Glory flew everywhere, and Americans displayed their fighting spirit. Congress appeared to unite and put aside its partisan differences, if only for a brief period. I fear, though, that with each terror-free day that graces our homeland, we as a nation lapse further into complacency and denial. Complacency and denial at this point in time is so very dangerous to our survival. Don't think for a moment that the likes of Osama bin laden are not taking notice. The clock is ticking. There will be another horrific attack. And another one after that.

Complacency is not an option, and denial is deadly. So assume the responsibility. Adopt the creed:

If not me, then who? If not now, then when?

BRIEFING # 2

A Run Down on the Bad Guys

Terrorist Numbers And Organizations

Contrary to the picture often portrayed in today's media, the bulk of the global terror threat does not come from Al Qaeda per se, but from the numerous Al Qaeda-trained, funded and sponsored splinter groups active in every corner of the globe.[24]

Speaking at the 2nd International Anti-Terror Conference, author of the international bestseller, *Inside Al Qaeda: Global Network of Terror*, updated his audience with respect to the latest terror threat estimates.[25]

Dr. Gunaratna stated that from the onset of the global War on Terror (GWOT) to present, Al-Qaeda's hardcore rank and file has been reduced significantly to between 2,000 and 3,000 core members. Al Qaeda's numbers have been whittled down

---

[24] A few of the more infamous Al Qaeda subsets are the Abu Sayyaf Group (ASG) and Jemaah Islamiyah strong in the Philippines and Southeast Asia island nations of Indonesia, Singapore, and Malaysia.
[25] Rohan Gunaratna is the Chief Director, International Centre for Political Violence & Terrorism Research, Institute of Defence and Strategic Studies, Nanyang Technological University, Singapore. He is the author of 10 books and a recognized expert on global terror threats.

markedly as a result of kills and captures in Afghanistan, Iraq, Pakistan, the Russian Federation, the United States, Southeast Asia, and Europe. This is the good news. The bad news is that beginning with the Soviet-Afghan war in 1979 through present day, Al Qaeda and its precursor, the mujahedeen, trained more than 20,000 terrorists in camps all over the world – including camps within the United States.

More than 600 known, functional terrorist organizations exist internationally. The National Memorial Institute for the Prevention of Terrorism (MIPT) – a non-profit organization created after the Oklahoma City bombing and dedicated to the prevention of terrorism on U.S. soil – lists a good number of them on its website www.tkb.org. Comprehensive lists such as these are normally placed at the end of a book for the reader's reference. I include the list here in the text not because I expect my readers to spend time examining each name, but because I want them to page through and grasp the magnitude of global terror in the 21st century.

Group

21 June

23rd of September Communist League

28 May Armenian Organization

2nd of June Movement

313

Abdurajak Janjalani Brigade

Abkhazian Separatists

Abu Bakr al-Siddiq Fundamentalist Brigades

Abu Hafs al-Masri Brigade

Abu Nayaf al-Afgani

Abu Nidal Organization (ANO)

Abu Sayyaf Group (ASG)

Accolta Nazinuale Corsa

Achik National Volunteer Council

Actiefront Nationistisch Nederland

Action Committee of Winegrowers

Action Directe

Action Front for the Liberation of the Baltic Countries

Aden Abyan Islamic Army (AAIA)

Aden Islamic Army

Affiche Rouge

African National Congress (South Africa)

Ahmadiya Muslim Mission

Akhmed Avdorkhanov

Al-Ahwal Brigades

al-Ali bin Falah

al-Arifeen

al-Badr

al-Borkan Liberation Organization

al-Doman Tribe

al-Faran

al-Faruq Brigades

al-Fatahal-Gama'a al-Islamiyya (GAI)

al-Hadid

al-Haramayn Brigades

al-Huqban Operation Martyrs Group of the Islamic Resistance

al-Intiqami al-Pakistani

al-Ittihaad al-Islami (AIAI)

al-Jihad

al-Madina

al-Mansoorain

Al-Mansoorien

al-Nasireen

al-Nawaz

al-Qaeda

al-Qaeda in the Arabian Penninsula

al-Qanoon

al-Quds Brigades

al-Sadr Brigadesal-Saiqa

al-Umar Mujahedin

al-Zulfikar

Albanian National Army

Alejo Calatayu

Alex Boncayao Brigade (ABB)

Alianca Libertadora Nacional (ALN)

All Burma Students' Democratic Front (ABSDF)

All Tripura Tiger Force (ATTF)

Amal

Amazonian Indians

Ananda Marga

Anarchist Attack Teams

Anarchist Faction

Anarchist Faction for Subversion

Anarchist Liberation Brigade

Anarchist Street Patrol

Anarchist Struggle

Anarchists' Attack Group

Andres Castro United Front

Angry Brigade

Animal Liberation Front (ALF)

Ansar al-Din

Ansar al-Islam

Ansar al-Jihad

Ansar al-Sunnah

Ansar Allah

Anti-American Arab Liberation Front

Anti-Armenian Organization

Anti-Authority Erotic Cells

Anti-Castro Cubans

Anti-Communist Command

Anti-Establishment Nucleus

Anti-Imperialist Cell (AIZ)

Anti-Imperialist Group Liberty for Mumia Abu Jamal

Anti-Imperialist Patrols for Proletariat Internationalism

Anti-Imperialist Territorial Nuclei for the Construction of the Fighting Communist Party

Anti-Mainstream Self Determination Faction

Anti-Olympic Flame

Anti-Power Struggle

Anti-Racist Guerrilla Nuclei

Anti-State Action

Anti-State Defense

Anti-State Nuclei

Anti-Terrorist Liberation Group

Anti-Zionist Movement

Anticapitalist Attack Nuclei

Apo's Revenge Hawks

Apo's Youth Revenge Brigades

April 19 Movement

Aqsa Group

Arab Commando Cells

Arab Communist Organization (ACO)

Arab Communist Revolutionary PartyArab Fedayeen Cells

Arab Liberation Front (ALF)

Arab Nationalist Youth for the Liberation of Palestine (ANYLP)

Arab Revenge Organization

Arab Revolutionary Brigades

Arab Revolutionary Front

Arab Unionist Nationalist Organization

Arabian Peninsula Freemen

Argentine Anti-Communist Alliance

Armata Corsa

Armata di Liberazione Naziunale

Armed Commandos of Liberation

Armed Communist League

Armed Forces of National Liberation

Armed Forces of National Resistance

Armed Forces Revolutionary Council (AFRC)

Armed Islamic Group

Armed Revolutionary Action

Armed Revolutionary Left

Armenian Red Army

Armenian Resistance Group

Armenian Revolutionary Army

Armenian Revolutionary Federation (ARF)

Armenian Secret Army for the Liberation of Armenia (ASALA)

Army of God

Army of the Corsican People

Army of the Followers of Sunni Islam

Arnoldo Camu Command

August 23 Movement

Aum Shinri Kyo

Autonomia Sinistra Ante Parlamentare

Autonomous Cells

Autonomous Cells of Rebel Action

Autonomous Decorators

Autonomous Intervention Collective Against the Zionist Presence in France

Autonomous Revolutionary Activity

Awami activists

Azad Hind Sena

Baader-Meinhof Group

Badr Forces

Bagramyan Battalion

Baloch Liberation Army (BLA)

Bangladesh Nationalist Party

Bani Hilal Tribe

Basque Fatherland and Freedom

Bersatu

Birsa Commando Force (BCF)

Black and Red Brigades

Black Brigade

Black December

Black Friday

Black Hand

Black Lebanon

Black Liberation Army

Black Panthers

Black Revolutionary Assault Team

Black September

Black Star

Black Widows

BLT

Boere Aanvals Troepe (BAT)

Bolivarian Guerilla Movement

Bolivarian Liberation Forces (FBL)

Borok National Council of Tripura (BNCT)

Breton Liberation Army

Brigades for the Defense of Holy Shrines

Brigades of Imam al-Hassan al-Basri

Brigades of the Mujahidin in Iraq

Brigades of the Victorious Lion of God

Brother Julian

Burning Path

Cambodian Freedom Fighters (CFF)

Canadian Hungarian Freedom Fighters Federation

Canary Islands Independence Movement

Carapaica Revolutionary Movement

Caucasian Front for the Liberation of Abu Achikob

Cell for Internationalism

Chadian People's Revolutionary Movement

Chaotic Attack Front

Charles Martel Group

Che Guevara Brigade

Chechyen Separatists

Children of Fire

Chilean Committee for Disarmament and Denuclearization

Chilean Committee of Support for the Peruvian Revolution

Christians for Peace and National Salvation

Chukakuha

Cinchoneros Popular Liberation Movement

Civilian Home Defense Forces (CHDF)

Clandestini

Clandestini Corsi

Coalition of National Brigades

Coalition to Save the Preserves (CSP)

Comando Alejo Calatayud

Comando Jaramillista Morelense 23 de Mayo

Combatant Proletarian Nucleus

Comité Argentino de Lucha Anti-Imperialisto

Commando Anarchist Group

Commando Internacionalista Simon Bolivar

Committee for Liquidation of Computers

Committee for the Security of the Highways

Committee of Coordination

Communist Combatant Cells

Communist Metropolitan Front

Communist Party of Nepal - Maoist (CPN-M)

Communist Revolutionaries in Europe

Communist Workers Movement

Communists Liberation Faction

Conscientious Arsonists (CA)

Consciously Enraged

Continuing Struggle

Continuity Irish Republican Army (CIRA)

Contras

Cooperative of Hand-Made Fire & Related Items

Corsican Patriotic Front

Corsican People's Army

Corsican Revolutionary Armed Forces

Council of Organizations for the Development of People (CODEP)

Counterrevolutionary Solidarity (SC)

Croatian Freedom Fighters (CFF)

Dagestan Liberation Army

Dario Santillan Command

de Fes

December 20 Torrijist Patriotic Vanguard (VPT-20)

Democratic Front for the Liberation of Palestine (DFLP)

Democratic Karen Buddhist Association (DKBA)

DHKP-C

Divine Wrath Brigades

Doku Umarov

Dukhta-ran-e-Millat

Eagles of National Unity

Earth Liberation Front (ELF)

East Turkestan Liberation Organization

Ecuadorian Rebel Force

Egypt's Revolution

ELJM

Enraged Proletarians

EPA (Ejercito del Pueblo en Armas)

Eritrean Liberation Front (ELF)

Ethiopian People's Liberation Front

Ethiopian People's Revolutionary Army

Ethiopian People's Revolutionary Party

Ethnocacerista

Eva Peron Organization

Ey Al (Fighting Jewish Organization)

Farabundo Marti National Liberation Front

February 28 Popular Leagues

Fedayeen Khalq (People's Commandos)

Federation of Armenian Revolutionaries

Fighters for Freedom

Fighting Ecologist Activism

Fighting Guerillas of May

Fires of Hell

First of October Antifascist Resistance Group

Five C's

For a Revolutionary Perspective

Francs Tireurs (Mavericks)

Free Aceh Movement

Free Greeks

Free Papua Movement (OPM)

Free People of Galillee

Free South Moluccan Youth's

Free Vietnam Revolutionary Group

Freedom for Mumia Abu-Jamal

Frente de Liberacion Nacional del Vietnam del Sur

Friendship Society

Front for Defenders of Islam

Front for the Liberation of the Cabinda Enclave

Front for the Liberation of the French Somali Coast

Front of Justice and Revenge

Fronte di Liberazione Naziunale di a Corsica (FLNC)

GARI (Internationalist Revolutionary Armed Groups)

Gazteriak

Generation of Arab Fury

Global Intifada

God's Army

Gora Euskadi Askatata

Gracchus Babeuf

Greek Anti-Dictatorial Youth (EAN)

Greek Anti-Regime Movement LAOS-11

Greek Bulgarian Armenian Front

Greek People

Green Brigades

Green Cells

Group Bakunin Gdansk Paris Guatemala Salvador

Group for Social Resistance to the State Mechanism

Group of Carlo Giuliani

Group of Guerilla Combatants ofJose Maria Morelos

Group of the Martyrs Mostafa Sadeki and Ali Zadeh

Group Revolutionary Reconstruction

Groups of Internationalist Communist

Guardsmen of Islam

Guatemalan National Revolutionary Unity (URNG)

Guerrilla Army of the Poor

Guevarist Revolutionary Army

Hamas

Harakat al-Shuhada'a al-Islamiyah

Harakat ul-Mudjahidin (HuM)

Harkat ul-Mujahideen al-Almi

Harkat-ul-Ansar

Hawks of Thrace

Hector Riobe Brigade

Heroes of Palestine

Hezbollah

Hikmatul Zihad

Hindu Sena Rashtriya Sangh Party

Hisba

Hizb-I-Islami

Hizbul Mujahadin

Hizbul Mujahideen (HM)

Holger Meins Kommando

Hotaru (Firefly)

HPG

HUGI & Asif Raza Commandos

Iduwini Youths

Immediate Action

Independent Armed Revolutionary Movement (MIRA)

Independent Kashmir

Indian Intelligence

Indigenous People's Federal Army (IPFA)

Indomitable Marxists

Informal Anarchist Federation

International Communist Group

International Justice Group (Gama'a al-Adela al-Alamiya)

International Revolutionary Struggle

International Solidarity

Internet Black Tigers (Tamils)

Iraqi Democratic Front

Iraqi Legitimate Resistance

Iraqi Revenge Brigades

Irish National Liberation Army (INLA)

Irish Republican Army (IRA)

Irish Republicans

ISI

Islam Chhatra Shibir (ICS)

Islamic Action in Iraq

Islamic Action Organization

Islamic Army in Iraq

Islamic Brotherhood

Islamic Defense Force

Islamic Front for the Liberation of Palestine (IFLP)

Islamic Golden Army

Islamic Great Eastern Raiders Front

Islamic Jihad Brigades

Islamic Jihad in Palestine

Islamic Jihad Jerusalem

Islamic Jihad of Palestine

Islamic Liberation Organization

Islamic Militants

Islamic Movement for Change

Islamic Movement of Holy Warriors

Islamic Movement of Iraqi Mujahideen

Islamic Movement of Uzbekistan (IMU)

Islamic Party of Egypt

Islamic Radicals

Islamic Renewal Movement

Islamic Resistance Brigades

Islamic Salvation Front

Islamic separatists

Islamic Shashantantra Andolon (ISA)

Islamic Society

Israeli Arab Islamic Movement

Jaime Bateman Cayon Group

Jaish-e-Mohammad (JEM)

Jaish-ul-Muslimin

Jamiat ul-Mujahidin (JuM)

Jammu and Kashmir Islamic Front

Janshakti

Japanese Red Army (JRA)

Jaysh Ansar al-Sunnah

JeM & SIMI

Jemaah Islamiyah (JI)

Jenin Martyrs' Brigade

Jewish boys

Jewish Defense League (JDL)

Jewish Settlers

Jihad Brigades

Jihad Committee

Jordanian Free Officers Movement

Jordanian Islamic Resistance

Jordanian National Liberation MovementJordanian Revolutionary and Military Committee (MOUAB)

Julio Guerra, Southern Operation

July 20th Brigade

June 16 Organization

Justice Army of the Defenseless People

Justice Commandos for the Armenian Genocide

Kabataang Makabayan (KM)

Kach

Kachin Independence Army (KIA)

Kahane Chai

Kakurokyo

Karbala Brigades

Karen National Union

Kayin National Union (KNU)

Kenkoku Giyugun Chosen Seibatsutai

Kenkokugiyudan Betsudotai Kokuzokseibatsutai

Khaibar Brigades

Khmer Rouge

Knights of the Torched Bank

Komando Jihad (Indonesian)

Kosovo Liberation Army (KLA)

Krause Group

Kuki Liberation Arm (KLA)

Kurdish Islamic Unity Party

Kurdish Patriotic Union

Kurdistan Freedom Hawks

Kurdistan National Liberation Front (ERNK)

Kurdistan National Union

Kurdistan Workers' Party

Laiki Antistasi

Laks

Lashkar-e-Jabbar (LeJ)

Lashkar-e-Jhangvi (LeJ)

Lashkar-e-Taiba (LeT)

Lashkar-I-Omar

Latin American Patriotic Army

Lautaro Youth Movement

Lebanese Arab Youth

Lebanese Armed Revolutionary Faction

Lebanese Liberation Front

Lebanese National Resistance Front

Lebanese Revolutionary Socialist Movement

Lebanese Socialist Revolutionary Organization

Leftist Nucleus

Liberating Communist Faction

Liberation Army Fifth Battalion

Liberation Battalion

Liberation Front of Quebec

Liberation Party

Liberation Tigers of Tamil Eelam (LTTE)

Liberia Peace Council

Lord's Resistance Army (LRA)

Loyalist Volunteer Force (LVF)

Loyalists

M-5Macedonia Dawn

Macedonian Revolutionary Organization (VMRO)

Macheteros

Mahdi Army

Mahir Cayan Suicide Group

Mano Blanca

Manuel Rodriguez Patriotic Front

Maoist Communist Center (MCC)

Maras Salvatruchas

Martyr Abu-Ali Mustafa Brigades

Martyrs of Baalbek

Maruseido (Marxist Youth League)

Masada, Action and Defense Movement

Maximiliano Gomez Revolutionary Brigade

May 15

May 15 Organization for the Liberation of Palestine

May 98

Meinhof-Puig-Antich Group

Melting Nuclei

Midnight Saboteurs

Military Liberation Front of Colombia

MLKP

Mohammed's Army

Montoneros

Moraza Nist Front for the Liberation of Honduras (FMLH)

Morazanist Patriotic Front (FPM)

Moro Islamic Liberation Front (MILF)

Moro National Liberation Front

Moro National Liberation Front (MNLF)

Moslem Commandos

Moslem International Guerrillas

Movement Against State Arbitrariness

Movement for Democracy and Development (MDD)

Movement for Democracy and Justice in Chad (MDJT)

Movement for the Struggle of the Jordanian Islamic Resistance

Movement of Islamic Action of Iraq

Movement of the Revolutionary Left

Movement of Youthward Brothers in War of the Palestinian People

Movimiento Armado Nacionalista Organizacion (MANO)

Movimiento Peronista

Movsar Baryayev Gang

Mozambique National Resistance Movement

MR-8 (Revolutionary Movement of the 8th)

Mujaheddin Army

Mujaheddin in Iraq

Mujaheddin Kompak

Mujahedeen Message

Mujahedin Al-Mansooran

Mujahedin-e-Khalq (MeK)

Mujahideen of the People

Mujahideen Without Borders

Mujahidin Division Khandaq

Muslim United Army

Muslims Against Global Oppression (MAGO)

Muttahida Qami Movement (MQM)

NADK

Narita Airport expansion opposition

National Army for the Liberation of Uganda (NALU)

National Democratic Front of Bodoland (NDFB)

National Front (Greece)

National Front for the Liberation of Angola (FNLA)

National Front for the Liberation of Egypt

National Front for the Liberation of Kurdistan

National Front for the Salvation of Libya

National Kurdish Revenge Teams

National Liberation Army (Bolivia)

National Liberation Army (Colombia)

National Liberation Front of Tripura (NLFT)

National Liberation Union

National Organization of Arab Youth

National Patriotic Front of Liberia (NPFL)

National Resistance Front

National Revolutionary Command (Omar al-Mukhtar)

National Warriors

National Youth Resistance Organization

Nationalist Group for the Liberation of Palestine

Nationalist Intervention Group

Nationalist Kurdish Revenge Teams

Naxalites

Neo-Nazis (Germany)

Nestor Paz Zamora Commission

New Armenian Resistance (NAR)

New People's Army (NPA)

New Revolutionary Alternative

New Revolutionary Popular Struggle

Night Avengers

Nihilists Faction

Ninth of June Organization

Norwegian National-Socialist (Nazi) Front

November 10 (Bolivia)

November 25 Anarchist Group

November's Children

Nuclei Armati Comunista

Nuclei Communist Combattants

Nuclei for Promoting Total Catastrophe

Nusantara Islamic Jihad Forces

Odua Peoples' Congress

OKE

Omar Torrijos Commando for

Latin American Dignity

ONLF

OPR-33

Orange Volunteers (OV)

Organization for Victims of Zionist Occupation

Organization of the Oppressed on Earth

Organization of the Sons of Occupied Territories

Organization of Victims of Occupied Territories

Orly Organization

Oromo Liberation Front (OLF)

Osama bin-Ladin

Other Group

Overthrown Anarchist Faction

Padanian Armed Separatist Phalanx

Palestine Liberation Front

Palestine Liberation Organization (PLO)

Palestinian Islamic Jihad (PIJ)

Palestinian Popular Struggle Front (PSF)

Palestinian Resistance

Palestinian Revolution Forces General Command

Pan-Turkish Organization

Partisans of Holy War

Partisans of the Iranian People of Hormuzgan

Patriotic Resistance Army (ERP)

Patriotic Union of Kurdistan (PUK)

Pattani United Liberation Organization (PULO)

Peace Conquerors

Pedro Leon Arboleda Movement

People Against Gansterism And Drugs (PAGAD)

People's Command

People's Defense Forces

People's Fighters Group

People's Liberation Army of Kurdistan

People's Liberation Forces (El Salvador)

People's Liberation Front (JVP)

People's Revolutionary Armed Forces (FRAP)

People's Revolutionary Army (Argentina)

People's Revolutionary Army (Colombia)

People's Revolutionary Front

People's Revolutionary Militias

People's Revolutionary Organization

People's Revolutionary Party (PRP)

People's Strugglers

People's War Group (PWG)

Peronist Armed Forces

Peykar

PKK/KONGRA-GEL

PLO Dissidents

Polisario Front

Polish Revolutionary Home Army

Popular Army of National Liberation

Popular Forces of April 25

Popular Front for the Liberation of Palestine (PFLP)

Popular Front for the Liberation of Palestine -- General Command (PFLP-GC)

Popular Justice

Popular Liberation Army

Popular Movement for the Liberation of Angola

Popular Resistance

Popular Resistance Committees

Popular Revolutionary Action

Popular Revolutionary Front

Popular Revolutionary Resistance Group

Popular Revolutionary Vanguard

Popular Self-Defense Forces (FAP)

Proletarian Action Group

Proletarian Combatant Groups

Proletarian Nuclei for Communism

Proletarian Reprisals

Proletarian Resistance

Proletarian Revolutionary Action

Front (FRAP)

Proletarian Solidarity

Protesting Miners

Pueblo Reagrupado

Puerto Rican Resistance Movement

Purbo Banglar Communist Party (PBCP)

Qaeda al-Jihad

Rappani Khalilov

Raul Sendic International Brigade

Real Irish Republican Army (RIRA)

Rebel Armed Forces

Recontra 380

Red Army Faction

Red Brigades

Red Daughters of Rage

Red Guerrillas

Red Hand Defenders (RHD)

Red Line

Regional Intendancy of the Sixth Region

Republic of New Africa

Research and Analysis Wing (RAW)

Resistance, Liberation and Independence Organization (AAA)

Resistenza Corsa

Revolution of the 1920s Brigade

Revolutionary Action Organization of the Arab Resistance Front

Revolutionary Action Party

Revolutionary Arab Youth Organization

Revolutionary Armed Corps

Revolutionary Armed Forces of Colombia

Revolutionary Armed Forces of the People

Revolutionary Army

Revolutionary Army of the People

Revolutionary Autonomous Group

Revolutionary Bolivariano Movement 200

Revolutionary Brigades

Revolutionary Cells Animal Liberation Brigade

Revolutionary Commandos of Solidarity

Revolutionary Eelam Organization (EROS)

Revolutionary Force Seven

Revolutionary Front for Communism

Revolutionary Front for Proletarian Action

Revolutionary Leninist Brigades

Revolutionary Liberation Action

Revolutionary Memory

Revolutionary Nuclei

Revolutionary Offensive Cells

Revolutionary Organization 17 November (RO-N17)

Revolutionary Organization of Socialist Muslims

Revolutionary Outburst Movement

Revolutionary People's Front

Revolutionary People's Struggle

Revolutionary Perspective

Revolutionary Popular Resistance Organization

Revolutionary Proletarian Initiative Nuclei

Revolutionary Proletarian Nucleus

Revolutionary Socialists

Revolutionary Solidarity

Revolutionary Struggle

Revolutionary Subversive Faction-Commando Unibomber

Revolutionary Torch-Bearing Run

Revolutionary United Front (RUF)

Revolutionary United Front Movement

Revolutionary Vanguard

Revolutionary Violence Group (RVG)

Revolutionary Worker Clandestine Union of the People Party

Revolutionary Youth of Ecuador

Rigas Fereos

Right Wing Extremists

Riyad us-Saliheyn Martyrs' Brigade

Roque Dalton Commando

Russian National Unity

Saif-ul-Muslimeen

Salafia Jihadia

Salafist Group for Preaching and Combat (GSPC)

Salah al-Din Battalions

Sandinistas

Saraya al-Shuhuada al-jihadiyah fi al-Iraq

Saraya Usud al-Tawhid

Sardinian Autonomy Movement (MAS)

Save Kashmir Movement

Secret Army Organization

Secret Organization Zero

Sekihotai

Self-Defense Groups of Cordoba and Uraba

September-France

Seventh Suicide Squad

Shahin (Falcon)

Shamil Basayev

Shining Path

Shurafa al-Urdun

Sihala Urumaya

SIMI

Simon Bolivar Anti-Imperialist Commando

Simon Bolivar Guerilla Coordinating Board (CGSB)

Sinhalese Janatha Vimukthi Peramuna (JVP)

SKIF

Social Resistance

Socialist-Nationalist Front (SNF)

Societa Editoriale Sarda

Solidarity for Political Prisoners

Solidarity Gas Canisters

Solidarity with 17N

Sons of the South

South Maluku Republic

South Moluccan Suicide Commando

South-West Africa People's Organization (SWAPO)

Southern California IRA

Southern Sudan Independence Movement (SSIM)

Sovereign Panama Front (FPS)

Spanish Basque Battalion

Spanish National Action

SPLM/A

Sri Nakharo

Sudan People's Liberation Army

Support and Jihad in Syria and Lebanon

Supporters of Horst Ludwig Meyer

Sword of Islam

Syrian Mujaheddin

Syrian Social Nationalist Party

Takfir wa Hijra

Taliban

Tanzim

Tanzim Qa'idat Al-Jihad fi Bilad al-Rafidayn

Tawhid and Jihad

Terra Lliure (TL)

Territorial Anti-Imperialist Nucleus

The Committee for Promotion of Intransigence

The Extraditables

The Holders of the Black Banners

The Inevitables

Third of October Group

Tibetan independence forces

Tigers

Tigray Peoples Liberation Front (TPLF)

TKEP/L

TKP/ML-TIKKO

Tontons Macoutes

Torrid Winter

Totally Anti-War Group

Tupac Amaru Revolutionary Movement

Tupac Katari Guerrilla Army (EGTK)

Tupamaro Revolutionary Movement - January 23

Tupamaros

Turkish Communist Party/ Marxist (TKP-ML)

Turkish Islamic Jihad

Turkish National Intelligence Organization

Turkish People's Liberation Army (TPLA)

Turkish People's Liberation Front (TPLF) (THKP-C)

Turkish Revolutionaries

Turkish Worker Peasant Liberation (TIKKO)

Uganda Democratic Christian Army (UDCA)

Ukrainian Reactionary Force

Ulster Defence Association/ Ulster Freedom Fighters

Ulster Volunteer Force (UVF)

Ummah Liberation Army

Uncontrolled Rage

Underground Government of the Free Democratic People of Laos

Unified Unit of Jihad

Union of Peaceful Citizens of Algeria

Union of Young Kurdish Revolutionaries

UNITA

United Anti-Reelection Command

United Arab Revolution

United Freedom Front (UFF)

United Kuki Liberation Front (UKLF)

United Liberation Front of Assam (ULFA)

United Nasirite Organizaiton

United Organization of Halabjah Martyrs

United People's Democratic Solidarity (UPDS)

United Popular Action Movement

United Popular Liberation Army of America

United Revolutionary Front

United Self-Defense Forces of Venezuela

United Self-Defense Forces/ Group of Colombia

United Tajik Opposition (UTO)

Unknown Group

Uygur Holy War Organization

VAR-Palmares

Venceremos

Vigorous Burmese Student Warriors

Vitalunismo

Waffen SS

Weather Underground Organization (WUO)

Weathermen

West Nile Bank Front (WNBF)

White Legion

Workers' Revolutionary Party

World Islamic Jihad Group

World Punishment Organization

World United Formosans for Independence

Yanikian Commandos

Young Cubans

Youth Action Group

Yunadi Turchayev

Zarate Willka Armed Forces of Liberation

Zero Point - People's Revolutionary Army

Zimbabwe African Nationalist Union (ZANU)

Zionist Action Group

Zoni Revolutionary Army (ZRA)

The MIPT Terrorism Knowledge Base, from which this list was extracted verbatim, is funded through the Department of Homeland Security's Office for State and Local Government Coordination and Preparedness (OSLGCP). The MIPT reports that between January 1968 and April 2005, these terrorist groups were responsible for 21,444 incidents, resulting in 71,626 injuries and 28,192 deaths.[26] During this same time period, 582 terror events occurred in North America, generating 1,835 injuries and 3,573 deaths. To think for a moment that the United States and its coalition partners possess the manpower and resources required to hunt down and eradicate all of the leaders and members belonging to more than 600 terrorist organizations worldwide is unrealistic at best.

Our twenty-first century war with global terrorists and insurgents, such as within Iraq and Afghanistan, cannot be won by destroying, killing and capturing. As long as the terrorist's cause lives, more warriors will follow in the footsteps of those removed from the fight. These wars can only be won by eradicating the causes around which the terrorists and insurgents rally, recruit, fight, and are willing to die. If we cannot kill the cause, we cannot win

---

[26] http://www.tkb.org/IncidentGroupModule.jsp.

the war. A correlation can be made between America's War on Terror and its war on drugs. We have been fighting the war on drugs for decades. We are no closer to winning it today than we were thirty years ago. Why? Because even though arresting and incarcerating dealers and users helps, we have yet to figure out a successful way to quell the demand. Until we can eliminate Americans' desire for illegal substances, we will never stand a chance of eradicating drug abuse. So it is with the global War on Terror; we have to figure out a way to stem the causes that fuel terror before we can begin to successfully eliminate it.

The Terrorist Targets of Choice

The primary targets that terrorists attack on a worldwide basis are listed below.[27] Note the 303 educational institutions on the list:

TARGET	Incidents
Abortion Related	5
Airports & Airlines	804
Business	3228
Diplomatic	2613
Educational Institutions	303
Food or Water Supply	9
Government	3057
Journalists & Media	461
Maritime	135
Military	792
NGO	282
Other	1410
Police	1198
Private Citizens & Property	3698
Religious Figures/Institutions	718
Telecommunication	111
Terrorists	213
Tourists	236
Transportation	862
Unknown	647
Utilities	652

What are the Primary Terror Tactics Employed?

Terrorists employ a wide variety of effective tactics:[28]

TACTIC	Incidents
Armed Attack	4657
Arson	603
Assassination	2132
198	198
Bombing	11555
Hijacking	234
Kidnapping	1661
Other	121
Unconventional Attack	55
Unknown	228

Terrorists overwhelmingly choose bombings as their tactic of choice: 11,555 of them in the past 36 years. Bombs can and have been creatively planted in a myriad of effective locations: cars, dumpsters, lunch boxes, shopping bags, under suicide bombers' clothing, toys, fire extinguishers, and even in watermelons. Bombs can be exploded at a time and choosing of the killer. Many bombs, such as those planted in parked cars, require no self-sacrifices, as they can be detonated remotely. Improvised explosive devices (IEDs) in Iraq continue to exact a toll in military and civilian lives and limbs, as well as inflicting severe psychological stress upon an Iraqi populace day-to-day.

This Enemy is Completely Ruthless

Terrorists exhibit some of the most abhorrent and revolting behavior ever witnessed. The notorious leader of the "Al Qaeda of the Two Rivers" in Iraq – Abu Musab al-Zarqawi – personally severed the heads of his kidnapped victims with a knife, filmed

---

[27] Ibid.
[28] Ibid.

the atrocity, posted the video on websites, and provided video to Middle Eastern television stations such as Al Jazeera.

In his book *Terror at Beslan*,[29] author John Giduck describes the brutal methods employed by some of these ruthless warriors. According to Giduck's report, the children held captive inside Russia's Beslan Middle School No. 1 for three days beginning September 1, 2004, were denied food, water and medical supplies by their captors. They were made to defecate and urinate where they stood or sat. The heat was so grueling inside the besieged school that the adult and child captives were forced to drink their own urine to keep minimally hydrated. Women and young girls were repeatedly raped. The few captive mothers whom the terrorists released were forced to choose which of their own children they wished to take with them, having to leave one or more of their offspring behind with those held hostage. Many of the children that mothers were forced to abandon in that Beslan school gymnasium perished in explosions and an ensuing inferno.

Giduck describes how the Chechen Muslim extremists abuse their Russian prisoners. John possesses copies of video made by the Chechens while they "gleefully tortured their captives."[30] I have seen these films. They are horrific. Some of the footage shows the "hapless victims being shot in different parts of their bodies, and then asked how it feels. . . others are made to hold their fingers out so that a gun can be put to them and the fingers shot off one by one. Most gruesome of all on the video, a Chechen places a knife to the captive's neck, pushes it in, and slowly saws the head off while the condemned gurgles on his own blood . . . ."[31] A severed head is even given to the children of the murderers to use as a soccer ball.

---

[29] Giduck, John. *Terror at Beslan – A Russian Tragedy With Lessons for American Schools* (Denver, Colorado Archangel Group, 2005). To this author's knowledge, his is the only eyewitness, accurate account of the school siege and massacre published to date. John Giduck was personally in Beslan on three occasions and spoke to the Russian Special Forces officers who engaged in close combat with the terrorists.

[30] Ibid, pages 266-267.

[31] Ibid.

This brand of inhumanity is extremely difficult for most Americans to comprehend. Driven by religious fanaticism and rarely demonstrating any mercy, pity or remorse, the most vicious of our terrorist enemies would do these same things to you, me, or our children if given the opportunity.

Islamist terrorists ironically murder more of their fellow Muslims than Christians or Jews, as anyone in the way becomes fair game. Michael Scheuer in his book *Through Our Enemies Eyes*,[32] says that "after the heavy casualties caused by the August 1998 attacks in Africa on U.S. embassies in Nairobi and Dar es Salaam, some Western and Islamic media commentators speculated that bin Laden would be deterred from similar attacks because of the large number of non-U.S. citizens, including African Muslims, killed or wounded in the attacks." NOT SO.

Osama bin Laden was interviewed in December 1998 by Pakistani journalist Rahimullah Yusufzai for ABC News. While discussing al Qaeda's attacks upon the U.S. embassies in Kenya and Tanzania, Yusufzai asked bin Laden, "If the targets of jihad are Americans, how can the death of so many Africans be justified?"[33] Osama bin Laden answered that deaths of these sorts, regrettable as they were, were unavoidable and "religiously permissible."[34]

The beasts who sever heads and offer them to their own children for soccer can only be effectively dealt with in one of two ways. They must be killed or captured. The reason is clear. With rare exception, any man or woman who is mentally and spiritually able to viciously and inhumanely kill innocents is too far gone to be redeemed. They must be neutralized, or they will kill again and again. Killing and capturing will not win the War on Terror,

---

[32] Scheuer, Michael. *Through Our Enemies Eyes* (Washington, D.C.: Brassey's Inc., 2003), p. 57.
[33] Ibid.
[34] Ibid.

but it will ensure that killers are taken out of the fight at every opportunity. One less killer is one or more fewer killed.

Our terrorist enemies view extended negotiations, concessions, sympathy, or any humanity afforded to them as signs of our Western weakness and lack of commitment to the fight. Each and every time a member of Congress complains publicly about the treatment of terrorists at U.S.-controlled facilities, you can score one for the bad guys, as it is yet another sign of the infighting and partisan selfishness among American congressional leaders. Each time military leaders fail to maintain good order and discipline among their subordinates, such as at Abu Ghraib prison in Iraq, score another one for the bad guys. It becomes a propaganda tool to be used for recruiting and turning more Muslims against us.

In June of 2005, a member of Congress demonstrated his inexcusable and utter ignorance on camera by comparing the U.S. treatment of prisoners at Camp Delta, Guantanamo Bay (Gitmo), Cuba, to the murder of six million Jews by the Nazis during World War II. If I was an Al Qaeda recruiter, I would have sent this "gentleman" a campaign donation and a note saying "thanks for making my job so much easier." When one compares U.S. treatment of prisoners to genocide of the Jews at the hands of Hitler, there can be no misspeak. There is no misinterpretation. A member of Congress aiding and abetting the enemy is shameful and inexcusable, and if the voters from the state that elected that unpardonable politician do not find a way to take him out of office for his reprehensible statements, then they share the shame and the blame along with him.

Ours is an open society, where pundits on TV and radio are quick to point out America's vulnerabilities and weaknesses on a daily basis. Terrorist leaders are avid television watchers, and they understand that one of the most exploitable weaknesses of our American society is, and will always be, our commitment to the free speech of all citizens. They use our free speech against us at every juncture. Prominent members of Congress who belittle the U.S. military in front of the television cameras provide more fuel for the enemy propaganda machines. Enemy resolve is fortified. More terror rank and file are recruited. Further attacks against our service men and women and innocent civilians are planned and executed.

Conclusions

Americans find it difficult to comprehend why the world cannot see things their way. We are most hesitant to recognize what other societies and cultures consider to be our damnable faults. We need to become much more aware of how we appear to others. To tens of thousands of Muslims raised in strict, fundamental Islamic settings, America – the "Great Satan" – is perceived as morally bankrupt, world dominating, arrogant, and insensitive. Though we Americans may not perceive ourselves as such, if others view us in this manner, then for all intents and purposes, we are just that. To ignore or denounce others' assessments of us offers no positive contribution at all. Perception becomes truth. Perception can be more powerful than truth. Once engrained, it is difficult to dislodge.

We must put forth greater efforts to learn about the world outside of the United States. Though other cultures, religions, and laws may be strange and questionable to us, we should endeavor to understand and respect them for what they are – other human beings' ways of life. America cannot single-handedly change the world. The world will change itself when it is ready. It may or may not ask for America's help at some point in its metamorphosis.

Complacency is not an option, and denial is deadly. So assume the responsibility. Adopt the creed:

If not me, then who? If not now, then when?

Know the Enemy: Think As He Does

The ancient Chinese philosopher Sun Tzu (circa 500 BC) remains one of the most respected military strategists in history. His teachings, titled *Art of War*, are held sacrosanct by adept soldiers and politicians to this day.

One of Sun Tzu's most profound maxims says that if we know the enemy and know ourselves, we need not fear the results of a hundred battles. We are all citizen soldiers in the War on Terror. We need to know our terrorist enemies and understand the world and the war from their perspectives. This briefing examines the terror leaders, and what I have come to recognize as their view of the United States and its exploitable vulnerabilities. I use Al Qaeda and Osama bin Laden as the textbook example of the terror mind.

Terrorist Leaders Are Educated Men

The misguided, easily manipulated terror rank and file who willingly strap bombs to their bodies and blow themselves up may not be the smartest members of their organizations. The real masterminds of terror, however, are generally intelligent, rational, well-educated men. The academic and professional credentials of many of Al Qaeda's leading members are fairly respectable:[35]

- Osama bin Laden: student of economics, construction engineering experience, voracious reader; extensive use of automation to include a data management team that travels with him, surrounds himself with well-educated men who are degreed and experienced in: science, medicine, teaching, engineering, computer sciences.

- Aiman al-Zawahiri, Egyptian Islamic Jihad (EIJ) leader and Al Qaida's number 2 man: medical doctor.

- Mustafa Hamza, commander of assassins for Al Qaeda: agricultural engineer.

- The late Abu Ubaydah al-Banshiri, aid to Al Qaeda number 2 man Aiman al- Zawahiri, captured Mamdouh Mahmoud Salim, a principal Al Qaeda delegate from Iraq and the late Mohammed Atef, Al Qaeda's emir and military commander: professional military or security officers. Salim is also an electrical engineer.

- Khalid al-Fawwaz, managed British and other foreign bank accounts for bin Laden: civil engineer.

- Abu Khaba al-Masri, Al Qaeda's explosives and chemical biological warfare expert (CBW): chemical engineer.

- Wadi El-Hage, one of bin Laden's chief operatives in Somalia in the 1990s: urban planner.

- Ramzi Yousef, Al Qaeda's chief bomb make in the 1990s: computer science professional.

---

[35] Scheuer, Michael. *Through Our Enemies Eyes* (Washington, D.C.: Brassey's Inc., 2003), pp. 72-73.

- Mohammed Jamal Khalifah, held and managed bank accounts for Osama bin laden in Dubai: successful international businessman and operator of non-governmental organizations (NGOs).

Terrorists are Adept Asymmetric Warriors

The ultimate in disposing one's troops is to be without ascertainable shape. Then the most penetrating spies cannot pry in nor can the wise lay plans against you.[36]
Sun Tzu

Terrorists know that they could never survive a conventional confrontation with U.S. forces on the open battlefield. Twenty-first century conventional, or "symmetric" warfare, is ruled by: night fighting, laser guided smart bombs, carrier battle groups, air superiority, advanced supply and logistics, integrated command, control, computer systems, reconnaissance and surveillance from space, and much more. Symmetric warfare is characterized by lines and shapes on battle maps that designate assembly areas, avenues of approach, axes of advance, enemy lines, friendly lines, rear areas, no fly and weapons free zones. It involves the assembly, movement, and commitment to battle of great numbers of warriors. Much of symmetric warfare is predictable, such as when the blue forces attacks here, the red forces will likely counter attack there. War fighting capabilities such as these can only be provided and sustained to large, massed fighting forces by their nation-states, and terrorists have no nation-states.

Unconventional, "asymmetric" warfare is none of these things. It is non-linear, and not predictable. There are no defined battle lines; where, when, and how the asymmetric enemy strikes is rarely known and extremely difficult to predict without timely, accurate human intelligence. The asymmetric warrior strikes

---

[36] Tzu, Sun. *Art of War* (Translated by Ralph D. Sawyer. Compact Disk. Recorded Books, LLC. New York, New York: Recorded Books, LLC., 2003).

unexpectedly and with devastating effect, inflicting shock and psychological trauma.

Asymmetric enemies blend easily into their surroundings. Travel to any major city on the globe and observe as people go about their daily business. There is no way to ascertain who among them are terrorists or terror supporters. There are no uniforms, no formations, no battle lines, and no outward signs of hostility. The enemy reveals itself only at a time and place of its choosing, and then strikes yet again with another improvised explosive device, car bomb or hostage grab.

Terrorists are not officially representing or fighting for any legitimate nation-state. One might call them rebels with a cause, but no country. As such, they have never agreed to international rules of war, conventions, treaties, or pacts such as the Geneva Conventions. Their treatment of the kidnapped, wounded, and imprisoned is open-ended. The asymmetric terrorist follows no rules. He makes up his own as he goes along.

Terrorists need not wait years for political approval, funding, acquisition, testing, certification, and procurement of arms and equipment. The bad guys can buy the latest and greatest Commercial Off-The-Shelf (COTS) technology and weapons from the global black markets today and pay cash money for all of it; asymmetric funding and acquisition.

Terrorist units that support or perpetrate attacks are not composed of rigid, garrison-based platoons, companies, battalions, and brigades made up of thousands of fighters. They are small operational cells that can consist of as few as two or three persons. The most clandestine of these cells are the "sleeper cells." Sleeper cells maintain low profiles, and blend into their surroundings. They endeavor to remain invisible to authorities, supporting terrorist activities or, when the time is right, launching their attacks. It easiest for them to assimilate into huge urban populations.

The hodgepodge of ethnicity within melting pots like New York, Chicago, and Los Angeles provides ideal surroundings for anonymity.

Small terror cells have no need for scores of supply and logistics professionals to procure, secure, ship, and distribute tons of food, clothing, and fuel for them. When our asymmetric adversaries get hungry, they can call out for pizza or walk down to the local sandwich shop. If they need clothes, they can drive to the nearest shopping mall, and when they are low on gas, all they need to do is drive into the nearest service station.

Cell members are instructed that when in Rome, they are to do like the Romans. Holed up in a city like Riyadh, Saudi Arabia, they may very well grow traditional Muslim beards, wear the native Arab garb, and comply with the strict Islamic laws. Residing in Boston, Massachusetts, on the other hand, they might shave their beards, frequent bars and nightclubs, drink alcohol and smoke publicly, and establish relationships with the neighborhood women. If they are going to be in one location for an extended period of time, they procure employment, and are good employees. They are careful to comply with local laws and converse in a courteous, polite manner. They draw no attention to themselves. They stay out of trouble, careful to avoid even a single traffic ticket.

Asymmetry affords terror organizations like Al Qaeda global freedom of movement and rapid decision-making. It enables them to remain flexible, changing and adapting real time as the operational situations dictate. Asymmetry affords a capability to completely decentralize worldwide attack planning and execution down to the lowest possible levels. Terror attacks may occur in days, months, or even years from when they are first conceived. Our enemies are content to wait for what they perceive to be the ideal time and circumstances to carry out their strikes. They want the biggest bang achievable: maximum death and destruction, psychological shock effect, and plenty of extended media coverage.

Terrorists are in this fight for life – literally until it kills or jails them. Remember that Al Qaeda waited more than eight years from the first World Trade Center bombing in 1993 until their successful execution of the 9-11 attack that finally got the job done: almost a decade of planning and waiting. Their patience, operational security, and sleeper cells got the job done.

Terrorist Leaders Are Not Crazy. They Are Committed. They Remain Ruthless

I speak to government and industry gatherings regularly. Based upon discussions I have with attendees, I have the notion that many hold erroneous impressions about Osama bin Laden and infamous men like him. They sense bin Laden to be an irrational, even insane killer, lacking normal mental functions, and perhaps even completely out of control. This is a total, and dangerous, misperception.

Osama bin Laden is not a madman; he is not crazy. Those who know him describe him as a devout Muslim, sound family man, articulate, educated, well read, a brave warrior, and natural leader of men. Osama bin Laden is, however, reported to have two faces: a public one which is displayed to his followers and the world media as pious, devout, gentle, and patient; and a very different, private, and genuine one, shared only within Al Qaeda inner circles. Doctor Rohan Gunaratna – leading expert on Al Qaeda - personally interviewed some of bin Laden's followers. They told him that "openly, he (bin Laden) is kind, compassionate, and evinces his love for all Muslims, whereas in private he is utterly ruthless, single-minded, never doubting that what he wants to happen will become a reality."[37]

---

[37] Gunaratna, Rohan Inside Al Qaeda: Global Network of Terror (New York, New York: Berkley Books, 2003), p.55.

The Osama bin Ladens of the terror underworld are driven and vicious. Right, wrong, or indifferent, they fervently believe - or successfully convey the belief - that the terror they perpetrate is in accordance with the will of their creator – Allah.

Osama bin Laden is as cunning as he is charismatic. His ability to rally support in the names of Allah and Islam is clearly proven. I suspect, however, that with such men as Osama bin Laden, the cause for which they fight is more about personal egos, agendas, and power than it is about religion. They strive to keep their followers convinced that all is for Allah. As long as they perpetrate the belief, whether they themselves truly embrace it or not, men will continue go to their deaths carrying out their orders.

The Osama bin Ladens of the world are ideologically opposed to American values such as religious tolerance and individual freedom of choice. They more vehemently combat what they believe to be the unacceptable American meddling into Muslim affairs, subsequent occupation of Muslim nations such as Saudi Arabia and Iraq, and collusion with Middle East monarchies, justified by America's need for oil. The bin Ladens are not senseless or foolish. They are fanatical and extreme, and view the world from a dangerously different perspective. In order to be victorious, they have no choice but to be the terrorists that they are - ingenious, asymmetric, secretive, persistent, and ruthless. There is no other recognizable path to victory for them.

People often make an observation that great terror masterminds such as bin Laden, who call others to martyrdom, are never the ones who personally pilot planes into buildings or strap bombs to their bodies and self-destruct. They ask me if I think this reflects hypocrisy or cowardice. I tell them not necessarily and offer an analogy. President George Bush deployed our military to Iraq. Tens of thousands of men and women remain in harm's way there. Should President Bush be labeled a hypocrite or coward for not picking up a rifle and joining the fight in Iraq? No, it's not his job. Some people such as kings, queens, prime ministers, presidents, elected politicians, and Osama bin Ladens - by virtue of their stations in life and leadership status - hover safely above the killing fray. Their loyal followers are not so lucky. Some get to lead and live, others must follow and die. Such is politics, war and life.

They Seek To Defeat Us By Wearing Us Down And Waiting Us Out

The Osama bins Ladens know that they can only defeat the United States of America economically, emotionally, or psychologically. It is essential that we acknowledge and defend our Achilles' heels.

Ours is a huge and vast land, and terrorists cannot physically kill a large enough number of us to win in a force-on-force scenario. They cannot demolish enough of our infrastructure to shut us down completely. America is too big, too complex, and too redundant. They can, however, destroy enough of it to seriously damage our economy, causing the stock market to drop many thousands of points, giving rise to massive layoffs, and eliminating millions of livelihoods. They could even, over a prolonged period, break our will to fight and win. The Democratic Republic of Vietnam (North Vietnam), and its allied National Liberation Front (the Vietcong), did just that in the Vietnam War. Al Qaeda leaders remember, but I am not sure America's leaders do.

The painful and drawn-out conflict in Vietnam turned father against son, and brother against brother. Our entire country appeared divided between those who were pro-war and those who vehemently opposed it. In 1967, after three years of heavy combat, Americans saw no exit strategy, no end to the death and destruction, out of control defense spending, and an autocratic Secretary of State, Robert McNamara, who called the shots carte blanche on behalf of the Oval Office. Sound familiar? The terrorists think so. They are betting that American history will repeat itself. When the cost gets too high in Afghanistan and Iraq, America will pull out.

Here are my facts and rationale behind what I think is Al Qaeda's firm belief that America will inevitably cut and run. Our investment in lives, limbs, and dollars in Afghanistan and Iraq is considerable. Operation Enduring Freedom in Afghanistan resulted in 259 American GIs dead and 676 wounded by the end of calendar year 2005.[38] January 17, 2006 Operation Iraqi Freedom statistics show 2,222 killed and 16,420 wounded in action.[39] The Congressional Research Service estimated in March 2005 that both wars would cost the American taxpayers approximately $250 billion by October 1, 2005.[40] Certainly the U.S. will not pull out until victory is won. Looking with retrospect to the Vietnam era, it both saddens and frightens me to admit that I'm not so sure.

The United States' political and military involvement in South Vietnam extended for decades. Harry Truman was the first American President to commit the United States to aiding that tiny nation by sending military advisors there in 1950.[41] United States troops entered Vietnam en mass in 1964, fighting for noble American causes to keep the Republic of South Vietnam free from North Vietnam's communist aggression and to stem the spread of communism in Southeast Asia and across the globe. Our troop strength in Vietnam peaked in 1968 to 1,200,000 in country (nearly ten times the number deployed in the much larger country of Iraq in 2006) and still, we did not persevere.[42]

There was no viable end in sight after years of fighting, and assurances from the administration and its defense department that we were

---

[38] http://icasualties.org/oef.
[39] Ibid.
[40] Amy Belasco. CRS Report to Congress: The Cost of Operations in Iraq, Afghanistan, and Enhanced Security (Washington, D.C.: Congressional Research Service, March 14, 2005), p. 1
[41] http://www.vietnamwar.com/presidentnixonsrole.htm.
[42] http://en.wikipedia.org/wiki/Vietnam_War.

making progress and getting the job done in Vietnam. American anti-war protests reached epidemic proportions. Congress fell into line with its voters, demanding an end to the war. The United States and Republic of South Vietnam entered into secret negotiations with North Vietnam in 1969 to effect a peace. Negotiations failed, and President Nixon pursued a peace settlement on his watch that would both honor the American and South Vietnamese military efforts, and protect the citizens of South Vietnam.

On January 27, 1973, a peace agreement was signed and the U.S. forces were hastily withdrawn from Vietnam. Our military was, in effect, ordered to abandon its South Vietnamese comrades, leaving them to the mercy of the North. Not unexpectedly, and even before our forces fully departed Southeast Asia, the North began to exact its revenge upon the South. It was brutal and merciless. The communists achieved their strategic objectives, but the U.S. failed.

One million, two hundred fifty thousand South Vietnamese soldiers were killed fighting alongside their U.S. "saviors."[43] Americans killed in Vietnam numbered a staggering 58,226, with 153,303, wounded in action.[44] Civilian casualties were estimated at between two and four million.[45] The fiscal cost of Vietnam was around $531.5 billion in 2005 dollars.[46] With millions killed, and half of a trillion dollars, spent, it was all for naught in the end.

The communists prevailed because they were politically in the fight for the long haul; whether ten years, twenty years or more, they would achieve their objectives. The U.S. was not as dedicated or driven. Al Qaeda understands that the U.S. military performed honorably in Vietnam, and that it did not fail America there. It knows that we, the American people, our Congress and

---

[43] Ibid
[44] Ibid
[45] Ibid
[46] Francis, David R. *"More costly than 'the war to end all wars."* Christian Science Monitor, August 29, 2005.

presiding presidents failed our military.   Al Qaeda asks itself if America's political resolve could once again grow weak, if the U.S. might eventually order its forces in Afghanistan and Iraq to cease, desist, and return home. The precedent was set. It happened once, it can surely happen again.

Al Qaeda Perceives That We Are Failing In Afghanistan And Iraq

When I examine the U.S. government's performance to date in Afghanistan and Iraq through what I perceive to be the eyes of Al Qaeda, I conclude that America is failing and will be unsuccessful in both countries. My rationale follows.

We began combat operations in Afghanistan in October 2001. We've been fighting in Iraq since March 2003. Anti-war rhetoric from our citizens and the halls of Congress is already growing strong. Americans and their media watchdogs are asking questions of their government similar to ones heard during the Vietnam conflict. What are our quantifiable national strategic and military objectives? What is our exit strategy? How will we stem the insurgent attacks? Why cannot the Afghani and Iraqi people defend themselves after so many years of training and funding? These are perfectly legitimate questions for democratic citizens to ask of their republic. The answers I hear to date from administration and DOD spokespersons appear to be just as murky and ill defined as those I remember from the Vietnam era. The outward inability or refusal to provide quantitative solutions sends the message to Al Qaeda that the U.S. is unsure of what it is doing in both Afghanistan and Iraq. This can only strengthen enemy resolve.

Slowly, but most assuredly, the post 9-11, "let's go to war," tide is turning. Al Qaeda hears. Al Qaeda listens. It looks back to Vietnam – America's first extended major war against terrorists and insurgents - and is confident that if it stays the course, the U.S. will keep bending until it finally breaks.[47]

My view is that Al Qaeda thinks America gave up on Afghanistan, believing that U.S. political resolve to keep commitments to the emerging Afghani democratic government ended the moment its defense department diverted troops and resources to Iraq.

Taliban fighters are alive and well in Afghanistan, despite what the current administration might have us believe. I received briefings from trusted associates who traveled to the Afghani capital of Kabul and the surrounding territories of Qandahar in 2005. My sources were guests of retired Afghani general officers, currently serving as high-ranking Afghani government officials. They confirmed what I already believed to be true: the Taliban is alive and kicking in Afghanistan.

Kabul is riddled with Taliban fighters who freely walk the streets by day disguised as Muslim women, wearing ladies' traditional burkas.[48] The Taliban rules the night in certain sectors of that capital city. The enemy we supposedly ejected from Afghanistan still controls vast segments of Afghanistan's countryside and small villages. My sources relayed that Afghani officials, speaking off the record, remorsefully stated if Afghanistan was to stand a chance of overcoming its tribal mentality and infighting, exchanging it for developing a national identity, embracing a central government, and keeping the Taliban out, the extended effort would require ten times the number of U.S. troops currently in Afghanistan and at least ten more years of U.S.– led presence. They acknowledged this will never happen. In failing

---

[47] I, as do many others, continually ponder the question, "Why has there not been another major attack on U.S. soil since 9-11?" The answer may well be that our enemies know that another mass killing would rekindle the same deep patriotism, cries for revenge, and support for the White House that followed September 11th, 2001. Americans in 2006 are tiring of war, suspect of the Bush Administration's competency and intentions, questioning the National Security Agency's eavesdropping boundaries, challenging all levels of government aspects of the Patriot Act, and bogged down in Iraq. It's all going so very well Al Qaeda. Why would they want to screw it up?

[48] The burka is the traditional Muslim woman's daily wear out-of-doors in Afghanistan. It consists of head to toe covering with only an open slit over the eyes to facilitate vision.

to commit the resources needed to complete the job, they view a U.S. withdrawal from Afghanistan as inevitable. They see their war-torn country as once again being an open and safe haven for the Taliban and Al Qaeda.[49]

The situation in Iraq is not looking good either, as the U.S. won the war but is struggling desperately to achieve a peace. The challenges in the forefront are numerous and possibly insurmountable. Al Qaeda recognizes this. Al Qaeda looks to Iraq's internal religious, cultural and political strife and smiles widely. Those who follow weekly news broadcasts from Iraq understand that: (1) Iraq is primarily composed of three diverse groups - Sunni Muslims, Shia (or Shiite) Muslims, and Kurds, (2) the three do not play well together, and (3) religion is inseparable from politics. It is the way it has been for many centuries. The U.S.-led coalition invaded Iraq, became an occupying force and inherited the entire mess. Al Qaeda has no problem with this.

Saddam Hussein is a Sunni Muslim. Sunnis were granted great privilege and political power over the oppressed and persecuted Shia and Kurds during his dictatorship. It was under the Sunni regime that Kurds were gassed by Saddam's forces and murdered in their villages. It was Sunni military forces that slaughtered thousands of their Iraqi Shia countrymen post-Desert Storm. The bottom line is that under Saddam, the Sunni Muslims ruled. It is not that way today.

The American invasion and subsequent formation of the new Iraqi government changed everything for the Sunnis. The Kurds now live in their geographic region of Iraq and basically run their

---

[49] I believe if the United States had concentrated its efforts and resources in Afghanistan and not taken on Iraq simultaneously, there might be hope for a free and democratic future for that war-torn nation Unfortunately, most of what America needed militarily to successfully accomplish its objectives in Afghanistan was pulled out much too soon and re-directed in support of Operation Iraqi Freedom. The United States simply does not possess sufficient ground forces or resources in-country to get the job done. Our senior military officers are fully aware of this. My bet is that they will tell us so someday, after they retire from active duty, have received their desired promotions, no longer work for Donald Rumsfeld, and write their best sellers.

own affairs, and it is "hands off" for the Sunnis. The Shia are now the numerical and political majority within the emerging Iraqi democracy, with Shia Iraqis outnumber their Sunni counterparts by about 3 to 2. Seeking their Shia revenge after decades of oppression and persecution by the Sunnis is not only fair game, but culturally expected; the Sunnis are not amused, but Al Qaeda surely is.

Al Qaeda understands that the social, religious, and political conflicts among Middle Eastern Kurds, Sunnis, and Shias have dragged on for centuries. Expecting United States' intervention and influence to change all of that in just five, ten, or fifteen years is extremely optimistic and perhaps totally unrealistic. Maybe, as Al Qaeda is betting, it is just down right impossible.

Our military is performing magnificently in Iraq just as it did in Vietnam. Al Qaeda recognizes that the U.S. forces cannot be defeated there, but knows that unless the U.S.-led coalition can establish security and stability (S&S) in Iraq, it cannot win either. Al Qaeda believes that the U.S. dropped itself right into a self-induced quagmire, characterized by: (1) insurgents continuing to cross Iraq's Syrian and Iranian borders, joining forces with those already fighting; (2) insurgents carrying on the killing, wounding, and kidnapping of military and Iraqi civilians; and (3) U.S.-led forces fighting back, killing and wounding insurgents and innocent Iraqis who become collateral damage. Al Qaeda sees all of this going on endlessly, until someone yells "Stop!" as happened in Vietnam.

Al Qaeda is convinced that the United States' volunteer military force is weakening under the strain of continual combat operations. As of January 2006, Army combat troops "are at a pace of about 1.5 years at home for every year in Iraq or Afghanistan."[50] Al Qaeda's beliefs are fueled by what they see and hear within the open U.S. media. A recent Pentagon-contracted study, highlighted by the Associated Press, headlined: "Army stretched too thin, report says - Insurgents might outlast U.S. deployments."[51] Andrew Krepinevich, a retired Army officer, concluded in his report that "the Army cannot sustain the pace of troop deployments to Iraq long enough to break the back of the insurgency."[52] Krepinevich highlighted the Army's 2005 recruiting slump; the first in six years. In one of his chapters titled "The Thin Green Line," he wrote that the Army is in a "race against time to adjust to the demands of war or risk 'breaking' the force in the form of a catastrophic decline in recruitment and re-enlistment."[53] Al Qaeda hears. Al Qaeda listens. It takes heart.

Al Qaeda is content to let this war play out over an extended period of time. It all works to its advantage. The U.S. remains in a quagmire, U.S. public support for the war wanes exponentially, and the 136,000 military men and women there can pose no threat to Al Qaeda outside of Iraq.[54] Perfect.

Just as Al Qaeda is suspicious of U.S. resolve in Iraq, so too are many Iraqis. They have every right to be doubtful. They, like Al Qaeda, know our history. If I were an Iraqi, I would ask myself, "Why should I risk my life to work side-by-side with the Americans or support the emerging Iraqi government?" I would reason that Saddam Hussein is still alive and well, as is the Baath Party. Americans cannot control the insurgency, just as they could not in Vietnam. The Sunni-Shia conflict will continue in Iraq, and may yet result in a full-blown civil war. The Americans cannot muster a military force capable of preventing armed conflict between millions of Iraqi Muslims should it ever come to that. Each Iraqi reasons: if I help the Americans, the Americans tire of their experiment here and withdraw, and everything goes to hell, I will be the one on the torturer's table or at the end of

---

[50] "Army stretched too thin, report says: insurgents might outlast U.S. deployments." Associated Press, January 25, 2006.
[51] Ibid.
[52] Ibid.
[53] Ibid.
[54] Ibid.

the executioner's rope. Better to tell the Yankees what they want to hear, remain neutral, and make no waves. Do not think for a moment that Al Qaeda and Baathist operatives in Iraq do not fuel these fears and apprehensions at every opportunity. They would be foolish and inept not to do so. They are neither.

The Administration did not foresee or plan to prevent a post-invasion insurgency movement in Iraq supported by hostile elements easily infiltrating across the vast Iraqi-Syrian and Iraqi-Iranian borders. To my way of thinking, the Joint Chiefs are just as guilty as the politicians they serve for this failure. Military planners (of whom I was one), Department of State Foreign Service officers, and our intelligence community were all were painfully aware of Saddam Hussein's close Bath Party ties with counterparts in Syria and Iran's fundamentalist, Islamic political and military support to the Shia Muslims in southern Iraq. I believe Secretary Rumsfeld was probably advised of the ramifications of not sealing the borders as part of Operation Iraqi Freedom, but disregarded it. I think that he Chairman of the Joint Chiefs of Staff and Service Chiefs "rolled" on this one. The exception was Army Chief of Staff General Shinseki, who advised that it would take several hundred thousand more troops to secure the peace than it would to win the initial fighting war against Saddam and his forces. General Shinseki estimated it would take 300,000 to 400,000 ground troops to secure and stabilize Iraq. Shinseki retired shortly after his statements. The press accused Rumsfeld of firing him. Rumsfeld said that Shinseki's service time was up and that he simply retired.[55] Al Qaeda must still be scratching its head over this lack of foresight. Iraq's 592-kilometer (355 mile) border with Syria[56] to the west and 1,280-kilometer (768 mile) border with Iran to its east remain porous, very similar to the U.S. border situation with Canada and Mexico. There is some

---

[55] For more details on the Shinseki affair, read from testimony of Secretary Rumsfeld and senior military leaders before the House of Representatives at
http://www.dod.mil/transcripts/2004/tr20040921-secdef1324.html.
[56] http://saroujah.blogspot.com/2005/09/bush-admits-syria-is-protecting-syria.html.

control, but not nearly enough to keep out those who are driven to enter and join in the fight against a free and democratic Iraq.

Al Qaeda judges the Bush Administration as having

> *Fueled the insurgency, missing an opportunity to rapidly build a security force when it disbanded the Iraqi Army. Though the Iraqi military was under the control of Saddam Hussein, Hussein loyalists did not comprise the majority of personnel, and many experts recommended removing only the top commanders and other loyalists. Instead, the Defense Department decided to disband all 400,000 members of the military. The consequences were twofold: (1) the U.S. neglected an opportunity to hasten the development of the Iraqi Security Forces (ISF) by drawing from a large pool of trained soldiers with a command structure and experience; and (2) the decision created a pool of 400,000 trained, professional soldiers with some degree of bitterness toward the United States from which the insurgency could draw.*[57]

When the U.S. disbanded the Iraqi Army it, in effect, sent four hundred thousand jobless Iraqi men back to their homes, with no means of supporting their families, no dignity, but with a lot of weapons and ammunition. This presented a target rich environment for Al Qaeda recruiters.

The U.S. chose to build an Iraqi Security Force (ISF) from scratch. It is not progressing well, no doubt to Al Qaeda's extreme delight. Iraqi Security Forces are not even close to the level of operational readiness necessary to defend their new nation. Gen. George Casey, commanding general of coalition forces in Iraq, testified in September 2005 before members of Congress that the number of Iraqi battalions capable of fighting without

---

[57] http://democrats.senate.gov/dpc/dpc-new.cfm?doc_name=fs-109-1-88, page 1.

American support dropped from three to one.[58] Only one Iraqi battalion is operationally ready after three years of training and tens of millions of dollars invested, offering even more encouragement to Al Qaeda to stay its course.

Prior to the U.S. invasion, Iraq had not experienced terrorist attacks on its soil. Now commonplace, weekly attacks take the lives of innocent men, women, and children. Al Qaeda is betting that continued bombings will wear down the Iraqi people to the point where they will pressure their government to order U.S. forces home if provided assurances from Al Qaeda that there will be no more indiscriminant killing and maiming.

An Overarching Reality In Iraq (That Al Qaeda Understands All Too Well)

I believe that an overarching reality exists in post-Saddam Iraq, one that Al Qaeda understands all too well, but our current administration and department of defense either cannot see or refuse to recognize:

> **As long as the likes of Al Qaeda continue to bomb, kill, take hostages, and reign down their terror in Iraq, that new nation can never and will never advance to become a thriving democracy and a participant in the 21st century's expanding, global economy. It will remain suppressed and stagnant, unable to go forward into the future, but always at risk of falling back into its past.**

It does not matter how long U.S. forces remain in Iraq; nor does it matter the number of forces and resources we commit to the fight. If we cannot stop the terrorist attacks, money and opportunities needed to raise the quality of life for future Iraqis and advance Iraq as a free and democratic nation will never

---

[58] http://www.msnbc.msn.com/id/9531843, page 1.

materialize. Globalization will pass them by. There will be no tourism, and there will be no robust trade, no international conventions, conferences, or industrial trade shows hosted in the capital city of Baghdad. All of the facets of international collaboration needed to advance economies, education, quality of life, and democracies themselves will never come to Iraq. The promises made to the Iraqis by the Americans – assurances of all of the wonderful things that will befall them under their new democratic government – will be seen as a blatant deception, not only to Iraqis, but other citizens of the Middle East who are watching and waiting. Al Qaeda understands this only too well.

I offer this discussion point to my readers. The next time you are debating the pros and cons of U.S. actions in Iraq, and the person with whom you are conversing maintains that it is all going very well, ask the hard question, "When will the U.S. Fortune 500 companies begin to extensively establish offices in Baghdad and other major Iraqi cities in order to exploit the growing Iraqi market?"

Closing Thoughts

We must stay the course in Iraq, whatever it takes for as long as it takes. If we do not, the Al Qaeda's of the world win a major public relations and propaganda victory, and there will be decades more hell to pay. We must re-engage with sufficient forces and resources in both Afghanistan and Iraq. Currently, our resources in both countries are woefully inadequate. This is not fair to the citizens of those nations, the American public, or – most importantly – our brave men and women who are sacrificing life and limb for the cause.

The most mortal of American sins would be to fail our military in Afghanistan and Iraq as we did in Vietnam.

We can win the War on Terror on all fronts, but only if we as voters press for: (1) achievable, U.S. strategic and military operational objectives, (2) sufficient ground forces and associated resources to get the job done, and (3) an unbreakable will on the part of the American people and its Congress to win at all costs.

The price in lives and dollars for Al Qaeda to perpetuate the terror attacks in Iraq, and thus keep Iraq from achieving significant political, social, and economic progress, is far less than America's cost in struggling to maintain security and stability there. Sustaining operations in Iraq costs the American taxpayer billions each month. Several suicide-homicide bombings in Baghdad each week for five or ten more years costs next to nothing in comparison, yet achieves the Al Qaeda goals and keeps the U.S. in its quagmire. Al Qaeda can maintain its operational pace indefinitely. It is betting that America cannot.

I fear that if we permit Al Qaeda to win in either Afghanistan or Iraq, we will surrender a part of America's precious will and national character that we will never be able to reclaim. It could even mark the beginning of our end as a reliable, respected, and trusted world power.

Complacency is not an option, and denial is deadly. So assume the responsibility. Adopt the creed:

If not me, then who? If not now, then when?

BRIEFING # 4

Knowing Ourselves

Briefing #3 was about knowing our terrorist enemy, but briefing #4 is introspective. It discusses several of America's shortcomings and vulnerabilities, which we as citizen soldiers must acknowledge and work untiringly to overcome. If we are not continually trying to evaluate and improve our performance in war, then we run the risk of either becoming or appearing stagnant and weak. We can ill afford to permit this to happen.

Righteous Nation, Heal Thyself

The United States Shares In The Global Guilt That Permitted Terror To Escalate

America can rightfully point fingers at nation-states all over the globe that are in the wrong for not doing enough to prevent terror from festering and growing exponentially in the latter part of the twentieth century. This global guilt is shared by Egypt, France, Great Britain, Saudi Arabia, Qatar, Kuwait, United Arab Emirates, Bahrain, Indonesia, Singapore, Malaysia, the Philippines, Pakistan, Afghanistan, Iran, Iraq, Syria, Libya, the

Sudan, Russia, Canada, Mexico and countless others. Though it is difficult for me to accept, near the top of the list of countries enabling, though I believe inadvertently so, the proliferation of global terror is my own United States of America.

I think that America's foreign policies and international actions are generally motivated by honorable intentions. Somewhere along the way, however, things often become convoluted and shortsighted to the point where the United States has all-too-often backed itself into a high visibility corner. Such is the case with some of our U.S. actions and policies with respect to global terrorism.

CIA Support to Al Qaeda: Our Tax Dollars At Work

In December 1979, the Armed Forces of the Union of Soviet Socialist Republics (USSR), or Soviet Union for short, invaded the tribal lands of Afghanistan. The Cold War was going strong. Anything that the U.S. could do in support of the defeat of its arch-nemesis it would do. The United States, spearheaded by its CIA, poured money and arms into Afghanistan for the Muslim, mujahedeen freedom fighters, led by men like Osama bin Laden. Only a few decades ago, bin Laden was an American ally who received countless millions of dollars in aid and arms from the CIA.

Muslims from all over the world that supported the Afghan resistance answered the call to arms, traveling to Afghanistan and Pakistan by the thousands to be trained, equipped, and sent into battle. A great many of them, such as bin Laden, came from Saudi Arabia and brought Wahhabism to the fight. The mujahedeen training included radical Islamist indoctrination, and the CIA knew what kind of men these freedom fighters were. One would assume that they had to know that the raising of a well armed, Islamist army would eventually come back to haunt the United States. However, the CIA's mission was clear and focused upon the defeat of the Soviet Union and an end to the Cold War. Nothing else mattered at the time.

Among the various arms provided to the resistance leaders Abdullah Azzam[59] and Osama bin laden were shoulder-fired, surface-to-air anti-aircraft missiles, known today as Man Portable Air Defense Systems (ManPADS). It is estimated that thousands of these aircraft killers were given to the Muslim fighters, with no request to "please return any missiles not used in your war." Such is the nature of covert operations. When our shortsighted government dumped hundreds of millions of dollars of arms into those Muslim war chests, they could not foresee that a decade later, the consequences of that kinetic handoff would be devastating. It would be naive to assume that Al Qaeda and other terror organizations do not possess some of the thousands of plane killers provided by our CIA. Further, it would constitute denial to doubt for one moment that Al Qaeda has not already smuggled some these ManPADS into the continental United States, given that less than five percent of ships' cargos and fewer than ten percent of all automobiles crossing into our borders are ever completely, physically inspected.

When you read about countries dealing in arms to terrorists, it is important to remember that the U.S. was one of the world's largest suppliers to the emerging Al Qaeda from 1979 through the late 1980s.

Negotiations With Terrorists And Financial Aid Provided Them

The United States is quick to lambaste other nations when it suspects that they contributed money directly or indirectly to terrorist organizations or their causes. America openly encourages its allies not to negotiate with terrorists. There appears to

---

[59] As earlier noted, Azzam was a great leader in the war who first conceptualized Al Qaeda. He was succeeded upon his death by Osama bin Laden.

be a clear double standard here, because the United States does negotiate with terrorists and does provide money to them and their causes.

The textbook example of U.S. hypocrisy in these matters is its relationship with, and support of, one of the most notorious terrorists the world has ever produced; Yasser (sometimes spelled "Yasir") Arafat. Also known as Abu Ammar, Arafat was the symbol of Palestinian nationalism for decades, until his death in 2004. Many believe that if one could "put a face on the terrible violence of the Middle East, that face would be Yasser Arafat's."[60] Yasser Arafat's life was characterized by his involvement in terror, his goal to destroy Israel, and his siphoning of hundreds of millions of dollars from money donated to help his Palestinian people into his own private accounts.

From February 4, 1969, when he was appointed Chairman of the Executive Committee of the Palestine Liberation Organization (PLO) through 2004, Arafat sanctioned a myriad of terrorist activities and other crimes. Events attributed to Arafat and organizations under his control include the following:[61]

- **Feb. 21, 1970**: SwissAir flight 330, bound for Tel Aviv, was bombed in mid-flight by PFLP, a PLO member group. Forty-seven people were killed.

- **May 8, 1970**: PLO terrorists attacked an Israeli school bus with bazooka fire, killing nine pupils and three teachers from Moshav Avivim.

- **May 1972**: PFLP, part of the PLO, dispatched members of the Japanese Red Army to attack Lod Airport in Tel Aviv, killing 27 people.

---

[60] Farah, Joseph. *"Arafat in the White House?"* WorldNetDaily.com. July 5, 2001, page 1.
[61] *"Yasir Arafat's Timeline of Terror."* (Online)
Available: http://www.camera.org/index.asp?x_article=795&x_context=7. November 13, 2004.

- **Sept. 5, 1972**: Munich Massacre – 11 Israeli athletes were murdered at the Munich Olympics by a group calling themselves "Black September," said to be an arm of Fatah, operating under Arafat's direct command.

- **March 1, 1973**: Palestinian terrorists took over the Saudi embassy in Khartoum. The next day, two Americans – including the United States' ambassador to Sudan, Cleo Noel – and a Belgian were shot and killed. James J. Welsh, an analyst for the National Security Agency from 1969 through 1974, charged Arafat with direct complicity in these murders.

- May 15, 1974: PLO terrorists infiltrating from Lebanon held children hostage in Ma'alot school. Twenty-six people, twenty-one of them children, are killed.

- March 1975: Members of Fatah attacked the Tel Aviv seafront and took hostages in the Savoy hotel. Three soldiers, three civilians and seven terrorists were killed.

- **March 1978**: Coastal Road Massacre – Fatah terrorists took over a bus on the Haifa-Tel Aviv highway and killed 21 Israelis.

- **Oct. 7, 1985**: Italian cruise ship Achille Lauro was hijacked by Palestinian terrorists. Wheelchair-bound elderly man, Leon Klinghoffer, was shot and thrown overboard. Intelligence reports note that instructions originated from Arafat's headquarters in Tunis.

- Jan. 3, 2002: Israelis intercepted the Karine-A, a ship loaded with 50 tons of mortars, rocket launchers, anti-tank mines and other weapons intended for the Palestinian war against the Israelis. The captain admitted he was under the command of the Palestinian Authority.

- September 2003: IMF report titled "Economic Performance and Reforms under Conflict Conditions," states that Arafat has diverted $900 million of public PA funds into his own accounts from 1995 - 2000.

Below are some of the attacks since September 2001 perpetrated by groups under Arafat's command:

- **Oct 4, 2001**: 3 killed, 13 wounded, when a Fatah terrorist, dressed as an Israeli paratrooper, opened fire on Israeli civilians waiting at the central bus station in Afula.

- **Nov 27, 2001**: 2 killed, 50 injured when two Palestinian terrorists opened fire with Kalashnikov assault rifles on a crowd of people near the central bus station in Afula. Fatah and the Islamic Jihad claimed joint responsibility.

- **Dec 12, 2001**: 11 killed and 30 wounded when three terrorists attacked a bus and several passenger cars with a roadside bomb, anti-tank grenades, and light arms fire near the entrance to Emmanuel in Samaria. Both Fatah and Hamas claimed responsibility for the attack.

- **Jan 17, 2002**: 6 killed, 35 wounded when a Fatah terrorist burst into a bar mitzva reception in a banquet hall in Hadera opening fire with an M-16 assault rifle.

- **March 2, 2002**: A suicide bombing by Al Aqsa Martyrs Brigade in an ultra-Orthodox Jewish neighborhood of Jerusalem killed 11 people and injured more than 50.

- **March 21, 2002**: An Al Aqsa Martyrs Brigade suicide bomber exploded himself in a crowd of shoppers in Jerusalem, killing 3 and injuring 86.

- **April 12, 2002**: Six killed and 104 wounded when a female Al Aqsa Martyrs Brigade suicide bomber blew herself up at a bus stop on Jaffa road at the entrance to Jerusalem's Mahane Yehuda.

- **Nov 28, 2002**: 5 killed and 40 wounded when two Fatah terrorists opened fire and threw grenades at the Likud polling station in Beit She'an, near the central bus station, where party members were casting their votes in the Likud primary.

- **May 19, 2003**: 3 were killed and 70 were wounded in a suicide bombing at the entrance to the Amakim Mall in Afula. The Islamic Jihad and the Fatah al-Aqsa Martyrs Brigades both claimed responsibility for the attack.

- **Jan 29, 2004**: 11 people were killed and over 50 wounded in a suicide bombing at the corner of Gaza and Arlozorov streets in Jerusalem. Both the Fatah-related Al Aqsa Martyrs' Brigades and Hamas claimed responsibility for the attack.

The record on Arafat is clear. He was a terrorist, murderer, thief, and liar. Yet America's representatives negotiated openly with him for many years. Presidents George H. W. Bush, Clinton, and George W. Bush hosted Arafat at the White House and Camp David. Here is an equally disturbing fact: The United States gave more than $1.5 billion to the Palestinian Authority in support of the Palestinian people since 1993.[62] Yasser Arafat exercised direct control over that money without any public record or accountability to the United States; at least none that I, in all of my research, could uncover. We will never know how much of that $1.5 billion dollars went to Arafat's personal bank accounts, the Hamas Sunni Muslim terrorist group that supported him, or to the families of suicide-homicide bombers as compensation for their sacrifices.

---

[62] *"Aid for Palestinians in jeopardy after election."* MSNBC News Service. (Online) available: http://www.msnbc.msn.com/id/11096260 , page 3.

In January 2006, Hamas won the majority of seats in the Palestinian government as a result of free elections. Hamas, which is publicly sworn to effect the destruction of the state of Israel, asked the international community not to cut aid to the Palestinian Authority. "We call on you to transfer all aid to the Palestinian treasury," stated Ismail Haniyeh, a Hamas leader in Gaza during a news conference following the Palestinian elections.[63] Addressing international concerns that aid would be used to fund violence, Haniyeh said, "We assure you that all the revenues will be spent on salaries, daily life, and infrastructure."[64]

There is no evidence to demonstrate that much of the $1.5 billion in U.S. aid was extensively used by Arafat to noticeably improve the life of his Palestinian people. There is no reason to believe that Hamas will use U.S. financial aid to better the lives of the Palestinian impoverished either.

Peoples of the world are not ignorant of U.S. hypocrisy. They recognize the double standards that damage our credibility and reliability. We must both acknowledge and put a stop to them now. We must not repeat mistakes of the past. Until such time as Hamas removes terror and the destruction of Israel from its charter, there should be no U.S. negotiations with it. Any thought of giving Hamas money must be immediately dismissed.

Now that we understand that we are not blameless in the terror negotiation, funding, and proliferation arenas, it's time to acknowledge our sins and work hard never to commit them again.

The U.S. Military Is Too Symmetric and Bureaucratic In Its Warfighting, With Too Many Chiefs And Not Enough Empowered Indians

Bureaucracies cannot help but be symmetric in nature. The American government and its supporting military infrastructure

---

[63] Ibid, page 1.
[64] Ibid, page 2.

are textbook symmetric entities. I remain deeply concerned about this inherent, American vulnerability. We know from earlier briefings that the terrorist enemy is asymmetric. Certain aspects of our symmetry must be somehow changed or circumvented if we intend to fight terror for the long haul.

Men like Osama bin Laden appear to possess endless patience. However, our government and military leaders, most especially those serving at the highest levels, have little patience. The bin Ladens of the world plan for the long term and are content to wait many years to see their plans come to fruition. The U.S. government and military hierarchy seek immediate gratification. Their report cards, promotions, political future, funding, salaries, etc., all ride upon their ability to achieve results on their watch. Exercising cautious judgment in an effort to never screw-up is just as critical to their success. Our bureaucracies appear to me to be more risk averse today than ever before. Too many within them are afraid to make a needed decision for fear of "blowback."[65] One way to avoid "blowback" is to not make any controversial decisions. Thus, decisions are tied up and delayed with countless emails, working groups, committees, steering groups, video teleconferences and the like. This has become a fine art within the Departments of Defense, State, and Homeland Security, and the Central Intelligence Agency. Our total symmetry works to our disadvantage in an asymmetric conflict such as the War on Terror.

Huge bureaucratic machines are infamous for sustaining a non-operational corporate culture, which is directly opposite the one embraced by our terrorist adversaries. Collapsing under their own obesity, immense bureaucracies such as DOD and DHS are for the most part combat ineffective.[66] They are riddled with painfully slow processes, legal regulation, administrative policies, fiscal constraints, political agendas, and tens of thousands of

---

[65] "Blowback" is the negative ramification that may result from a suggestion, plan, decision, or action.
[66] "Combat ineffective" is a term used by military professionals to describe units that, for whatever reason, are unable to perform their assigned or implied missions.

middle-management decision non-makers whose duties and responsibilities overlap and conflict. It is often difficult for action officers to determine which specific civilian or military officer within their chain of command is definitively in charge - or will assume ultimate responsibility for - a given mission area. This all too often makes it impossible for the minority of competent, dedicated commanders and staffers to excel in their duties and effect positive change. I attest after decades of first-hand experience that innovative, timely initiatives will tend to fester within the walls and halls of the DOD, until they die of natural causes or are crushed to death by the sheer volume of the review and approval processes. This is good for our enemies. It is certainly not good for us.

I returned to serve the DOD in November 2002, as an executive consulting contractor to offer my information operations and counter-terror expertise in support of Operations Enduring Freedom and Iraqi Freedom. I served on-site within the headquarters of three of the nine unified commands: United States Space Command (USSPACECOM), United States Strategic Command (USSTRATCOM), and United States Northern Command (USNORTHCOM). I remain stunned by the excessive number of Army, Air Force, and Marine colonels and Navy captains who trip over each other in the walls and halls of these commands, creating an "all chiefs and no Indians" environment; an insurmountable military bureaucratic infrastructure. I speak from personal experience.

One joint staff organization I supported at USSTRATCOM in Omaha, Nebraska - then designated the "Joint Task Force-Information Operations" or JTF-IO, summer 2003 – consisted of four full colonels, two lieutenant colonels, three navy commanders, two majors, a few DOD civilians and about nine contractors, most of whom were retired field grade[67] military

---

[67] Field grade officers in the army, air force, and marines are majors, lieutenant colonels, or colonels. Their navy equivalents are lieutenant commanders, commanders, and captains.

officers such as me. When I would ask which senior officer was in charge of this or that project or operation, I usually received an answer such as, "Well, they are working on it together" (meaning two officers of equal rank). I would always follow-up with, "OK, but which one is in charge and has the final approval authority?" The answer would come back, "Both of them" or "I don't know." Ours was a military operation by committee. It was symmetric and dysfunctional. It failed miserably.

Our decision making and approval process within our information operations joint task force (JTF) at USSTRATCOM was completely stalled. Instead of buckling down and concentrating on helping United States Central Command (USCENTCOM) and United States Special Operations Command (USSOCOM) to fight the wars in Afghanistan and Iraq, USSTRATCOM's leadership placed a different colonel in charge of our JTF roughly every 120 days. The "new guy" would no sooner get his feet on the ground, and then be transferred. From April 2003 through October 2004, I personally witnessed the leadership of our JTF change hands no less than seven times, with one Marine colonel, five Air Force colonels, and one Navy rear admiral each taking a shot at running the team within that eighteen month period. Not only were we assigned a new leader every few months, but USSTRATCOM reorganized our task force no less than four times during that same eighteen month period. Morale went to hell after about our third reorganization and fourth leader. Effectively fighting an asymmetric enemy such as al Qaeda is virtually impossible within a negative working environment such as this.

I implored the senior officers to stabilize the organization and its leadership for at least a year and a half so we could all settle down and concentrate on supporting the war effort. One would assume, which is erroneous, that seasoned military men and women who rise to general and flag rank[68] fully understand that any team of

---

[68] One-stars through four-stars in the army, marines and air force are called "general officers." Navy equivalents are called "flag officers."

men and women exposed to such turbulence can never bond as a cohesive, productive military team. This is not rocket science. Personnel turnover and organizational turbulence will destroy any organization, military or civilian.

Much to my dismay, even United States Central Command's (USCENTCOM) information operations team – information practitioners fighting two wars - suffered the same fate as their brethren at USSTRATCOM. Central Command placed no less than four colonels in charge of its information operations staff and reorganized that staff at least three times between April 2003 and September 2004. Its information operations campaign left much to be desired in Iraq and the Middle East at large, despite several world-wide, classified video-teleconferences each week, during which many outstanding ideas were discussed and discussed and discussed some more.

I work alongside countless military officers who, in private conversation, agree fully with everything I stated above. Regrettably, I observed precious few willing to stand against the system and force positive change. Too many choose to not make waves. They appear far more concerned about their longevity, promotions, assignments, or pending retirements than they do about supporting their fellow warriors in harm's way. This was the case within the information operations directorate at USSTRATCOM in the first two years of Operation Iraqi Freedom. It remains the case within the information operations directorate at USSNORTHCOM today. It is sad. It must change. The military must rekindle the ideal of selfless service among much of its officer corps.

I firmly believe that dysfunctional, unified military commands and staffs must get back to time-proven basics. I implore our troubled commands - and they know who they are - to consider the following in order to provide maximum support to the ongoing combat efforts:

1. At the senior officer level (pay grade 0-6 and above which are colonels and navy captains and higher), cease placing these men and women in critical positions of leadership and responsibility when they have announced, or are preparing to announce, their retirement from active military service. It is a disservice to the mission and to the dedicated action officers who strive to accomplish the missions. It has been my experience that the vast majority of these designated retirees placed in key positions render less than stellar performances, indicative of what we old timers call "ROAD soldiers" - Retired On Active Duty.

2. Before placing an 0-6 in charge, ensure that he or she has at least eighteen months to devote to that same job. Get a commitment from them to stay in the job and then keep them there. Make them perform, or fire them, regardless of their seniority.

3. Place only qualified leaders and action officers into requisite jobs. If you must put officers into positions for which they are not qualified - as is often the case with military assignments – ensure that: (a) the individuals receive subject matter education immediately; (b) the individuals are dedicated to learning their new jobs as quickly as possible; and (c) the individuals are performing satisfactorily within the first 90 days. If performance problems are uncorrectable, reassign the individuals. If attitude problems persist, fire them.

4. Decide how each directorate and staff section is to be organized and stabilize it for at least eighteen months. A stable organization is bound to perform much better than an unstable one.

5. Clearly designate who is in charge and ultimately responsible for each and every task and mission. Place one person in charge and ensure that everyone else supporting the effort understands who the final authority is. Avoid military operations by committee.

The military must begin experimenting now with asymmetric staffing procedures. This is a massive stretch requiring colossal policy changes. This concept is so far off in the distance that it is not yet a topic of discussion. Asymmetric staffing is a process by which operationally sound, yet time sensitive ideas can be surfaced, staffed, and approved for execution in a fraction of the time usually required. The process requires senior officers to identify their "shit hot"[69] staff officers and NCOs. We will refer to them here as "super staffers." Super staffers are the hard-charging, dynamic, effective officers and NCOs within a command that maintain a reputation for total reliability and getting it right the first time. Senior officers then empower their super staffers to jump the chain of command if they deem the operational situation warrants such action in order to complete a time-sensitive mission effectively.

Here's an example of how my asymmetric staffing concept would work. Let us say that I am an Army Major (0-4) in USSTRATCOM and the command's expert in counter-terror, possessing Special Forces combat experience in Bosnia, Afghanistan, Iraq, and classified places others know about but cannot discuss outside of highly classified circles. I work for an Army Lieutenant Colonel (0-5), who works for a Marine Colonel (0-6). The Marine Colonel reports to a more senior Air Force Colonel (0-6). This Air Force Colonel works for a Navy Rear Admiral (0-7) who is under the big boss, the Air Force two-star Director of Operations (0-8). As a Major, this would be my proper chain of command. (This is a very common scenario within Unified Commands.)

Normal symmetric staffing would require me, a mere major, to laboriously work my way up the chain of command through four superior officers, before approaching the two-star for a decision. Usually, a staff officer does not skip links in the chain of command. I would not go to the marine colonel, for example, until I briefed my immediate superior, the Army lieutenant colonel. It's the way it is.

---

[69] "Shit hot" is common tern used throughout the military to denote an absolutely outstanding commander, staff officer, or NCO. A superior compliment from fellow officers would be, "He is a shit hot commander!" or "She is a shit hot aviator!"

Let us say that I am recognized as a super staffer. A call comes into my desk from the Special Operations folks at USCENTCOM headquarters in Baghdad. The call is over a secure line so that we can talk at the top secret level without compromising our conversation. I know and trust the person on the other end. He tells me that a large counter terror operation is being planned for execution within a week or so. Basically it's a solid plan, but there are some rough spots that need to be ironed out and they need my expertise in-country. I am asked, "Can you be here and how soon?" I tell him I will get back to him ASAP. I think to myself that it is going to take a few days to make flight arrangements and get into Baghdad. Time is short. I need a decision immediately.

I am working on three big projects at present. I assess that none are as important as supporting men and women in a combat operation in Iraq. My immediate boss – the lieutenant colonel is out of the office until late afternoon. His next two bosses – the Marine and Air Force colonels, are away on temporary duty, attending meetings at the Pentagon. I decide to go to the rear admiral's office and brief him on what I think needs to be done. When I get to his office, the door is closed and his executive officer says that he is not to be disturbed. I tell the admiral's "exec" that, with all due respect, I need five minutes of the admiral's time immediately. She picks up the phone and tells the admiral I need to see him now. The admiral, knowing I am one of the designated super staffers, sees me immediately. I tell him that no one else my chain of command was available and that I need his decision. I brief him on the situation and the time sensitivity. I recommend to him that I be put on the first flight out to Baghdad to assist as requested. I mention I have three big projects ongoing. Two can wait until I get back. One is due in two days and I will get another staff officer to cover for me and finish it up. The admiral tells me to pack my bags, get orders, and go to Baghdad. He assures me that he will back brief the two full colonels and my immediate boss, the lieutenant colonel, and tell them what transpired in their absence. Within fifteen minutes, I am able to call Baghdad and tell them that my trip is approved and I am on the way. Within six hours I am on the first flight towards Iraq. **This is my idea of asymmetric staffing: the ability to make decisions and effect actions as rapidly as necessary to keep pace with, or a step ahead of, the enemy.**

America's Critical Infrastructure – The Biggest Target in the World

In knowing ourselves and recognizing our vulnerabilities, it is important to address our massive U.S. critical infrastructure that always presents a lucrative target set for the terrorists. The critical infrastructure, as defined in President Bush's introductory letter to the February 2003 National Strategy for the Physical Protection of Critical Infrastructure and Key Assets, is the "infrastructures and assets vital to our public health and safety, national security, governance, economy, and public confidence."[70] We need to remain cognizant of three points.

First, it is impossible to prevent future terror attacks upon components of this nation's critical infrastructure. Our nation is so huge that its critical infrastructure is simply too immense to be completely protected. There is simply not enough money, resources or people to safeguard it all twenty-four hours each day, seven days a week, indefinitely. Our critical infrastructure is staggering, which the government so aptly calls the "protection challenge."[71] The following is a list;

- 1,912,00 farms
- 1,800 federal reservoirs
- 1,600 municipal waste treatment plants
- 5,800 registered hospitals
- 87,000 U.S. emergency services

---

[70] http://www.dhs.gov./dhspublic/display?theme=32.
[71] "National Strategy for the Physical Protection of Critical Infrastructure and Key Assets." February 2003, p. 9.

- 250,000 defense-based firms in 215 distinct industries
- 2 billion miles of telecommunications cable
- 2,800 conventional power plants
- 300,000 oil and natural gas producing sites
- 5,000 public airports
- 120,000 miles of major railroads
- 590,000 highway bridges
- 2 million miles of pipelines
- 300 inland/coastal ports
- 500 major urban public transit operations
- 26,600 FDIC-insured institutions
- 66,000 chemical plants
- 137 million delivery sites
- 5,800 historic buildings
- 104 commercial nuclear power plants
- 80,000 damns
- 3,000 government owned and operated facilities
- 460 skyscrapers

Second, even if the United States possessed all of the resources, money and personnel required to guard all facets of our critical infrastructure around the clock, the "human factors" would inevitably come into play. Human beings are imperfect. Terrorists know this. Our imperfect species is subject to fatigue, forgetfulness, political pressures, family strain, personal trauma, job stress, intimidation, bribes, blackmail, and a host of other weaknesses and frailties. More than one door (or back door) remains open for the terrorists who are committed to perpetrating the dastardliest of deeds.

Human beings can also be duped. They can be tricked into aiding the terrorists when they do not even realize they are doing so. Let us take a night watchman, for example, who is paid near minimum wage to walk around outside a locked facility at night. Someone who befriends this night watchman might be able to convince him or her – aided by some badly needed cash - to "look the other way" for a few moments while he and a friend enter the building for what is portrayed as a mundane and not too harmful purpose. Human nature is a vulnerability widely exploited by terrorists, especially by those adept at social engineering.[72] Everyday people are regularly used and taken advantage of by terrorists.[73]

And finally, as President Bush often points out in his stump speeches around the country, we have to be right one hundred percent of the time. The terrorists only need to get lucky once. The chance of our being right one hundred percent of the time is nil. The chances of the terrorist getting lucky on more than one occasion are considerably higher.

Our *National Strategy for the Physical Protection of Critical Infrastructures and Key Assets* is right on the money when it assigns shared responsibilities for safeguarding of America's economic lifeblood, its critical infrastructure:

> *Homeland security, particularly in the context of critical infrastructure and key asset protection is a shared responsibility that cannot be accomplished by the federal government alone. It requires coordinated action on the part of federal, state, and local governments; the private sector; and concerned citizens across the country.*[74]

Expect more and increasingly lethal attacks upon our critical infrastructure. These incidents are inevitable. But never forget that one or more of them may very well be thwarted by you or me, our eyes and ears ever vigilant, unafraid to take appropriate action.

Complacency is not an option, and denial is deadly. So assume the responsibility. Adopt the creed:

If not me, then who? If not now, then when?

---

[72] "Social engineering" as used in this book is the art of playing against a person's weaknesses in order to get him or her to unwittingly assist in the perpetration of an illegal act. Social engineers often target a victim's vanity, looks, accomplishments, importance, hobbies, and/or accomplishments.

[73] Maria Ressa's book, *Seeds of Terror*, cites some excellent examples of how terror cell leaders duped women whom they had met in bars (and subsequently courted) into opening bank accounts for them, securing apartments, and assisting with other necessary logistics support activities.

[74] "National Strategy for the Physical Protection of Critical Infrastructure and Key Assets." February 2003, p. vii.

Terrorists Always Welcomed Here!

America's porous borders with Canada and Mexico, coupled with its criminal-friendly immigration policies and practices, pose a clear and present danger to our national security and personal safety. Heightened awareness of, and concern about, these problems is placing increased pressure upon the administration and its Department of Homeland Security to get serious about controlling and monitoring the flow of foreigners into our country. Not nearly enough is being done to significantly improve the situation.

With respect to the continuing influx of illegals into the southwestern United States via Mexico, it appears that the Department of Homeland Security cannot even be embarrassed into stopping the flood. In 2005, an assembly of volunteers called the Minutemen grew discontent with what they perceived to be government inaction. They took matters into their own hands on the Arizona-Mexico border. Establishing a 24/7 watch, these common citizens effectively stopped illegal border crossings on the stretch of land that they guarded. Ordinary citizens took up the cause and proved to their elected and appointed officials that our international borders can be effectively secured given resources, personnel and resolve.

Further attention was drawn to America's troubled southern boundary that same year when the governors of both Arizona and New Mexico declared states of emergency to free-up federal funds to enhance their states' border security. International news anchors continue to report live from troubled spots, underscoring the need for more guards, patrols, and high tech equipment. Still the illegals come, and we do not stop enough of them from entering.

I think that if our government refuses to secure our international boundaries, they should at least erect signs along the unprotected stretches of our borders that truly tell it like it is:

WELCOME TO THE USA, WHERE CHEAP LABOR
AND POLITICAL CORRECTNESS MEAN SO MUCH
MORE THAN OUR CITIZENS' LIVES!

CONGRATULATIONS ON YOUR BORDER CROSSING!
THE OTHER 10 MILLION ILLEGAL ALIENS ALREADY
HERE WELCOME YOU!

WELCOME TO AMERICA!

REMEMBER TO ASK ABOUT OUR CATCH AND
RELEASE POLICY!

We have 4,000 miles of Canadian border, 1,940 miles of Mexican border, and as many miles of coastline. A terrorist would have to be just plain stupid and incompetent not to be able to get into the United States, maintaining a low profile until it was time to kill.

I am not naïve; I fully understand why politicians from local through national levels are happy to keep America's doors wide open: votes, special interests, cheap labor, and money. And did I mention cheap labor and votes?

I cannot understand what it is about the need for strict immigration laws and their enforcement, especially post September 11, that so many of my fellow Americans simply cannot grasp. I have heard their arguments: "They (illegal aliens) have rights too," "We have no right to prevent them from seeking a better life," "Why would you deny their families the incomes they need to survive?"

My position is simple and straightforward. I do not deny the right to seek a better life to anyone, anywhere, as long as that path to prosperity is a legal one. Let me make it clear that I do not fault impoverished and otherwise law abiding Mexican citizens from attempting to cross the U.S. border in search of employment that they cannot find in their native country. I would do the same for my family if the need was as great. They do what they feel they must in order to survive. We, as Americans, must also do what we must to survive, and that means keeping border violators on their side of international boundaries.

While I agree that "they" have a right to earn a living and feed their families, the key word here is "legally." I am an American, born and bred. I am not allowed to break the laws. I am not permitted to earn a living illegally. Why shouldn't the same laws that apply to a homegrown American apply to those entering my country illegally? It makes absolutely no sense to me why Americans are content to permit illegals more freedom than they themselves are afforded.

Illegal aliens should have no rights in my country; illegal aliens are criminals. They have no more the right to break into my country than they do to break into my house, car, or business. We not only possess the right to keep illegals out of our country, but post 9-11 we have a responsibility to do so.

There are a myriad of ways for foreigners to legally enter the United States. As a matter of fact, the 9-11 airplane hijackers and homicide bombers ALL entered this country LEGALLY—welcomed with open arms by our U.S. Immigration and Naturalization Service (INS). If the terrorists that killed thousands of people in New York, Pennsylvania, and Washington, D.C. can enter the U.S. legally, there is certainly hope for law-abiding persons who want to gain entry.

Osama bin Laden tells us that more attacks are coming. He says that these attacks will be progressively more brutal, making previous ones pale in comparison. The U.S. has been put on notice that bad people will enter its homeland to do bad things to its citizens. It is only sane, prudent and cautious to take minimum precautions to keep them at bay.

Here is an analogy. Let us say that my next door neighbor continually threatens me and my family. Comments passed weekly include such menacing words as, "One of these days I'm going to kick down your front door and beat the snot out of you!" Let us say that this neighbor has already physically assaulted two other men in the neighborhood. The threat is real. I would be neglectful if I did not take measures to prevent his entry into my home and any ensuing assault. One measure I would immediately take would be to check the locks on my doors and windows and be sure they were secure at all times. Another would be to notify local law enforcement of the threat, so that the police are aware of the man who threatens me by name and face. I may decide to invest in a home security and alarm system. I might even keep a weapon close to my person at all times in case my neighbor actually kicked in my door and came after me or my family members. I certainly would not leave my front door wide open, and I doubt my readers would do so either. Yet this is, in effect, what America does with its borders. It leaves them wide open to those who pledge to cross them and destroy us.

If we collectively do not convince our government to commit the personnel and resources needed to lock our international doors, then we are inexcusably ignorant, and share the blame for whatever happens as a result of our disregard.

The Government's Rampant Dereliction of Duties

Our open borders are just a part of our problem in keeping terrorists and other undesirables out of the United States. The inaction and incompetence of our own immigration authorities are just as much to blame.

Conducting research for this book, I was shocked to discover precisely how inept some top officials of the former Immigration and Naturalization Service (INS)[75] remain post 9-11. The stories stagger the imagination. Michelle Malkin, author of *Invasion: How American Still Welcomes Terrorists, Criminals, and Other Foreign Menaces to Our Shores*, sums it up so succinctly: "Americans must realize that the government has failed to carry out its most basic constitutional duty: to 'provide for the common defense'."[76]

A Washington Post article in February 2002 (five months after the attacks in New York, Pennsylvania, and Washington, D.C.) reported that more than 300,000 illegal aliens ordered deported were "lost" within the "system." Six thousand of them were of Middle Eastern decent.

A USA Today investigation discovered that undercover government officials at thirty-two of our nation's airports were able to sneak knives through security checkpoints seventy percent of the time. They were able to bring simulated explosives through sixty

---

[75] On March 1, 2003 the responsibility for providing immigration-related services and benefits such as naturalization and work authorization were transferred from the Immigration and Naturalization Service (INS) to the U.S. Citizenship and Immigration Services (USCIS), a bureau of Homeland Security. Accessed at http://www.dhs.gov/dhspublic/theme_home4.jsp.

[76] Malkin, Michelle. *Invasion –How America Still Welcomes Terrorists, Criminals, and Other Foreign Menaces to Our Shores* (Washington, D.C.: Regnery Publishing, Inc., 2002), p.xiii.

percent of the time, and guns, thirty percent. This was between November 2001 and February 2002 – again, post- 9-11.[77]

At Miami International Airport, top INS bureaucrats released criminal aliens from their custody in order to relieve jail over-crowding before visiting members of Congress arrived at their detention facility. These top officials are still employed in sensitive positions.[78]

Michael Cochran, Los Angeles Deputy Port Director, issued a February 12, 2002, memo ordering inspection agents as follows: "Unless there is some special, extenuating circumstance, we are not to respond to calls from airlines requesting that we examine the documents of suspected illegal aliens. . . even if something 'special' does come up, i.e., suspected terrorists, kidnapping, slavery or other, we should not go and arrest groups of people."[79]

Harried, overworked and lazy airport inspectors at JFK Airport in New York City admit that they do not even look at visas before stamping their approval nor do they request required documen-tation, because it would take too much time.[80]

At Los Angeles International Airport (LAX) inspectors reported that their supervisors told them NOT to respond to concerns from airlines about illegal immigrants elsewhere within the airport, because it would distract them from their number one duty of processing passengers.[81] It is a safe assumption that after dozens of unanswered calls, airline personnel would simply stop calling.

On April 2, 2002, in Hawaii, nine Chinese men were rescued from an Indonesian oil tanker when it caught fire, and placed into

---

[77] Ibid, p. 5.
[78] Ibid.
[79] Ibid, p. 4.
[80] Ibid.
[81] Ibid.

a hotel. They fled from the hotel in which they were supposed to remain and disappeared into the population. Donald Radcliffe, district director for the INS office in Honolulu, said that the INS did not take them into custody because "we thought they'd play by the rules."[82] We all know that the Chinese are supposed to play by the rules, and so are the Russians, and Saudis, and Koreans, and Indonesians, and French, and Germans, and Afghans, and even the Americans. I would expect public servants like Radcliffe to possess a realistic, as opposed to idealistic, view of humanity.

The U.S. intelligence community knew that terrorists were plotting to use airplanes to kill Americans as early as 1995 when, in the Philippines, a freak apartment fire and subsequent police investigation led to the capture of three terrorists and a computer showing Al Qaeda plans to blow up eleven U.S. airliners. These men – Abdul Hakim Murad, Wali Khan Amin Shah, and Ramsi Yousef – were extradited to the United States, interrogated, and subsequently convicted in a New York court.[83] Five years later, a poorly functioning INS allowed Mohammed Atta – the pilot of the first plane that crashed into the World Trade Center – to enter the U.S. for flight training on a temporary student visa.

Not only did the then-INS permit Atta to enter the U.S. – apparently unaware of his questionable reputation and suspicious prior travels and activities - but six months after Atta and his 9-11 colleagues flew to their deaths, the INS upgraded Atta's temporary student visa to student status, and sent notification to his flight school that his visa had been approved.[84] Even if the immigration and naturalization databases remained outdated and untimely, I would expect the INS employees that processed and approved the post 9-11 student visa for Atta to at least recognize his name from numerous media reports and ask the appropriate questions.

---

[82] Ibid, p. 5.

[83] Ressa, Maria A. *Seeds of Terror* (United States of America: Free Press, 2003), p. xv and 40-44.

[84] Brandt, Ben. "Securing U.S. and Minnesota Borders: Plugging Breaches in a Free Nation of Immigrants." American Experiment Quarterly. Winter 2002-2003, p. 62.

Bureaucrats will give you a handful of reasons why immigration authorities experience great difficulty in doing their jobs. At the top of the list is the extreme political pressure – spurred by airline lobby groups - for inspectors to shorten their inspections in order to expedite processing and air travel. This pressure to speed up service results in absurdity. Often, inspectors have sixty seconds or less to process an individual – little time to do the job properly and in the manner in which they were trained.[85]

Let's not forget the VISA Waiver Program (VWP). "The Visa Waiver Program (VWP) enables nationals of certain countries to travel to the United States for tourism or business for stays of 90 days or less without obtaining a visa. The program was established in 1986 with the objective of promoting better relations with U.S. allies, eliminating unnecessary barriers to travel, stimulating the tourism industry, and permitting the Department of State to focus consular resources in other areas."[86] In a nutshell, this generous loophole provides a final way to gain entry into the U.S. when all of the existing, protective restrictions prevent that entry. It is this program that is responsible for Mohammed Atta being allowed into the country. With no other legal way to permit him entrance into the U.S., authorities granted him entrance under this waiver program.

Let one point remain clear throughout this book. I mostly blame the senior leadership of our government for the wrong doings, NOT the vast majority of dedicated civil service men and women on the front lines who endeavor to serve us in the best manner they can despite paralyzing restrictions, conflicting regulations and policies, improper resources, insufficient numbers of co-workers and extraordinarily long hours. The reality is that these folks have families to feed, kids to raise, and bills to pay. I implore these people to never forget that

---

[85] Ibid.
[86] http://www.travel.state.gov/visa/temp/without/without_1990.html#1.

they are a critical part our first line of defense. Our lives are often in their hands.

The President Shares the Blame

As long as I'm castigating some of our government officials, let me include President George W. Bush. Mr. Bush's 2004 push to legalize between eight and ten million illegal aliens at a time when our nation is at war with some 20,000 Islamist terrorists globally was incredibly irresponsible and potentially lethal. As reported by Bill Sammon in his Washington Times article titled, "Bush revives bid to legalize illegal aliens,"[87] President Bush moved aggressively within days of his re-election to resurrect his plan to relax rules against illegal immigration. "The president met privately in the Oval office with Senator John McCain to discuss jump-starting a stalled White House initiative that would grant legal status to millions of immigrants who broke the law to enter the United States."[88] Thanks to Congressional opposition, the President's plan went nowhere. The Founding Fathers' system of checks and balances saved the day.

President Bush's lackadaisical attitude with respect to our nation's unsecured international boundaries with Canada and Mexico borders on criminal, as his refusal to lock down our threatened nation violates his oath to "protect and defend."

Our Leading Congressmen Share the Blame

Massachusetts Senator Ted Kennedy certainly does not appear concerned about our porous borders. He championed a visa lottery program as a way for Irish illegal immigrants to gain amnesty.[89] "Tens of thousands of foreigners can gamble for a shot at one of America's highly coveted permanent resident immigrant visas (green cards) every year."[90] From 1997 through 2002, 7,409

[87] http://www.washtimes.com/national/20041110-123424-5467r.htm.
[88] Ibid.
[89] Dunn, Ashley. "U.S. Plans Lottery With Jackpot of Legal Residency." Los Angeles Times, May 6, 1991: A1

lottery visas were awarded to applicants from Iraq, Iran, Syria, Libya, Sudan, and Afghanistan. In 2002, Saudi Arabia had 38 lucky green card winners. Egypt had 1,551 winners. Yemen, an Al Qaeda stronghold where our USS Cole was attacked, had 44 lottery recipients. Afghanistan, home to the Taliban and training ground for Al Qaeda, claimed 45 winners. Official state sponsors of terrorism to include Iran, Iraq, Libya, Syria, and Sudan clinched a grand total of 2,259 visa lottery winners.[91]

In February 2002, Democratic House Majority Leader, Dick Gephardt, who is supported by Senator Ted Kennedy and President Bush on this matter, gave a speech on an Hispanic radio station in which he said that, "We need to expand and extend programs like 245(i)." This legal provision, actively championed by Hispanic activists, permits illegal aliens to "adjust" their unlawful status in order to eventually become legal and permanent residents of the United States without ever having to leave our country for having entered it illegally in the first place.

City officials, like the Mayor of New York, appear to be place politics over their cities' security. On November 19, 2001, just two months after 9-11, New York City Mayor-elect Michael Bloomberg reassured immigrants that the city would remain a sanctuary for illegal aliens when he stated that "people who are undocumented do not have to worry about the city government going to the federal government. It is the federal government's job to make sure we get control of our borders and have an appropriate immigration policy."[92] Terrorists welcomed here.

In the city of Colorado Springs, Colorado, mayoral candidate (now elected mayor) Lionel Rivera said during a local, pre-election, post 9-11, radio interview that illegal immigration was not the city's concern, and that illegal immigrants should be able to obtain driver's licenses and employment based upon Mexican

---

[90] Malkin, Michelle. *Invasion –How America Still Welcomes Terrorists, Criminals, and Other Foreign Menaces to Our Shores* (Washington, D.C.: Regnery Publishing, Inc., 2002), p.19.
[91] Ibid.
[92] Ibid, p. 47.

identification papers (matricula consulares) obtainable from the Mexican consulate in Denver. One could argue that the safety and security of Colorado Springs' residents – especially its large military population – is not high on the mayor's priority list. Perhaps someone should remind the mayor that in his city:

- Critical global positioning satellites (GPS) needed by our combat soldiers to navigate on the battlefields and drop precision guided munitions upon our Islamist enemies are controlled from Schriever Air Force Base, in Colorado Springs.

- United States Northern Command – the military homeland defense command for this nation – is headquartered at Peterson Air Force Base, Colorado Springs.

- NORAD, the North American Aerospace Defense is headquartered at Peterson Air Force Base, Colorado Springs.

- The United States Air Force Academy that graduates the pilots who drop bombs on terrorists and insurgents (and sometimes, regrettable as it is, innocent Muslim civilians who become collateral damage victims) is located in Colorado Springs.

- The Army's 10th Special Forces Group, that has killed terrorists and insurgents by the truckloads, is located along with its families in the city of Colorado Springs.

- Cheyenne Mountain Air Station – housing the guardians of Canadian and American air space, is located adjacent to Fort Carson in Colorado Springs.

Terrorists welcomed here.

Our States Are Also To Blame

In recent years, many state legislatures, under pressure from special interest groups, passed laws that made it easier for illegal aliens to obtain driver's licenses. These states included: Tennessee, Virginia, Utah, North Carolina, New Mexico, Missouri, Washington, and California.

Some of the legislation passed to make it more convenient for illegals to get driver's licenses included the following provisions:

- Documents other than social security cards are valid proof of identification to obtain a driver's license;

- License applicants need not prove residency;

- Identity for driver's licenses can be proved with a tax identification number instead of a Social Security number; and,

- Residency certification forms can be accepted as proof of residency to obtain a driver's license.

Terrorists welcomed here.

We Even Have Illegal-Friendly Banks

In November 2001, with the tragedy of 9-11 just two months old, California-based banking leviathan Wells Fargo, announced that it planned to loosen identification requirements for illegal aliens from Mexico who desired to open savings or checking accounts in any of its branches in more than 20 states. Banks normally require foreign customers to show passports or driver's licenses as primary forms of ID. Today, illegal immigrants from Mexico can open their accounts at U.S. banks such as Wells Fargo by showing their matricula consulares (Mexican citizenship ID) as their primary form of identification.

Terrorists welcomed here.

Some Final Thoughts

City dwellers that leave their front doors wide open when no one is home could be called naive or just plain stupid. Countries at great risk that leave their borders open where no one is watching are not naïve. They are felony ignorant. Citizens who allow people to step into their residences without knowing who they are, where they come from, or anything about their backgrounds could be considered inexperienced and placing themselves at risk. Countries under threat that still permit questionable persons to enter through their ports are not inexperienced. They are asking for it.

Until Americans demand that their leaders place border control, immigration policy and enforcement among the highest of national security concerns, this nation will remain at risk, and our foreign enemies will continue to easily enter and perpetrate their dastardly deeds on American soil.

Complacency is not an option, and denial is deadly. So assume the responsibility. Adopt the creed:

If not me, then who? If not now, then when?

BRIEFING # 6

Our Leaders Have Some Issues

The Government Will Not Get it Right Without Citizen Persistence

Our government bureaucracies are like the universe after the theorized "Big Bang." They expand continuously and without any discernable control. Bureaucracies operate at a snail's pace, bogged down with layer upon layer of redundant middle and upper management. Inefficiency is the rule rather than the exception. Deadwood is stacked so high that our competent, dedicated civil servants spend an inordinate amount of time attempting to clear it, move around it, or succeed despite it. In order to maintain a "neck-and-neck" pace with a decentralized, sleek operation like Al Qaeda, Americans need to effect change from the grassroots level. Everyday Americans must pick up both the slack and the pace, because our government at large appears unable, incapable, or unwilling to do so. Permit me to build my case.

The Bush Administration's immediate reaction to Al Qaeda's asymmetric attacks on 9-11 was a resounding cry for more bureaucracy, added symmetry, additional micromanagement, and countless more decision makers, known today as our Department of Homeland Security. Forget about firing people in positions of authority who failed us prior to 9-11. Never mind a radical idea like admitting where and how our existing terror-fighting organizations screwed-up, and subsequently redirecting efforts with more manpower, training, and resources as required. Instead, let's take billions upon billions of dollars and create a new, mega bureaucracy such as the world has never known; so big, in fact, that it will take decades to mold it into an efficient government entity.

The last thing we needed was the Department of Homeland Security. This nation already possessed enough organizations and activities to effectively fight terrorism. The CIA, NSA, FBI, DEA, DOD, U.S. Customs and Border Patrol, and a myriad of law enforcement agencies (LE or LEA) just to name a few. All we had to do was force them to talk to each other and work together, provide them the requisite personnel, training, resources, and hold their leaders accountable.

Instead of moving expeditiously to force existing activities to do their damned jobs, our government saw fit to create several more centralized, indecisive, and inefficient bureaucracies. Among my favorites are the Department of Homeland Security (DHS), its Transportation Safety Administration (TSA), and the Office of the Director of National Intelligence (DNI).

DHS: Our New Mega Bureaucracy

In past briefings, we discussed the absolute advantage that an asymmetric enemy such as Al Qaeda maintains while fighting a linear, overburdened, process-bogged government such as ours. The DHS, by virtue of its gargantuan size, charter, and number of senior decision makers, is yet another Al Qaeda dream come true. The creation of the DHS represents the largest federal reorganization since World War II. I submit that creating the DHS, the merging of 22 government agencies and activities and more than 180,000 government employees at a time when our nation was already fighting three wars, was not necessary or prudent.[93] Let's examine the DHS, our government's stalwart response to our asymmetric, terrorist enemies, in more operational and financial detail.

Anyone who has ever been unfortunate enough to be part of a major government or private sector merger or reorganization knows that it usually takes many years for the dust to settle, the turmoil to subside, and the new organization to begin working at acceptable levels of efficiency and effectiveness.

The creation of DHS represents a merger and reorganization of the greatest magnitude. Here is a list of some of the entities and functions transferred from existing organizations to the new DHS:[94]

ENTITY	Transferred From
Critical Infrastructure Assurance Office	Department of Commerce
National Communications System	FBI
National Infrastructure Protection Center	FBI
National Infrastructure Simulation and Analysis Center	Dept of Energy
Energy Assurance Office	Dept of Energy
Federal Computer Incident Response Center	General Services Admin.
U.S. Coast Guard	Dept of Transportation
U.S. Customs Service	Its Own Separate Entity
Transportation Security Administration	Its Own Separate Entity
Federal Protective Service	Its Own Entity

---

[93] Afghanistan, Iraq, and the Global War on Terror.
[94] Taken from the "Department of Homeland Security Reorganization Plan," November 25, 2002.

Functions of the Immigration & Naturalization Service (INS)	INS
Office of Domestic Preparedness	Its Own Entity
Federal Law Enforcement Training Ctr	Its Own Entity
United States Secret Service	Its Own Entity
National Bio-Weapons Defense Analysis Center	DOD
Federal Emergency Management Agency	It's Own Entity
Integrated Hazard Information System Of the National Oceanographic & Atmospheric Administration (NOAA)	NOAA
National Domestic Preparedness Office	FBI
Domestic Energy Support Team	Dept of Justice
Metro Medical Response System	Dept Health & Human Svc
National Disaster Medical System	Dept Health & Human Svc
Office of Emergency Preparedness & Strategic National Stockpile	Dept Health & Human Svc
Plum Island Animal Disease Center	US Dept of Agriculture

The new sub-bureaucracies created within DHS include five new directorates:[95]

- Border and Transportation Security
- Emergency Preparedness and Response
- Information Analysis & Infrastructure Protection
- Science & Technology
- Management (includes Coast Guard, U.S. Citizen & Immigrations Services, and the U.S. Secret Service)

All of this reorganization, merging and re-naming results in new policies, new procedures, more complicated processes, more regulations, new bosses, office re-locations and reorganizations, and last but not least, the early retirement of some of our more sterling and experienced government men and women who are fed up with yet another major employment and lifestyle change.

DHS: The Costs

The Congressional Budget Office (CBO) estimated that establishing and administering the new department, DHS, would cost about $150 million in fiscal year 2003 and about $225 million each year thereafter.[96] Simply taking these cost estimates at face value (i.e., assuming that they remain accurate over the years and do not increase), we taxpayers are spending $600 million from 2003 through 2006 just to keep DHS operating as a 180,000-person, government monolith.

Department of Homeland Security is sluggish and overburdened with chiefs and decision processes, like any other enormous government entity. Just look at the number of senior decision makers within the DHS headquarters alone. The DHS website organizational chart shows one Secretary, a Deputy Secretary, five Undersecretaries, five Assistant Secretaries, one Special Assistant, one Commissioner, eight Office Heads, and four Office Chiefs. And that's just within the Washington, D.C. headquarters structure.

Let's talk about some of the more creative ways in which the DHS spends our tax dollars. Of all the questionable expenditures, I had to put this one forth. Colorado Representative Marilyn Musgrave revealed that our stellar DHS officials paid $136,000 to former actress Bobbie Faye Ferguson "to review TV and movie scripts, with the possibility of offering technical advice."[97] Musgrave pointed out to her constituents that the money paid to the former actress could have been used to purchase badly needed bullet-resistant vests for her son-in-law's police department – 165 of them to be exact. I will admit that in the grandiose scheme of things, one hundred thousand dollars or so is not a lot of money, but to a cop who is wearing outdated body armor,

[95] http://www.whitehouse.gov/omb/budget/fy2005/homeland.html.
[96] H.R. 5005, Homeland Security Act of 2002, accessed at
http://www.cbo.gov/showdoc.cfm?index=3592$sequence=0
[97] Soraghan, Mike. "Musgrave sees star over cost." The Denver Post, March 21, 2004.

expenditures such as this are legitimately questionable.

Here's my bottom line, and I am sticking to it. September 11, 2005 marked four years since the 9-11 tragedy. After the creation of DHS, its mergers and reorganizations, dollar expenditures into the billions, and the efforts of tens of thousands of government bureaucrats, the average citizen is not markedly safer from the threat of terror attacks than he or she was on September 10, 2001:

- Still, less than five percent of the tens of millions of shipping containers offloaded at U.S. seaports each year is ever one hundred percent inspected by our port authorities;

- Still, less than ten percent of all cargo loaded into the bellies of our commercial passenger jets is ever one hundred percent inspected by the TSA;

- Still, our borders with Canada and Mexico are among the most porous and unguarded of any industrialized nation; and,

- Still, it is questionable whether or not our intelligence and law enforcement agencies share all of their critical and time-sensitive information.

Is our nation any more prepared at the federal level to deal with the next major terror attack against our homeland? After observing the feds' less than stellar handling of the Hurricane Katrina aftermath, I have serious doubts.

Many Americans remain less than impressed with the federal government's DHS response to Hurricane Katrina and the subsequent fiasco in New Orleans. A lack of situational awareness, indecision, and power politics remained the order of the day, while our fellow Americans – told to rally at the New Orleans Superdome – suffered without food, water, sanitation, or medical assistance. Many perished. Granted, there is plenty of blame to go around at all levels, from the New Orleans mayor himself, to the Louisiana State governor, right on up through DHS and into the Oval Office. The direct and proximate result of this negligence at so many levels is that the City of New Orleans became a third world nation overnight. Hundreds of thousands were homeless. Young and old alike dehydrated in the stifling heat. Mothers struggled to keep their young babies alive. While all the king's horses and all the king's men sat back, argued, and debated, our brethren perished on American soil.

Where was the workable disaster relief plan at the city and state levels? Why didn't the governor bring the feds in to bail out Louisiana's sorry state of affairs before the suffering and death escalated to such an unacceptable level? When it was obvious that the City of New Orleans and the State of Louisiana were ill-prepared and ill-equipped to respond to a disaster the magnitude of Hurricane Katrina, why didn't President Bush immediately federalize the situation and take control? A large part of the answer is "politics." Could President Bush have taken complete control of the rescue and response from the state of Louisiana at anytime? Yes. Why didn't he? For a president to basically supersede a state's rights to its own sovereignty is a risky political move with potentially grave ramifications come election time. It was better that Americans be allowed to suffer and die. After all, the city and state are ultimately responsible for their citizens, not the federal government.

The global media gobbled up Hurricane Katrina aftermath coverage. The world saw the pathetic and inexcusable manner in which the greatest nation on Earth was unable to render immediate and effective assistance to tens of thousands of its own suffering citizens. As the world press harshly criticized our nation for its inability to function responsibly, yet another recruiting tool for the likes of Al Qaeda was born. Now terror recruiters could turn their lies into recruiting ads and slogans by showing news footage and applying their own spin. "Americans leave their own black citizens to suffer and die." "The American government permitted its own elderly men, women and babies to die in the hot Louisiana sun with no water or food."

Were I a terrorist leader and planner, the Katrina debacle would have served to motivate and encourage me to plan and execute "The Big One." I know now as a terrorist that America is unable to handle major disaster response and recovery in the larger but predominantly less affluent cities. Handling "water events" is obviously not America's forte. Maybe flying a big airliner into a major damn structure and flooding out the cities below is an idea worth pursuing.

Numerous foreign press reports in reaction to the Katrina calamity were highly and rightfully critical of our government's inability to get it right the first time. Do our leaders have homeland security issues? After Hurricane Katrina, much of the world thinks so:

> *Katrina, the "political hurricane" that struck the United States, exposed the weakness of the American model for dealing with natural disasters. . .one would have expected U.S. agencies to handle the crisis . . .with a greater measure of success than the agencies of other countries do. What actually happened, however, was a total failure in dealing with this crisis in a scientific and appropriately professional way.*
> – "The American Model Is Shaky: Katrina, the Political Hurricane, Has Not Blown Over Yet," Sep 17, 2005, by Ali Bin-Shuwayl, Al Jazeera Television, QATAR.

> *The world has been horrified at the American response to Hurricane Katrina and its aftermath in New Orleans. Four years after the terrorist attacks of September 2001, with billions of dollars allegedly spent on preparedness for*

another emergency, America has shown the world that it is not prepared even for an event that came with ample warning. – "Lessons Learned from the Black Tsunami," Sep 17, 2005, The Nation, THAILAND

Chinese officials tasked with disaster relief have been closely observing fallout from Hurricane Katrina with shock. It is not just the apparent ineffectiveness of the federal government response. Their greatest concern is they have been adopting Federal Emergency Management Agency procedures for years, assuming they knew best.— "Mr. Bush's Glass House Shatters," Sep 20, 2005, South China Morning Post, CHINA

Washington's incompetence and sluggishness in dealing with "natural calamities" and consequently the awful awkwardness and failure of authorities to carry out rescue and relief operations and help the mainly poor and coloured people of the area has turned into a political crisis on the scene of U.S. domestic politics. – "Excuse by Name of Katrina," Sep 7, 2005, The Reselat, Tehran, IRAN

America is a maximalist state viewed from the outside and a minimalist state when the perspective is from within. Tellingly, Washington had to bring troops back from Iraq to deal with the crisis in Louisiana. While there seems to be no limit to the resources the U.S. can deploy abroad, at home it appears to be ill equipped to deal with calamity. The U.S. is not a Third World country, yet it suffers from a desperate shortage of domestic institutions. – "The American Way of Death," Sep 19, 2005, by Azmi Bishara, The Daily Observer, Oman, JORDAN

America's struggle to win the minds and hearts of the Muslim world in our fight against global terror is a full time proposition. There is no "off" switch. In an age of immediate information at the speed of satellite links, America keeps few secrets. Our kimono always remains partially open, and the world is continually peeking in. After Katrina, the world questions our post-9-11 anti-terror readiness posture. Frankly, I do also.

The TSA

Let's talk about transportation security. It did exist before 9-11, although obviously lacking in effectiveness. After September 11, we should have poured big bucks into more personnel, training, and technology for those organizations and security personnel already performing transportation security duties at our air, ground, and sea ports. Instead, the Bush Administration created yet another massive and questionably effective organization called the Transportation Safety Administration. Maybe there is someone who can follow the logic in standing up TSA, but I cannot.

As Texas Republican Congressman, Dr. Ron Paul, so eloquently stated: "TSA was created in the wake of the September 11, 2001, terrorist attacks. Although the National Guard, DOD, FBI, CIA, NSA, and FAA utterly failed to protect American citizens on that tragic day, federal legislators immediately proposed creating yet another government agency."[98]

Problems with TSA are becoming legendary. In the rush to hire the post 9-11 new TSA workforce, 28,000 screeners were put to work without having undergone background checks. Some turned out to be convicted felons. Others were drug abusers. Many were young and uneducated, with little job experience. Overnight, these folks were federally empowered to make any and all calls in the airport. At Kennedy and LaGuardia airports in New York, police arrested dozens of TSA employees who were stealing valuables from the luggage they were assigned to

---

[98] "TSA-Bullies at the Airport," is a castigating article by Rep. Ron Paul, MD. Accessed at http://www.lewrockwell.com/paul/paul220.html

inspect.[99] Today, the only locks approved for travelers' suitcases are TSA-approved locks, which the TSA inspectors can open at will. Apparently, here is how the luggage security game is played. Transportation Safety Administration inspectors - many of whom possess questionable backgrounds - can take things out of our suitcases or put things into them. They have complete control. The traveling public has none.

The Government Accounting Office (GAO) and private consulting firms report that the TSA is bureaucratic and unresponsive, plagued with morale problems, understaffed, overworked, and possessing poorly articulated guidelines.

I travel regularly and find most of the TSA inspectors to be friendly and courteous. Every now and then one of them verbally crosses the line, being rude, abrupt, or impolite. I deal with it firmly and politely, but I don't let them get away with it. I'm the taxpayer. I'm an American. I will not be abused by a federal screener in a public airport when I have done nothing wrong.

I question some of the routine TSA actions in airports. I observe little old ladies and five-year-olds being led away from the crowds for more detailed search, while other travelers who look quasi-suspicious to me, pass through the security screening with ease. I know persons who have unwittingly taken razor blades and mini-box cutters, removable from their key chains, through TSA airport screenings and onto aircraft without detection or confiscation. While these weapons still find their way into passenger cabins, well-endowed women are told to strip to the waist, so that TSA authorities can "examine" them for bombs (I don't mean visually, I mean manually).

We all have to remove our shoes and send them through the scanning machine or be subjected to a personal search. Yet as of

---

[99] Ibid.

January 2006, only a few U.S. airports have technology on-site that enables TSA personnel to detect such dangerous items as liquid nitroglycerin that passengers may be attempting to take onboard.[100]

Knives and scissors have been banned from airplane carry-on luggage since shortly after 9-11. Rightfully so, I believe. I have flown regularly for more than 35 years. I cannot think of even one time when I needed scissors or a knife to survive the flight (a stiff drink or a barf bag at times, but never a knife or scissors). It took a few years, but the flying public adjusted and accepted the TSA's "no knives, no scissors" ruling. No knives, no scissors, no problem. All of a sudden in 2005, the TSA announced it was moving to permit knives and scissors to once again be carried onto aircraft by passengers. Why? No one needs them onboard a flight except the bad guys. Where is the logic? What happened to common sense? Where is the adult leadership? I all-too-often cannot find it within the TSA. Al Qaeda must certainly remain puzzled and amused by our TSA policies.

I believe that most TSA screeners in our airports – the ones doing the day-to-day grunt work, dealing face-to-face with the traveling public - are dedicated, hardworking civil servants who are trying their best to keep us safe. I have heartburn with the TSA leadership that establishes policy, procedure, and priorities for the screeners.

I argue that the biggest threat to airline safety today is the un-inspected luggage and packages loaded into the cargo holds of passenger airliners, especially the big ones. As packages that might contain timed bombs, radioactive materials, or harmful toxins are stacked into the belly of my 7 a.m. flight, I am taken once again aside by a TSA inspector and asked to unbuckle my belt and take off my shoes. I simply do not get it. I don't think TSA does either.

---

[100] Ramsi Yousef, Al Qaeda's chief bomb-maker in the early 1990s, did just that and managed to time-detonate a bomb that blew a hole in a 747-jet liner over the Pacific.

The Director of National Intelligence

Among the breakdowns leading up to 9-11, I remain convinced that our intelligence community-at-large failed us in many respects. The agencies did not employ and train enough human intelligence (HUMINT) assets (spies) who spoke Arabic and Farsi and could penetrate Islamist radical and terror organizations. "Firewall" laws[101] between the supposedly cooperating agencies that make up our intelligence community, forced them to remain at odds and in competition with one another. Information was not shared on a timely basis, especially between the CIA and FBI. The bottom line is that the leaders within the intelligence community – especially the Director of Central Intelligence (DCI) himself – failed to properly execute their duties. The first step towards a solution – and ensuring that our top officials did not abrogate their duties in the future - should have been to fire those in charge who failed to thwart the 9-11 terror attacks. They, and those under their direct supervision, ignored the warnings leading up to the 9-11 attacks.

It would appear that to hold a failed government official accountable for poor performance is virtually unthinkable in this day and age. I know of no top-ranking government official who lost his or her job over the 9-11 tragedy. Not one. Instead of firing, hiring, and holding feet to the fire, the Bush Administration's solution was to create yet another new layer of intelligence bureaucracy: Office of the Director of National Intelligence (DNI). As President Bush himself explained to Congress: "The National Intelligence Director will serve as the President's principal intelligence advisor and will oversee and coordinate the foreign and domestic activities of the intelligence community."[102]

---

[101] By this I mean certain policies and procedures – especially within the CIA and FBI - set in place with, I am sure, was the best of intentions: to keep each organizations working within legal charter, so as not to cause conflicts of interest or redundancies.
[102] President's remarks on intelligence reform, accessed at http://www.whitehouse.gov/news/release/2004/08/200408902-2.html.

The reality surrounding the creation of this new cabinet position is that the DNI has no real power or control over organizations such as the Central Intelligence Agency, the National Security Agency, the Defense Intelligence Agency, or the National Reconnaissance Office. Why? Because the DNI does not possess budget control or hire and fire authority over any of the dozen or so organizations and activities that make up our intelligence community. The DNI is a cabinet post that, once again, places an additional layer of taxpayer-subsidised bureaucracy between those who own and operate the intelligence community and the White House. The next time a successful terror attack in the U.S. is attributed to an intelligence community failure we can blame the new and virtually powerless DNI, the executive branch of government that created it, the Congress that approved it, or we can create yet another position of authority within our intelligence community to supposedly do it right the next time.

Do our leaders have some issues? I believe that they do indeed.

What Is It About 'Planes Should Not Be Permitted To Fly In No Fly Zones' That Our Government Refuses To Confront?

Remember 9-11? The big airplanes? The crashes? The destruction at the Pentagon? The fact that the flight that plummeted into a Pennsylvania field was probably targeting the White House or Capitol Hill? Just checking.

It appears that our national leadership does not grasp the fact that they are supposed to protect our nation's capital and other cities from air attacks. They still do not get it. Almost five years after September 11, airplanes continue to violate our capital's air space with little or no ramifications and not one "shoot-down" to date.

Here is my going-in position, and I'm sticking to it: *Any person licensed and trusted to fly an airplane over the continental United States should be smart enough to know about the post-9-11, no-fly zone over Washington, D.C.* If they cannot grasp the concept of "no-fly," then they SHOULD NOT FLY, EVER!

On May 5, 2005, a single-engine plane flew into restricted air-space over Washington, D.C. The White House and Capitol Hill were evacuated. Subdued panic was the order of the day on the downtown streets. Former Secretary of Homeland Security –Tom Ridge – was quoted as saying, "They (authorities) saw it was a Cessna, saw it was a single-engine plane and took care of it."[103] My interpretation of Ridge's comments is that this small plane was not much of a threat, and was permitted to fly through Washington's restricted air space for many minutes without being shot down.

Took care of it? I don't think so. Got lucky once again? I believe so.

It was just a single-engine plane. Does Mr. Ridge understand that with today's state-of-the-art explosives, a Cessna single-engine aircraft can wreak a massive amount of damage and destruction if crashed into a populated target or national landmark by a homicidal pilot? Do Mr. Ridge and other men and women in positions of responsibility understand that a little Cessna, packed with radioactive materials and conventional explosives can become an RDD – radiological dispersion device? Has everyone in charge of our defense forgotten the Cessna that crashed onto the White House lawn during the early days of the Clinton presidency?

The pilot was reported as "lost" over the nation's capital. How the hell does a pilot become "lost" on a clear day over our nation's capital? From 20,000 feet in the air, one can clearly see such Washington landmarks as the Washington Monument, Jefferson

---

[103] NBC's Today Show. May 13, 2005.

and Lincoln Memorials, White House, the Capital Building, and the Reflecting Pool. Nothing from that altitude can be more recognizable than the Pentagon. Post 9-11, any pilot noticing he or she is within miles of the heart of Washington, D.C. should immediately divert without being told to do so.

This Cessna failed to respond to a Homeland Security helicopter scrambled to stop it.[104] It was necessary for military jets to fire four warning flares at the single-engine aircraft before it turned away from our national landmarks.

According to the timeline of events as reported by MSNBC,[105] authorities did not react to the air intrusion in enough time to have stopped a terrorist at the stick from crashing the Cessna into the heart of our nation's capital.

The MSNBC News account reported that:

- The incident began at 11:28 a.m. when the Federal Aviation Administration radar picked up the small plane. At 11:28 the plane was 21 miles – about 17 minutes flying time – from Washington, D.C.

- One Black Hawk helicopter and one Cessna Citation jet belonging to the U.S. Customs and Border Protection were dispatched at 11:47 a.m. from Reagan National Airport. The nineteen-minute gap was completely unacceptable.

- At the White House, the Secret Service did not raise the alert level to "red" until 12:03 p.m., with the intruder Cessna just 10 miles from the White House. Thirty-five minutes transpired from the time the FAA picked up the plane until the time the Secret Service moved to red alert.

---

[104] From an Associated Press report of May 12, 2005, posted at http://www.msnbc.msn.com/id/7828525.
[105] Ibid, p. 2.

- The Capitol Police put the Capitol on red alert at 12:04 p.m., 36 minutes after the airspace violator was detected.

- Authorities said the Custom's Citation established communication with the small plane's pilot at 12:06.

- It took 47 minutes to notify President Bush that a plane was headed in the direction of the White House.

- The Departments of Defense and State did not even evacuate their personnel.

- FOX News reported that at the height of the incident, the plane was only 90 seconds flight time from the general vicinity of the White House.[106]

Let's do some math on this one. At 11:28, the plane was 17 minutes flying time from the nation's capital. Contact was established with the violating pilot at 12:06 p.m. THIRTY-EIGHT (38) minutes transpired from the time the FAA picked the plane up on radar until the interceptors made contact and diverted the plane to Frederick, Maryland. Only 17 minutes to the heart of D.C. at 11:28 a.m., a terrorist piloting that small plane could have successfully crashed it into a D.C. landmark in the 38 minutes it took for our authorities to take action. To the bureaucrats' ways of thinking – the Tom Ridge's of the world – the system worked well. All's well that ends well. I do not agree at all. All ended well despite our response, and not because of it.

How should this intrusion into restricted airspace have been handled? The only option is crystal clear to me. It was a clear day, and the weather was good, so as soon as the plane neared

---

[106] FOX & Friends reporter E.D. Hill, 8:08 a.m. EDT. May 13, 2005.

a course into restricted airspace, attempts should have made to contact the pilot and divert the plane. Simultaneously, armed fighter jets should have been scrambled. Once the aircraft entered the restricted airspace, it should have been shot down – no questions asked. We are at war. This is not a made-for-TV movie. Any pilot ignorant enough in this day and age to even threaten restricted air space over our nation's capital deserves to be shot down.

Perhaps the June 9, 2004 near downing of Kentucky Governor Fletcher's plane over Washington, D.C. and near tragedies like it, are one reason why authorities hesitate to order a shoot down.[107] Military and civilian powers fear the political and legal ramifications of a possible "mistake." If we deal with the facts, though, there can be no "mistaken" shoot downs. If a plane is ordered shot down within a U.S. city's no-fly zone, NO MISTAKE IS MADE. Planes in a post 9-11 no-fly zone are subject to being taken out of the air, period. Every pilot should know this, and, in fact, all pilots do. If innocents die when a plane is brought down inside a no-fly zone, the result may be rightfully described as "tragic," or "unfortunate," but the word "mistake" could not be used. The general officer who orders a shoot down is doing the job that your tax dollars pay him to do – protect us and "provide for the common defense." It's as simple as that.

In reality, if you are a general or flag officer authorized within strict rules of engagement (ROE) to shoot down an aircraft over U.S. airspace, and you don't possess the guts to do so when the ROE justifies such a shoot down, then resign and let someone else protect us, as you are no value in the fight. During the editing of this book two more planes were permitted to enter Washington, D.C. restricted air space. One incident occurred on the evening of Wednesday, June 29, 2005 and

---

[107] The Kentucky governor was flying to Washington, D.C. for President Ronald Reagan's funeral. His aircraft violated the city's airspace. Had this plane been shot down within the no-fly zone, the officer giving the order would have inadvertently killed an American governor.

received very little publicity. President Bush was "hurried from his residence to a safer location and lawmakers were evacuated from the Capitol."[108] Then on Sunday, July 3, 2005 the Associated Press reported that a small Cessna passenger plane "entered restricted air space in the Washington area before two fighter jets forced it to land."[109] How many more intrusions will be permitted before the terrorists figure out that small planes are the only way to fly?

If one reads voluminously from the Department of Homeland Security (DHS) website – http://www.dhs.gov – it becomes clear that DHS believes that a key component for defeating terror is immediate response and information sharing among federal, state, and local officials. On May 12, 2005, however, our government officials demonstrated their inability to immediately respond and inform all parties concerned.

Washington, D.C. Mayor Anthony Williams reported that city officials were not told about the Cessna threat until the "all clear" was sounded, "more than 10 minutes after the White House and Capitol were evacuated."[110] A city government building that houses the mayoral and District of Columbia council offices, located only two blocks from the White House, was not evacuated. "Sharing" critical information has yet to become a manageable homeland security task. As taxpayers, we should not be amused.

What if the Cessna pilot was a terrorist who spoke flawless English? What if the Cessna pilot was stringing authorities along – just long enough to plunge the small plane into a national landmark? What if the general officer authorized to direct a shoot down – the memory of Governor Fletcher's near catastrophe in 2004 still glaring – hesitated to give the order just long enough

---

[108] FOX NEWS Web Site-posted article "Plane Forced to Land After Air Space Scare." Associated Press. Frederick, Maryland. July 3, 2005. http://www.foxnews.com/story/0,2933,161440,00.html.
[109] Ibid.
[110] Associated Press report of May 12, 2005, posted at http://www.msnbc.msn.com/id/7828525.

to enable the terrorist to succeed? Do we think for a New York minute that terrorists don't fully comprehend our weaknesses and work to exploit them? Surely, they do. I believe that our enemies can force our leaders into situations that make them hesitate and think twice before issuing orders, just long enough to enable an attack to be successful.

I believe that the terrorists have at least one more solid chance of executing a 9-11-type scenario involving the use of small aircraft over the nation's capital or other U.S. metropolis.

What is it About 'Our Borders Must Be Sealed' that Our Government Simply Cannot Understand?

On May 13, 2005, both FOX News and The Washington Times reported that, "U.S. border patrol agents have been ordered not to arrest illegal aliens along the section of the Arizona border where protectors[111] patrolled last month because an increase in apprehensions there would prove the effectiveness of Minuteman volunteers."[112]

More than a dozen border agents – all of whom asked the Washington Times reporter that they not be identified for fear of retribution – said that orders issued from Border Patrol supervisors at the Naco, Arizona station made it clear that arrests were "not going to go up" along the 23-mile section of the border that the Minuteman volunteers monitored with great success. Border agents reported that new arrests were being kept to an absolute minimum in order "to offset the effect of the Minuteman

---

[111] "Protectors" makes reference to the Minutemen – average men and women who volunteered their time in April 2005 to maintain what turned out to be an extremely effective watch over this infamous stretch of the Arizona border with Mexico.

[112] Seper, Jerry. "Border patrol told to stand down in Arizona." The Washington Times, May 13, 2005 @ http://www.washingtontimes.com/national/20050513-122032-5055r.htm

[113] Ibid.

vigil."[113] Patrols along this famous stretch of Arizona border have also been severely limited in order to reduce the number of new arrests.

Border Patrol Chief David V. Aguilar at the agency's Washington, D.C. headquarters called the accusations "outright wrong."[114] Does the Chief think that the taxpayers he supports are stupid? This is not a case of just one disgruntled employee complaining. More than a dozen experienced and frustrated agents – putting their careers at risk even speaking off the record – are telling their fellow citizens that the border patrol supervisors are not taking national security seriously.

I would expect Chief Aguilar, our number one border patrol authority, to say something like, "I'll look into these allegations immediately," or "Something is obviously not right in Arizona, and I'm going to the Naco station to personally investigate these allegations." But he said the accusations were "outright wrong." DENIAL. DENIAL. DENIAL.

In my opinion, the chief either: (1) knew there was a problem, but for political reasons was not going to stop the local officials from issuing "no arrest" orders, (2) the chief or one of his cronies directed the actions on the 23-mile stretch of border for political reasons, or (3) when the chief's supervisors in Naco told him "we didn't give those orders," he blindly accepted their statements as ground truth. Any one, or all of the above, reasons for his statement are totally unacceptable in my opinion. We are a nation at war, and yet it appears that our Chief of Border Patrol either does not care enough to fix a serious problem in Arizona or does not want

---

[113] Ibid.
[114] Ibid.

to see his department embarrassed by the more effective border control implemented by the Minuteman citizen volunteers.[115]

Still think that our government leaders are looking out for us? I think they are looking out for themselves first. After all, that's politics, is it not?

The 4,000-mile stretch of Canadian border also remains a serious problem for both the U.S. and Canada. In 1999, the car driven by would-be "Millennium Bomber" Ahmed Ressam was fortunately stopped for random inspection when driving over the Canadian border into Port Angeles, Washington. Ressam had nitroglycerin and four timing devices concealed in the car's spare tire wheel well. He was later convicted of plotting to bomb Los Angeles International Airport.

Although the number of border patrol agents was doubled after September 11, large expanses of Canadian border still remain unmanned. Fox News reported that, "The union representing Canadian customs agents identified 225 roads along the U.S.-Canadian border that are currently unguarded, 50 of them in British Columbia."[116] Why did the Millennium Bomber go through a guarded crossing when he could have crossed via one of the hundreds of unmanned roads? Your guess is as good as mine. Perhaps he was just plain stupid. God help us if the likes of him wake up and smell the coffee.

In October 2005, Homeland Security Secretary Michael Chertoff stated during various radio and TV interviews that the U.S. needs to account for the millions of illegal aliens in our country. When asked by reporters how the DHS would keep track of ten million-plus persons illegally in the United States,

---

[115] These 850 + volunteers in effect shut down illegal border crossing along the 23-mile section they purveyed. The Minutemen alerted Border patrol authorities when they observed illegal crossing, resulting in the arrests of 349 illegal aliens.
[116] Fox News. "Canadian Border Security Needs Boosting." July 3, 2005. www.foxnews.com/story/0,2933,161446,00.html.

Secretary Chertoff stated that their addresses will be placed into a large data base. I have a problem with this proposed "solution." Call me a skeptic, but I just don't see every illegal man and woman notifying the DHS when they change residences and addresses so that our national database can remain current and accurate. Secretary Chertoff obviously believes that they will. Is yet another government data base the government's solution to controlling illegal aliens within the United States? I think some of our leaders need a reality check.

Badges? We Don't Need No Stinkin' Badges

During the second week of May 2005, agents from the Immigration and Customs Enforcement (ICE), another of the many divisions of the Department of Homeland Security, "seized more than 1,300 'high-quality counterfeit' badges representing officials from 35 different federal, state, and local law enforcement agencies."[117] Among the fake credentials nabbed in the raid were those resembling identification cards from the FBI, Secret Service, Drug Enforcement Administration, New York Police Department, and Federal Air Marshals. Immigration and Customs Enforcement has no idea how many of these near perfect fake badges and credentials are already in the hands of the bad guys.

Our government officials tell citizens to be on the lookout for persons showing these fake badges and credentials. I ask: "How?" Could most Americans pick out a real FBI credential from an almost perfect fake? Even after three decades of government service, I could not. Once again, the government direction looks good on paper: "Be on the lookout for fake law enforcement IDs." Their butts are covered, but ours are left swinging in the breeze.

---

[117] Meeks, Brock N. "Counterfeit badges pose 'serious' security." May 11, 2005 @ http://www.msnbc.msn.com/id/7818052

We Must Hold Our Leaders Accountable

Our national leaders at the highest levels of government ignore or fail to effectively perform their duties with impunity. Former Director of Central Intelligence, John Deutch, placed highly-classified CIA files on several unclassified, unprotected computers in and around the Washington, D.C. metropolitan area. As an Army lieutenant colonel, or a civilian defense contractor, the price I would pay for such blatant disregard of security regulations is very severe. At best, my government security clearances would be revoked as would have my ability to earn money on any government contract requiring a security clearance. Worst case, I would end up in prison. Top government officials appear to be immune from any penalties. They remain well above the laws that apply to me and other common citizens.

Director of Central Intelligence, George Tenet, was at the helm of the intelligence community during its failures leading up to 9-11. He should have been relieved of his duties soon after. He was not. America went to war with Iraq based primarily upon "facts" provided to the President by his intelligence community, headed by Director Tenet. George Tenet told President Bush that Saddam Hussein had weapons of mass destruction. In the Oval Office, Tenet assured the President it was a "slam dunk." The intelligence proved to be dead wrong. Still, the President did not relieve Director Tenet of his duties.

Another example of our government's tolerance of the misdeeds of its senior officials is President Clinton's National Security Advisor, Sandy Berger, who blatantly and illegally stuffed his clothing with classified documents from our National Archives. He remains a free man today who received a mere slap on the wrist for his deliberate disregard for our national security. There are rarely any serious penalties levied against senior government officials who knowingly and intentionally compromise our security. This is wrong. This must stop. When it involves blatant compromises of national security, justice should be administered regardless of seniority, duty position, rank, and time in grade.

In executing Operation Iraqi Freedom, Secretary of Defense Donald Rumsfeld violated one of the time-honored and sacred principles of war: unity of command. When the official hostilities ended and the job of stabilizing, securing, and rebuilding Iraq began, the only one in charge of Iraq was the Secretary of Defense himself, almost half a world away from the day-to-day occurrences and realities there. The Combatant Commander of United States Central Command (USCENTCOM), General Abizaid, was solely in charge of the armed forces fighting in Iraq. A politician, Ambassador Paul Bremer, was in charge of the Coalition Provisional Authority (CPA) in Baghdad performing the day-to-day governing roles. No one individual was placed in charge inside Iraq. The "buck stopped nowhere." Confusion always existed between both staffs as to whether a decision was Abizaid's call or Bremer's. The conflict and consternation between the two staffs often caused a good plan or necessary action to be tabled or side-stepped because it was simply too painful to work through the convoluted chain of command and the politics of it all. Americans and Iraqis paid the price. Insurgents organized, supported by Al Qaeda. Fighters streamed across the unprotected Syrian and Iranian borders. Iraqis came to view the Americans as an occupying power with its Iraqi puppets placed in charge of the new Iraqi government. Security and stability was never seized and achieved from the get go.

I was working with the DOD at that time. I can personally vouch for the lack of communication and coordination between the USCENTCOM and the CPA staffs, as well as the disjointed operations and chaos that resulted from no one person being "physically" in charge of the U.S. effort inside Iraq.

What can we do about "leaders" who refuse to properly execute their duties and responsibilities? How do we deal with high-ranking public servants who are in no hurry to "get it right?" How do we effect change while remaining clearly within the limits of the law at all times? It is difficult. My contributions include voicing and writing my opinions privately and publicly, and advising my government clients in a totally honest manner when I serve them in a consulting role. I also voice my opinions at election time. Everybody can do something. Writing to local, state and national politicians, working petitions and referendums, and getting involved with local citizens' groups are just a few possibilities. In order to stay on top of it all, we must discipline ourselves to:

- **Stay Educated.** Many Americans do not read enough to keep apprised of what is or is not being done on their behalf by their elected and appointed officials. Knowledge of current events is so very important. Web sites such as those operated by MSNBC and CNN[118] can be quickly scanned several times each day to maintain what the military calls "operational awareness." Try to keep your knowledge base "an inch deep across the entire lake." Then, do "deep dives" on those stories which require more attention to detail.

- **Share Knowledge.** Sharing knowledge with family and friends benefits everyone. Recommend books to read, web sites to visit, and news events or documentaries to watch on television.

- **Impart Opinion and Influence at Every Opportunity.** Attend and vocalize at local school, city council, and state level meetings when issues important to the cause are at stake. Exercise freedom of speech: that's

---

[118] www.msnbc.com and www.cnn.com.

what it's there for! If you feel strongly enough about an issue, ask to be interviewed by local newspapers and television reporters. It is surprisingly easy to get publicity for your cause.

- **Vote Always.** Vote whenever the opportunity presents itself. If elected officials do not live up to your expectations, then vote them out of office. If appointed officials are making poor decisions, lead campaigns to have them removed from office.

- **Teach Our Children.** Don't ignore the kids. Kids are tough. Kids are smart. We need to raise the next generation to be aware, concerned, and active. Let your children know what you are fighting for, how you are going about it, and what you are attempting to achieve. These are important life skills that they must learn, and grade school age is not too early to begin the teaching.

Complacency is not an option, and denial is deadly. So assume the responsibility. Adopt the creed:

If not me, then who? If not now, then when?

Our Own Kids Can Be Terrorists Too

Child - On - Child Violence

Just a few decades ago, the very notion that children would be murdered in their schools by other children was unthinkable. Sadly, it is not only a reality of 21st century American life, but remains a uniquely American epidemic. Whether an Islamist terrorist is pointing an AK-47 or a student is wielding a .44 Magnum handgun, both are equally capable of killing a son or daughter, a brother or sister, a teacher, administrator, or coach. In the final analysis, terrorists are terrorists, bullets are bullets, and we must find a way to keep them out of our schools.

As of the 2006 printing of this book, not one American school, thank God, has fallen victim to an international terror attack. Until that sad day arrives, one of the greatest threats to the safety of our children remains gun violence perpetrated by fellow students in school. We have to accept this and deal with it in an effective manner. Just as with the global Islamist terror movements, if we cannot identify the root causes of domestic child terror and eradicate them, we will never stop the attacks in our schools.

The Sources of Child Violence & Killing . . .
What the Studies Show Us

Lieutenant Colonel Dave Grossman, a retired U.S. Army Ranger, degreed psychologist, and a recognized expert on killing,[119] reminds us that, "for the first time in human history we are dealing with a large scale epidemic of preteen and teenage mass murders."[120] The pre-teens and teens who commit these murders are domestic terrorists.

Grossman blames much of the new preteen and teenage violence on the video game industry, Hollywood movies, and TV shows that desensitize our children to violence from a very young age. In his books *On Killing*, and *On Combat*, Grossman makes a definitive link between teens who murder and the extremely violent video games that they play. Some of the most popular video games that too many young children are permitted to play award points for the greatest number of crimes committed in the shortest period of time. Kids are rewarded for perpetrating illegal acts including murder, and are penalized if they fail to inflict enough death and destruction within an allotted time frame. Hours upon hours of this type of play can be extremely detrimental to a young mind.

Some of the more popular video games that end up in the gaming machines of preteens and teens reward them for performing such entertaining acts as:

- Stealing cars, selling drugs, making money, then buying and having sex with a prostitute;

- Once the sex with the prostitute is over, shooting the prostitute, and watching as she bleeds and pleads for her life; and,

---

[119] Lt Col Grossman's has published several books on the subject of killing and why people kill. His Web Site is www.killology.com: it is well worth a visit! His books are a 'must read.'
[120] Grossman, Dave, Lt. Col. *On Combat: The Psychology and Physiology of Deadly Conflict in War and in Peace*. (United States: .PPCT Research Publications, 2004), p. 80

- Shooting a cop, and then, while the cop is dying, urinating into his mouth.

Even though a game such as Grand Theft Auto: San Andreas contains "graphic violence and brutal murders of women" it was rated "M" (Mature) by the Entertainment Software Rating Board (ESRB) instead of "AO" (Adults Only).[121] On July 11, 2005 ABC Evening News reported that explicit pornographic scenarios are now available to players of Grand Theft Auto: San Andreas. "The player is able to direct scenes of explicit sexual activity."[122] Ten-year-olds can now create their own graphic sexual interludes, in addition to the normal fun of killing prostitutes and urinating into a dying cop's mouth.[123]

The video game companies appear to have no problem peddling this all-to-realistic, high-tech garbage to our kids. This is America. It is all about competition, market share and profit margins.

We can remain in denial as parents and guardians or face what is now scientifically proven fact. Lieutenant Colonel Grossman reports that, "In July 2000, the American Medical Association (AMA), the American Academy of Pediatrics (AAP), the American Psychological Association (APA), and the American Academy of Child and Adolescent Psychiatry (AACAP) . . . made a joint statement to both Houses of Congress. They said that, 'Well over 1,000 studies point overwhelmingly to a causal connection between media violence and aggressive behavior in children.' The report continued, 'Preliminary studies indicate that the negative impact of interactive electronic media (violent video games) may be significantly more severe than that wrought by television, movies, or music'. "[124]

---

[121] 121 National Institute on Media and the Family website: http://www.mediafamily.org "Media Influence on Children."

[122] 122 Ibid.

[123] Grand Theft Auto: San Andreas and the porn download scandal was picked up by the major media –especially FOX News – in summer/fall of 2005. Largely because of the pressure brought upon the manufacturers and sellers by the media and child advocate groups, some of these extremely violent video games are now rated as "adult only."

[124] Grossman, Dave, Lt. Col. On Combat: The Psychology and Physiology of Deadly Conflict in War and in Peace. (United States: PPCT Research Publications, 2004), p. 78.

Grossman documents several studies that make the connection between violent play and violent kids:

- In 2001 the National Institute for Media and the Family released its report on research involving over 600 8th and 9th grade students from four schools. The study concluded "children who are the least aggressive in nature but are exposed to violent video games are more likely to get into fights than children who are very aggressive but do not play violent video games."[125]

- "This study found that children who play violent video games:
  - See the world as a more hostile place;
  - Argue with teachers more frequently;
  - Are more likely to be involved in physical fights; and,
  - Don't perform well in school."[126]

Medical science is showing us that continued exposure to violence and killing at a young age, in video games, in movies, and on television, adversely affects our kids. The ball is in our court.

Studies show that kids who are involved in healthy, adult-supervised extracurricular activities -- such as sports, hobbies, martial arts, hunting, school clubs, drama, art, and dance – are not the ones who walk into their schools or churches with guns and begin blowing away innocent people. As a matter of fact, profile studies on similarities among school shooters show that kids who target shoot or hunt with family members ARE NOT the ones who turn out to be school shooters. Rather, it is those who spend countless hours playing violent video games that train them to dole out random violence and death who are much more likely to snap.[127] I firmly believe that what people do with weapons is

---

[125] Ibid.
[126] Ibid.
[127] Ibid.

a direct result of how they are trained. I reached this conclusion after commanding both U.S. and British combat units.

I considered myself to be a fair and equitable, but very strict, commanding officer. I administered non-judicial punishment regularly for offenses such as theft, failure to obey a lawful order, assault, conduct unbecoming, etc.[128] One training day on the M-16 rifle range, I was walking up and down the firing line behind my soldiers, observing as they shot at the silhouette targets. As I trooped the line, I was reminded of the stern punishments I recently handed down to a few of my more problem soldiers, the ones who never stayed out of trouble. I was convinced that these individuals disliked me at best, or at worst hated me enough to kill me.

I remember thinking how easy it would be for any one of them to point their loaded M-16 my way and simply pull the trigger. I was surrounded many times in my career by my "bad apples" carrying loaded, Army-issued weapons, but I never once felt threatened by them. Not one of them ever took a shot at me, nor at my officers, or my non-commissioned officers (NCOs).

I truly believe that the reason why none of them ever tried to kill their company leaders is because they were disciplined and NEVER trained to kill the good guys. They were trained hard to take care of one another, fight as a team, and focus on killing the enemy.

The Amount of School Violence is Shocking

The School Violence Resource Center website provides a comprehensive list of school shootings in America current through mid-2005.[129] I extracted the list from their website for my readers:

---

[128] Article 15, Uniform Code of military Justice permits commanding officers in all services to reduce soldiers in rank, fine them, restrict them to the barracks and give them extra duty for offenses that are not referred to military Courts Martial.

[129] http://www.svrc.net/ShootingsMap.htm.

February 2, 1996: Moses Lake, Washington

A 14 year-old shot a teacher and two students with a rifle.

February 29, 1996: St. Louis, Missouri

A 30 year-old man fired into a school bus where two were injured including a pregnant teenager and the bus driver.

February 19, 1997: Bethel, Alaska

A 16 year-old shot and killed his principal and a student. Two other students were injured.

October 1, 1997: Pearl, Mississippi

A 16 year-old killed his mother, then went to school and shot nine others. Two died.

December 1, 1997: West Paducah, Kentucky

A 14 year-old shot eight students as they prayed in school. Three died and one student was left paralyzed.

December 15, 1997: Stamps, Arkansas

An eighth grader was arrested and charged as an adult after he confessed to shooting and wounding two of his fellow students as he hid in the woods outside of a high school.

March 24, 1998: Jonesboro, Arkansas

Two boys ages 11 and 13 shot fourteen students and one teacher. The teacher and four of the students died.

April 24, 1998: Edinboro, Pennsylvania

A 14 year-old student shot a teacher to death at a graduation dance.

April 28, 1998: Pomona, California

A 14 year-old shot three boys. Two are killed.

May 19, 1998: Fayetteville, Tennessee

An 18 year-old shot and killed a classmate just three days before graduation.

May 21, 1998: Onalaska, Washington

A 15 year-old took his girlfriend from a school bus at gunpoint, and forced her to go to his house where he used a gun to commit suicide.

May 21, 1998: Springfield, Oregon

A 15 year-old shot and killed both parents before going to school and opening fire in the cafeteria. Two students were killed.

June 6, 1998: Columbia, South Carolina

A 14 year-old student was arrested after a school shooting that wounded a teacher and elderly volunteer aid.

June 15, 1998: Richmond, Virginia

A 14 year-old student was charged as an adult after opening fire in a crowded high school hallway, wounding a 45-year-old social studies teacher and a 74-year-old volunteer.

April 20, 1999: Littleton, Colorado

Two boys, ages 16 and 17, shot 35 students and 1 teacher before committing suicide. Twelve students and the teacher died.

May 20, 1999: Conyers, Georgia

A 15 year-old wounded six classmates.

November 19, 1999: Deming, New Mexico

A 12 year-old shot a classmate in the back of her head. She died the next day.

December 6, 1999: Fort Gibson, Oklahoma

A 7th grader brought a handgun to school and opened fire. Four students were wounded.

February 29, 2000: Mount Morris Township, Michigan

A 6 year-old boy brought a .32 semi-automatic handgun to school, and killed a first grader.

March 10, 2000: Savannah, Georgia

Two students were killed by a 19 year-old student while leaving a Beach High School dance.

May 26, 2000: Lake Worth, Florida

A 13 year-old sent home from school returned with a handgun and killed a teacher.

September 26, 2000: New Orleans, Louisiana

A student fought with another student, went home, returned with a gun and killed that student in the high school gymnasium.

October 24, 2000: Glendale, Arizona

A teenager held a teacher and 32 students hostage for an hour before surrendering.

January 10, 2001: Oxnard, California

A 17 year-old entered school and took a girl hostage in an attempt to persuade police to shoot him. After the SWAT team arrived, he was shot dead.

January 17, 2001: Baltimore, California

One student was shot and killed in front of Lake Clifton Eastern High School.

March 5, 2001: Santee, California

A 15 year-old opened fire from inside a school bathroom shooting 15 and killing 2.

March 7, 2001: Williamsport, Pennsylvania

A 14 year-old brought his father's handgun to school and shot a classmate in the shoulder.

March 22, 2001: El Cajon, California

A student shot three teens and two teachers at Granite Hills High School.

March 30, 2001: Gary, Indiana

A student was shot in the head while waiting for a class to begin.

January 15, 2002: New York, New York

A teenager wounded two students at Martin Luther King Jr. High.

November 19, 2002: Hoover, Alabama

Two 17 year-old males were reportedly fighting in a hallway when one student pulled a knife and stabbed the other to death.

November, 22, 2002: Dallas, Texas

A 15 year-old male high school student was shot as he and fellow students tried to wrestle a gun away from another 14-year-old student.

December 12, 2002: Seattle, Washington

A 13 year-old male fired a rifle in his middle school, injuring two students with broken glass, and then used the gun to kill himself, according to police reports.

December 16, 2002: Chicago, Illinois

An 18 year-old male high school student was fatally shot outside of Englewood High School, while trying to protect his sister from two other male students.

January 22, 2003: Providence, Rhode Island

A 12th-grade male student was arrested for allegedly firing a .22 caliber gun inside the school's cafeteria after an assistant principal had broken up a fight. The shot was fired toward the ceiling and no one was injured.

February 5, 2003: Westminster, Colorado

A 14 year-old male freshman was taken into custody after several shots were fired in a high school courtyard.

March 17, 2003: Guttenberg, Iowa

A 17 year-old walked into his high school principal's office, thanked the principal for listening to his problems stating "talking would no longer help," pulled out a .22 caliber rifle from underneath his coat, and shot himself in the stomach.

April 1, 2003: Washington, DC

A 16 year-old male high school student was shot in the leg during a lunchtime argument with another 15-year-old student who fled afterwards and later turned himself in to police.

April 24, 2003: Red Lion, Pennsylvania

A 14 year-old male junior high school student shot and killed his principal inside a crowded cafeteria and then killed himself with a second gun according to police.

September 24, 2003: Cold Spring, Minnesota

One student died and another was hospitalized after a shooting in a Minnesota high school. A physical education teacher, Mark Johnson, talked the student into surrendering.

August 14, 2003: Columbus Georgia

A 14 year-old girl went back to her middle school to visit her old teachers. While she was there, a fight broke out between two boys, each 13, in the woods behind the school. Several students went into the woods to watch and the girl went with them. During the fight, one of the boys pulled out a gun and opened fire. As the students fled, one of the bullets struck the girl, killing the high school co-ed.

November 22, 2004: Philadelphia, Pennsylvania

An 18 year-old former student was shot and killed, and two current female students were injured, in a shooting outside of a North Philadelphia high school.

November 24, 2004: Valparaiso, Indiana

James Lewerke, a 15 year-old student at Valparaiso High School in northern Indiana, pulled two knives and stabbed seven of his classmates.

December 10, 2004: Nine Mile Falls, Washington

A 16 year-old male high school junior shot himself in the head and later died in the high school's entryway around 1:20 PM during a school day. The school was placed in lockdown and students were later released. A canister holding fireworks, shotgun shells, and rifle cartridges was found in a backpack belonging to the student around 3:30 p.m.

March 21, 2005: Red Lake, Minnesota

Jeff Weise, 16, killed his grandfather and a companion, and then arrived at school where he killed a teacher, a security guard, 5 students, and finally himself, leaving a total of 10 dead.

The youngest of the school murderers was a six-year-old boy who killed a fellow first grader with a .32 semi-automatic handgun in 2002. If we can't keep a six-year-old from bringing a gun into a first grade classroom and perpetrating terror upon his fellow students, what possible chance do we have of preventing well-trained Islamist terrorists from doing worse things?

These school shootings are no longer random anomalies. Twenty-six (26) states and the District of Columbia experienced school shootings from 1996 through mid-2005. Casualties included 9 teachers/principals/staffers killed and 7 wounded, 46 students killed, and 97 students wounded. With more than one half of the United States suffering from the pain and anguish of kid-on-kid and kid-on-teacher violence, it appears that America has a growing epidemic on its hands: child domestic terrorism.

In May 2002 a report entitled *The Final Report and Findings of the Safe School Initiative: Implications for the Prevention of School*

Attacks in the United States[130] was jointly published by the U.S. Department of Education and the U.S. Secret Service. Though it is a few years old, the report findings[131] are still relevant today:

- **Key Finding:** Incidents of targeted violence at school are rarely sudden, impulsive acts. Students perpetrating acts of violence in school do not simply "snap" one day. Their acts are carefully planned and calculated.

- **Key Finding:** Prior to most of the recorded incidents of school violence, other people knew about the attacker's ideas or plans to attack. Though adults rarely expected what was about to occur, the information was usually known by other friends, classmates, or siblings.

- **Key Finding:** Most school attackers did not threaten their victims directly prior to perpetrating the attacks.

- **Key Finding:** Most of the school attackers engaged in some aberrant behavior prior to the incident that caused others concern or indicated a need for help.

- **Key Finding:** Most attackers had difficulty coping with significant losses or personal failures. Many had attempted or considered suicide.

- **Key Finding:** Many attackers felt bullied, persecuted, or injured by others at their schools prior to the attacks.

- **Key Finding:** Most attackers had access to and had used weapons prior to the attack.

---

[130] The report can be found at http://www.ed.gov.offices/OESE/SDFS and http://www.secretservice.gov/ntac.
[131] *"The Final Report and Findings of the Safe School Initiative: Implications for the Prevention of School Attacks in the United States"* ED pubs, Education Publication Center, U.S. Department of Education, P.O. Box 1398, Jessup, Maryland 20794-1398, pp.32 – 38.

- **Key Finding:** In many cases, other students were involved in the attacks in some capacity (they knew that something bad was going to happen).

- **Key Finding:** Despite prompt law enforcement responses, most attacks were stopped by means other than law enforcement intervention, such as by teachers, principals, or fellow students, or by the high school shooters themselves upon committing suicide.

What Can We As Parents and Guardians Do?

Parents and guardians should take responsibility for their children. This includes knowing where they are, who they are "hanging with," what they are doing, and what may be bothering them. It goes without saying that kids should not be permitted access to weapons in the home.

Knowledge is power. Adults as well as their children need to be advised of the key government findings noted above. We must educate and encourage parents, teachers, and students to observe and act when they suspect that something bad may be going on in their schools. Everyone needs to be assured and that negative ramifications WILL NOT befall them if what they report, in good faith, results in a false alarm. Better a false alarm than dead students and teachers in our schools. Kids need to be trained and trusted with "ownership." By this I mean that students must take responsibility for the safety of their schools and each other – every bit as much as teachers, administrators, parents and guardians.

Our kids need to be taught not to bully others. They need to be taught that every human being has value, possesses talent, and is capable of making a great contribution to others somewhere along life's path.   Students themselves should be instilled with a zero tolerance for bullying: no excuses and no exceptions.

Schools need to be able to "lock down" when violence strikes. Lock down drills should be as common as fire drills in all of our schools.   Schools should have contingency plans.   They must coordinate with local law enforcement by providing police blueprints, surveillance plans, and doorway measurements, even films of every hallway, classroom, storage, sports, and activity room.

The government established a website that addresses various emergencies including natural disasters, school violence, and terrorist attacks. The site is www.ready.gov and is to be updated regularly for the benefit of those charged with the safety and protection of our school children.   Go to this website every so often. Read and heed its guidance. It's good stuff.

If we cannot thwart our own unorganized, untrained, homegrown kids from perpetrating domestic acts of terror, how will we prevent dedicated and trained international, Islamist terrorists from doing the same when they enter our schools in the not-so-distant future?

Complacency is not an option, and denial is deadly. So assume the responsibility. Adopt the creed:

If not me, then who? If not now, then when?

Anti-Terror Awareness & Planning in Our Schools

We as parents, guardians, and teachers endeavor to be the protectors of our school-aged youth. Our challenges are daunting; times have changed for the worse, bringing new threats and a greater level of violence.

In Briefing #7, we discussed the reality of child-on-child and child-on-teacher domestic terrorism in America. Unfortunately, our kids live in a world that poses a double terror threat to them, domestic and international. Though it is probably the farthest thing from their minds, American students are endangered by what I believe to be inevitable Islamist terror attacks upon our schools in the not-too-distant future. We must be prepared mentally and emotionally for the worst that is yet to come. More importantly, we must strive to thwart these pending attacks.

Terrorists Kill Children

Terrorists kill children. Not only do terrorists kill Christian and Jewish children, they also kill large numbers of Muslim ones as well. Young girls and boys often become collateral damage in car bombings and, suicide-homicide killings in crowded, public places. To the terrorist, the unintentional death of children is simply the cost of doing business. Not all terrorist-related youth killings are unintentional, though. If the terrorist's objective is to achieve deep psychological impact and damage to an adult population and its community, killing kids is a proven way to get the job done effectively and with long-term psychological damage.

Terrorists kill kids in their schools. They have done so in Israel, Russia, Pakistan, Turkey, and elsewhere, and they pledge to do so in America. We have no reason to doubt their word or question their resolve.

The most horrific example of a terror attack on a school to date is the Beslan, Russia tragedy (previously cited in this book). *Terror at Beslan* author John Giduck notes, "Though they cannot say it openly, or to the public or news media, for most American law enforcement officers and school security officials, the likelihood of an incident similar to the terrorist siege of hundreds of children in Beslan, Russia in September 2004, happening in America is more a question of when than if."[132] Terror is coming to American schools. It is time to regroup and reevaluate the way we have traditionally viewed school safety and crisis planning. We need to get our act together quickly. The lives we save may very well be those of our own children.

There are several reasons why it makes sound operational sense for terrorists to attack our schools. The motives offered by the National School Safety Center sum it up fairly well:[133]

- Such an attack would instill fear and panic nationwide. Consider the effects of the student attack at Columbine High School.

---

[132] Giduck, John. *Terror at Beslan: A Russian Tragedy With Lessons for American Schools.* (United States: Archangel Group, 2005), p. 37.
[133] *"Safeguarding Schools Against Terror,"* published by the National School Safety Center, 2004, p.4.

- An attack on a school could promote the reputation and power of a terrorist group.

- Schools provide an essential community service. About one-quarter of the nation's population attends school each day. (Disrupt this service, and you disrupt the community.)

- An attack on a school would warrant national media coverage. (Terrorists need the extended media coverage to publicize both their causes and their lethal capabilities.)

- Schools symbolize America and America's future.

- Many schools remain easy targets due to their accessibility, vulnerability, and prominence in the community.

- There are more Americans in school today than in America's history.[134]

The logic and reason behind the terrorist mind is not always easy for us as Westerners to grasp. Major terror organizations such as Al Qaeda and their spin-offs embrace varying ideologies, causes, and objectives. They may differ on the extent to which they will go to kill for their cause. Some terrorists will target children, while others care not to do so. We must remain focused on the reality of the threat. Children have been killed in the past. They are targeted today, and remain threatened tomorrow.

Understanding That Changes Must Be Made

Lieutenant Colonel Dave Grossman researches causes of child injury and death in our schools.[135] He makes a very interesting point in his seminars and books, which is most relevant to

---

[134] *"Student population soars."* The Associated Press. June 2, 2005.
[135] Dave Grossman's verbal presentation to the Archangel Group's 2nd Annual International Anti-Terror Conference, Denver, Colorado, April 2005..

what we are discussing in this briefing. Grossman suggests that with respect to today's looming terror threats, our priorities on school safety may be misdirected. He is concerned, as am I, this nation lacks definitive, mandatory guidance pushing schools to prepare for the worst case scenarios. Some schools conduct lock down drills; some do not. Some coordinate closely with local law enforcement, others have not yet pursued the liaisons. A number of American school districts have actually trained with local law enforcement and first responders in simulating a Beslan-type attack for purposes of training, team building, and honing responses in a real world situation. Most have not yet progressed to the planning stages for such an assault.

Anti-terror preparedness, training, and drills in our schools should be of concern to all of us. If we could just get the emphasis on anti-terror drills up to the same level of attention as fire drills, that would constitute significant progress. Dave Grossman points out that there has not been an American child killed in a school fire in more than half a century. Not one. Though the chances of our children being injured or killed in a school fire remain absolutely miniscule, every school embraces fire alarms, fire suppression systems (sprinklers), wall-mounted fire extinguishers, fire exits, and fire drills. It's the law. We would not send our kids to a school that wasn't well prepared within code to handle a school fire. As taxpayers, we are happy to spend millions of dollars each year to prevent an incident that has not happened in at least fifty years. Yet we appear to have no problem sending our children to schools that are not in the least bit prepared to deal with today's growing threats of child violence and international terror. Grossman is right to question our collective reasoning.

Schools have procedures for handling bomb threats. In all of his years of research, Lieutenant Colonel Grossman cannot find one example of an American school that actually experienced an explosion after a bomb threat was phoned in. Schools and local responders are trained to handle bomb threats, even though the chance of a bomb threat coming to fruition is almost nil. When it comes to the ever-increasing and much more likely threats of domestic and international terror in our schools, we have no universal "codes" that schools must follow. We do not have federally-mandated, anti-terror compliance requirements for our schools. Our homeland defense authorities are painfully slow in providing definitive guidance. So will we wait until something bad happens and then complain, or act now? Sometimes, if we wait for others to get things done, nothing ever gets done. Remember our creed: If not me, then who? If not now, then when?

Schools must re-examine procedures that have been in place for decades upon decades. Let's take fire drills, for example. Watch how schools conduct fire drills. The type of school does not matter. The city and state does not matter either. When school buildings are evacuated, for whatever reasons, the people inside the facility are moved outdoors and herded into what amounts to a holding area, oftentimes the adjacent school parking lot. They are kept there until the "all clear" is sounded, at which time they are paraded back into the building and returned to their classrooms.

To terrorist operational planners, school parking lots full of hundreds of evacuated students and teachers constitute a perfect military "kill zone." All that the terrorists need do is simply observe area schools conducting their beginning-of-the-year mandatory fire drills. The terrorists can note where the kids are grouped outside of the buildings from a nearby vehicle or even on foot at a street corner. The bad guys then make an assessment of which school procedures, terrain, access roads, parking areas, and numbers of children in single groupings present the most lucrative targets. At a later date, the terrorists simply call in a bomb threat or set off the fire alarms, causing the very predictable mass exodus. **When the teachers and students are "safely" outside, in the kill zones, the pre-positioned car or bus bombs are detonated. Maximum body counts for the**

terrorists, and they did not even have to enter the school to kill the kids. **Our own unwitting teachers will have delivered all of the victims to the terrorists on a silver platter.** The "herding" of students also presents a lucrative opportunity for domestic school shooters. School security experts Michael and Chris Dorn point out that, "there have been at least four school shootings carried out by students in the United States where the shooter or shooters first activated the school fire alarm and shot evacuees when they were outside of the building."[136]

What Needs to be Done?

Schools must rethink the manner in which students are evacuated. In all of the U.S. government's anti-terror guidance for educators and schools that I researched, I cannot find ANY guidance that addresses the need to keep our kids out of the kill zones. The U.S. Department of Education's August 2004 "Practical Information on Crisis Planning: A Guide for Schools and Communities" does not address kill zones. The Department of Education's April 2003 Campus Public Safety: Weapons of Mass Destruction Terrorism Protective Measures" does not address them either. Nor does the Department of Homeland Security (DHS) 2004 "Safeguarding Schools Against Terror" guidance on the DHS website. Much of the assistance provided by these documents is very sound and should be implemented, but in typical bureaucratic fashion, the direction provided falls short of the level of detail required to satisfactorily address such things as the way terrorists might exploit school standing operating procedures.

The Department of Education's "Campus Public Safety: Weapons of Mass Destruction Terrorism Protective Measures" provides typical, macro-level guidance to campus administrators,[137] such as:

---

[136] Dorn, Michael and Chris. *Innocent Targets: When Terrorism Comes to Schools* (Canada: Safe Havens International, Inc., 2005), p. 114.
[137] http://www.ed.gov/admins/lead/safety/emergencyplan/campussafe.html.

- "Establish a working relationship with the Supervisory Agent in charge of your nearest FBI office."

- "Establish a management team responsible for directing the implementation of your campus emergency operations plan."

- "Update your most recent risk assessment inventory."

- " . . .institute 100% identification checks."

Many of the things that various governmental departments suggest our campuses and schools do are quite sound. Here's the rub: government guidance is put forth without regard to the resources, personnel, and money that may be required to implement terror prevention, deterrence, mitigation, and response in the manner prescribed by these helpful government organizations.

I am strongly recommending that our schools immediately take measures which do not require a quantitative leap in personnel, resources, or money, but rather, a reallocation or re-prioritization of additional duties, time, and wherewithal already available. Schools – under the supervision and direction of school boards – should institute plans, procedures, and policies for sound, all-hazards crisis planning. With respect to the threat of terror, school actions should include, but certainly not be limited to:

- **Terror awareness training for students of appropriate age (middle school and above).** This training can be as simple as a one-hour school assembly quarterly where students are asked to help keep a watch over the school and its premises. It is about teaching students to be vigilant, not paranoid. These awareness sessions for kids need to be upbeat and positive. They need not be threatening to them.

- **Awareness training for parents, faculty, and administrators.** These briefings can deal at a more adult level with the actual threats. Parents and educators can discuss collectively what should be done to mitigate, prepare for, and most importantly prevent terror attacks against their schools. The more community minds that are brought together, the more creative, resourced, and financed the possible solutions will become.

- **Review of school procedures (reactions to threats & evacuations).** School procedures that may not be valid in light of today's threats – such as evacuation of students and faculty from the school – must be reviewed and amended as required. It cannot simply look good on paper. They must have a reasonable chance of actually being properly and successfully executed. Procedures need to be simple, understood by all, embraced and rehearsed on a regular basis.

- **Anti-terror drills inside the schools to include lock downs.** These drills should be designed, coordinated, and practiced with the advice and assistance of professionals. Police and sheriffs' departments, the local FBI field office, and state departments of homeland defense or public safety should offer the expertise required.

- **Liaison with local law enforcement, to include providing the police and sheriffs' departments with blue prints and pictures of the school.** Local law enforcement, fire departments, medical first responders, and others would certainly be aided in a crisis situation by possessing the layout of the school facilities.

School safety experts Michael and Chris Dorn agree that schools should develop safe schools plans for **all hazards**, of which the anti-terror piece is a part. The Dorns point out "most schools have incomplete safe school plans. For example, many school systems have a detailed emergency operations plan but lack a written prevention plan that fully addresses the four phases of emergency management:"

- Mitigation/prevention
- Preparedness
- Response
- Recovery[138]

The Dorns reviewed many safe school plans from around the nation. They concluded that less than one in one hundred school systems and private schools have a plan that properly addresses the four phases of emergency management listed above.

A good reference that will aid in developing four-phased all hazards plans for schools is found on the Department of Education website. Called "Practical Information on Crisis Planning: A Guide for Schools and Communities." This August 2004 planning tool provides an outline that tells planners what topics need to be addressed within each of the four phases.

One of the most comprehensive and detailed textbook-sized guides is the *Jane's Safe Schools Planning Guide for All Hazards* (www.janes.com). Scott Hayes, Director of Public Safety for Jane's, describes the approach used in the development of this series as "an incredible and ambitious effort to expand upon the excellent work of the United States Department of Education to provide school and public safety officials with the most comprehensive approach to the topic to date."[139]

Get involved with parent-teacher groups and school associations, and attend school and school district public meetings and forums.

---

[138] Dorn, Michael and Chris. *Innocent Targets: When Terrorism Comes to Schools* (Canada: Safe Havens International, Inc., 2005), pp. 84-87.
[139] Ibid, p. 87.

Seek out local security experts able to provide their time and talents, organize an awareness campaign, and offer to assist school principals, their staffs, and student bodies. Move to educate first. Then follow-up with plans, policies, procedures, training, and exercises. Everyone can do something. Let's take charge and get the job done.

Complacency is not an option, and denial is deadly. So assume the responsibility. Adopt the creed:

If not me, then who? If not now, then when?

We Are All Citizen Soldiers

We are all citizen soldiers in the War on Terror. All of us share common responsibilities to protect our families, each other, our infrastructure, and our nation. We did not ask for these duties. Rather, they defaulted to us by virtue of the type of enemy we are fighting. In not knowing when, where or how the terrorists will strike next, Americans are forced to become lookers and listeners: the first line of defense for their homeland.

Vigilance, Not Paranoia

Smart Americans "buckle up" when they get into an automobile. They do so not because they are scared or obsessed by the thought of being killed or mutilated in an auto wreck. Americans buckle up because they have been properly educated, trained, and conditioned over time to do so. It was the National Safety Council's decades-long public awareness campaign, characterized by slogans like "Buckle Up for Safety" and "Seat Belts Save Lives," that convinced our nation's drivers that employing a seatbelt was the intelligent and vigilant thing to do. People buckle seatbelts because they are vigilant, not paranoid.

There has not been a child killed in a school fire in the United States in more than 50 years. State-of-the-art technologies that include fire suppression and alarm systems, combined with mandatory fire drills, keep the possibility of injury or death by school fire extremely remote. With respect to preventing school fires, Americans are vigilant, not paranoid.

Thousands of neighborhoods establish and maintain the now famous "Neighborhood Watch" programs. They do so not because they are paranoid about break-ins and thefts. Neighborhoods institute these programs because they desire to prevent local crime rates from rising. Neighborhood watch programs are designed to discourage the bad guys from perpetrating crimes because the residents there are trained to be vigilant and everyone is on the lookout. Hundreds of pairs of alert citizens' eyes and ears are far superior to just a few cops on patrol. So it is with the War on Terror. Millions of pairs of eyes and ears are far more likely to identify and thwart a serious terrorist incident than just the comparatively few belonging to members of law enforcement and our other valiant first responders.

Establishing Conditions Necessary for Vigilance

American vigilance in the war against terror demands five indispensable requisites:

- **Education:** Citizens must be trained to know what to look and listen for day-to-day.

- **Observation:** Citizens must actually look and listen. They need to maintain a comfortable yet effective operational awareness of what is going on around them.

- **Action**: Citizens must be ready and willing to act in the common defense when the situation demands.

- **Empowerment:** Citizens must be empowered by federal and local government and law enforcement to act when necessary until first responders arrive on the scene and take charge.

- **Legal Protection:** Citizens must be able to react quickly in an anti-terror situation. They cannot and should not be mentally burdened by thoughts of criminal and/or civil legal ramifications that could cause them to hesitate, or not act at all, in a moment of crisis.

Let's examine each of these requisites in more detail.

Education

During the Cold War between the United States and the U.S.S.R., and the near nuclear exchange between the two during the Cuban Missile Crisis of 1962, Americans were educated as to what they had do to prepare for and survive a nuclear exchange between the two super powers. I can remember performing "duck and cover" drills as a first grader. These drills initially scared us. But as we repeatedly drilled, we became quicker and better able to meet our survival requirements. The fear factor declined with time and practice. As naïve as these drills were in terms of actual protection from a nuclear attack, they helped us become mentally stronger and more able to come to grips with the harsh realities of life during the Cold War. We children of the 60s survived those stressful years mentally and emotionally intact.

Children today are much more aware of the dangers that surround their everyday lives than we were at their age. Kids are tough, resilient, and thirsty for the facts. They are most capable of dealing with the harsh realities of the War on Terror if the information is presented in the proper doses and in the appropriate format and venue, tailored to the various age groups. Young men and women will be no more emotionally scarred by participating in school anti-terror lock down drills than they would be by participating in fire drills or bomb threat evacuations.

Think back to the concepts of asymmetric warfare discussed earlier. The enemies of our state are on our soil and have already destroyed thousands of us. They are indoctrinated into the martyr's cause. They are armed. They are plotting. They are committed to our demise. We have to get it right now. If we fail to "be all that we can be" in this fight, more of our fellow citizens will pay the very highest price.

The education and awareness requisites necessary to comprehend and cope with the War on Terror are significantly greater than in past wars. This is because unlike past wars, we are all potential targets. In contrast with past armed conflicts, we all play an important defensive role to protect our homeland and each other. I am waiting for the federal and state governments to initiate public awareness and education programs through the television, radio, and print media. Where are the government efforts to bring and keep us up to speed? I do not see them.

Nearly five years after 9-11, I can find no government-sponsored public awareness campaign to combat terror. I observe no coast-to-coast billboards along federal highways reminding us to "OBSERVE, LISTEN, REPORT: ANTI-TERROR IS EVERY CITIZEN'S RESPONSIBILITY." I see no government-distributed posters in shop windows stating: "WE ARE DOING OUR PART IN THE WAR ON TERROR." High schools display no banners proclaiming: "THIS IS A TERROR-AWARE AND PREPARED SCHOOL." I have yet to read even one sign welcoming me into a small town with the assurance: "WE ARE A TERROR AWARE AND PREPARED COMMUNITY." I long for the day when I see full page, anti-terror ads in magazines like *Newsweek*, *Time*, and *Sports Illustrated*, paid for by the Department of Homeland Security.

I am anxiously awaiting the day when I turn on my television and see an anti-terror public service announcement (PSA) brought to me by my Department of Homeland Security and the National Ad Council. I want to view a 30 second spot in which a young man is delivering a pizza to an apartment building in a big city. He knocks on the door. The door opens half way. The camera angle is from the delivery boy's view. We peer into the apartment. There is little furniture: a mattress, laptop computer on the floor, some throw pillows. We do not see the face of the man paying for the pizza, but we hear his voice: a Middle Eastern accent. The man opens the door a bit wider to take the pizza. The boy's eye briefly catches a glimpse of what appears to be a large sack of fertilizer against a corner wall. The man thanks the boy for the pizza, hands him money, tells him to keep the change, and quickly closes the door. We then see the delivery boy exiting the building onto the street, where he hails two beat cops. The PSA ends with the boy telling the policemen that something strange may be going on in that apartment.

Another example could be two high school students, a boy and his girl friend walking hand-in-hand from the parking lot into school. They are greeting other kids and talking about a test that they are ill-prepared for during third period. The girl's eye catches a parked car on a street adjacent to the school. There are several persons in the car, although we cannot clearly see their faces. As seen from the young lady's viewpoint, there is a camera lens pointed at the school from a half-lowered car window. She draws her boyfriend's attention to the car and the camera. He agrees that the car looks suspicious. The kids agree to drop into the principal's office before homeroom and report what they saw. The PSA ends with a voice saying, "School security is everyone's responsibility. Do your part. Stay alert. Report suspicious activity."

These are just two examples of PSAs that I believe would be short, simple, to-the-point, and extremely effective. Neither would be difficult or expensive to produce. Their unquestionable value as terror-fighting tools is a "no brainer" to me. Your guess is as good as mine as to why authorities have not already pursued an aggressive public awareness campaign. Perhaps they are waiting until after the next big attack.

I would like to see anti-terror awareness programs that involve our high school students. These programs, which I call Operation Terror Aware and Prepared (OPTAP) programs, could be tailored to suit individual communities. My concept is simple. Teenagers today need community service hours to meet high school graduation and even some college admission requirements. Cities and communities need anti-terror awareness and preparedness information. We all need to be a part in the War on Terror and assume ownership. The OPTAP programs would be a win-win-win situation. The community would develop OPTAP brochures or pamphlets updates as required with the assistance of local, or state homeland security officials. Teenage volunteers, through their local high schools enrolled in the OPTAP program, would cover malls, businesses and neighborhoods handing out these awareness guides. These young people could wear OPTAP t-shirts and sweatshirts provided by the program sponsors (local businesses, chambers of commerce, church groups, etc.). These programs would not be difficult or expensive to enact.[140]

This glaring lack of education to promote public awareness is only part of the problem. There is also the absence of any state or nationwide programs that provide common citizens with a sense of ownership in the War on Terror. During World War II, for example, American families sacrificed fuel, fruit, meat, sugar, eggs, and tobacco that were desperately needed overseas for our fighting men and women. The citizenry-at-large was required to surrender comfort items and food stuffs for the war effort,

---

[140] I proposed such an OPTAP program to the Homeland Security officials in my home state of Colorado. Colorado officials are apprehensive that such a program will alarm or frighten residents. Perhaps after the first big attack in Colorado, they will reconsider.

and that made them part of the fight. Families were issued ration cards that controlled amounts of foodstuffs, gasoline, and other items needed in the European and Pacific theaters of war. It created a sense of unity and personal contribution towards victory and national success; even among America's youth. Instilling ownership among our fellow citizens is something that we can effect in our communities today. We need not wait for our state and federal governments to move off dead center.

Americans need to command much more from their local and state officials. Communities across this nation should be demanding public awareness, education, and training venues. In order to be vigilant, Americans must possess a working knowledge of such things as:

- The very latest terror tactics, techniques, and procedures employed in recent successful attacks;

- The policies, procedures, technologies, drills and plans needed to effect due care and diligence in our schools, churches, businesses, malls, and entertainment facilities; and

- How a nation such as Israel – that has had its schools, malls, and restaurants attacked for decades – trains and equips its citizens to deal with and respond to terror threats and events.

America's civilians have a right to know the ground truth surrounding the War on Terror; specifically, how bad the fight will get right here at home. It is impossible to do our parts as citizen soldiers without it. Our government officials do not think we can handle the truth. If they did, they would be telling us more. I believe we CAN handle the truth, no matter how disturbing and painful it may be. We will assimilate it. We will cope. We will prepare mentally and physically for the very worst that can befall us, hoping to breathe a sigh of relief if the most terrible of possible scenarios never come to fruition.

The truth that I have come to know, embrace and mentally prepare for I share here with my fellow citizen warriors:

- There will be subsequent terror attacks on American soil that make 9-11 pale in comparison with respect to injury, death, destruction, affect on the economy, and psychological impact on our citizens-at-large. The question is not "if" but "when?"

- Suicide bombers will eventually make their way into American public places such as restaurants, family fun parks, movie theaters, and sporting events.

- Terrorists will come after our children. They will kill them in their schools.

- If not a nuclear detonation, a radiological dispersion device (RDD) – known more commonly as a "dirty bomb"[141] – will be exploded in a U.S. port or densely populated area. The psychological affect upon America will initially be devastating.

- Americans who are sympathetic with or indoctrinated into the terrorist ideologies will assist, participate in, and even perpetrate acts of terror upon their own citizens (similar to Timothy McVeigh and Terry Nichols, who were assisted by Al Qaeda explosive experts in their planning and execution of the Oklahoma City Bombing).[142] Undoubtedly, some of these home-grown

---

[141] An RDD or dirty bomb is basically a conventional explosive device around which radioactive materials have been packed. When the explosion occurs, radioactive materials are spread onto the land and into the air and water surrounding the detonation.

[142] Sufficient evidence exists to more than suggest an Al Qaeda connection with the Oklahoma City bombers. Want more? Read *The Third Terrorist"* by Jayna Davis, Nelson Current Press, 2004 & *Seeds of Terror* by Maria Ressa, Free Press, 2003.

terrorists will be products of the Saudi-sponsored mosques and madrassas in Washington, D.C., New York City, Alexandria, Virginia, Chicago, Los Angeles, Miami, and many other U.S. cities.

• Communities that do not take responsibility for their own education, prevention, and preparedness programs will remain the most vulnerable to attack.

• Airplanes will, yet again, be used to kill Americans.

• ManPADS (Man Portable Air Defense Systems) shoulder-fired surface-to-air missiles will be used to down aircraft over U.S. soil.

• Our open borders with Mexico and Canada will be the death of many of us.

• It will take a U.S. body count of at least 10,000 from a single terror attack or series of coordinated attacks before our politicians put border security and other vital homeland defense needs ahead of partisan politics, special interest groups, re-elections, and the almighty dollar.

• Only when our government seals the borders, rounds up and expels illegals, and enforces immigration laws, will Americans know that its government is finally serious about fighting terror on our homeland.

Observation

Observation for the everyday citizen means maintaining a comfortable, conscious level of operational awareness. Living and working day-to-day in our communities, we tend to become creatures of habit. We park in the same spaces at work, drop the kids off here and there, and make quick stops at the local convenience store for bread or milk. We buy gas, shop regularly at the neighborhood mall, and recreate in local gyms, on nearby playing fields, or along community jogging paths. In doing so, we are subconscious observers of what constitutes normality within our immediate surroundings. Honing a sense of awareness within ourselves will increase the likelihood that we will take notice of events out of the ordinary. I offer a few personal examples.

I served as master of ceremonies for my daughter's annual dance studio recital at a local high school in Colorado Springs, Colorado, just a few weeks after the Columbine school massacre. The event was held on a Friday night in a local public high school auditorium which seated about 500 attendees. An acquaintance notified me that when the house lights came on at the break, a briefcase was resting behind a seat in the second row, a briefcase that he was sure had not been there when the show began. He saw something out of the ordinary. He was aware of his immediate surroundings in that theater. He did not hesitate to report it.

When the audience returned to their seats after intermission, I stepped up to the stage microphone and asked if anyone claimed the briefcase. No one admitted ownership. I knew that the chances of a bomb being in that briefcase were slim to nil. But on the remote chance that the Columbine massacre motivated another wacko in Colorado to kill children, I was determined that such an attack would not happen on my watch. Having coordinated during the intermission with the director of the dance studio, I informed the audience that their children would be escorted out of the back of the school and moved several hundred yards from the building. I directed the crowd to exit the school from the auditorium doors in an orderly fashion, and to move across the street from the school while I notified the authorities.

The second half of the show was delayed for about an hour and a half while authorities arrived and determined that the briefcase was a cruel hoax. No one was injured. No one was killed. There was no bomb. A hand written note in the brief case said, "I bet you thought this was a bomb!" My young daughter was completely mortified. I felt for her. But no one's kid was going to die on my watch. End of discussion. Some parents were quite perturbed at me. I didn't care. Others told me they appreciated what I did on behalf of their kids. I valued their support.

On another occasion, I was walking from the parking lot towards the entrance to the headquarters building of United States Space Command, Peterson Air Force Base, Colorado Springs, to attend a classified counter-terror intelligence briefing a few months after the September 11 events. As I approached the building, I observed a familiar lawn chemical company vehicle, with its 250 gallon truck-mounted tank, parked not 20 yards from the four-star general's headquarters and adjoining command center. The truck was unmanned, with no one in the cab or in the vicinity of the liquid storage and dispensing truck. I was incensed that neither the military police (MP) nor the hundreds of employees entering the building that morning noticed the abandoned, potentially deadly truck. Forgetting for the moment that I was no longer an active duty Army lieutenant colonel, I ran into the foyer of the headquarters and told the MP on duty that he had one minute to find the owner of that truck and get it moved, or I would make him regret the day he raised his right hand and signed up with the Air Force. The truck driver was quickly found and the truck moved away from the headquarters. The truck was legitimate. It was never a threat, but it could have been. Why didn't anyone else become alarmed over the parked truck, especially so soon after 9-11? Lack of awareness? Lack of education? Apathy? "It could never happen here" syndrome? Probably a combination of "all of the above."

Here's the bottom line. Gym bags or shopping bags left unattended in malls, people wearing heavy full-length coats into buildings on hot summer days, an abandoned truck parked up against the side of the local courthouse, or someone taking snapshots of the entrance to a high school from a car parked in front, may or may not be occurrences out of the ordinary. **Those who live, work, attend classes, and shop regularly in their hometowns are in the best position to know when something looks out of place and suspicious.** Folks simply need a little awareness training and occasional reminders to keep them pumped up to do their parts.

Action

"Action" means doing what needs to be done before something bad happens. Action is tough. It requires self-confidence and guts. It often means placing the common good ahead of one's apprehensions and fears.

There is often a natural hesitancy to act when suspicions are aroused. "Will people think I'm paranoid if I call the authorities?" "Will I get in trouble if the police arrive on the scene and this is simply a forgotten gym bag full of gym clothes?" "With all of the people who have passed here today, why am I the only one who thinks there may be something wrong?" There are many who would really like to act but regrettably elect not to do so because of the politically-correct, careful not to offend, everyone-sue-everyone-else environment in our country today. America's growing obsession with political correctness and risk averse behavior often puts us all at risk in this War on Terror.

Terror is nasty business. Both the perpetrators of it and the defenders against it must be able to act swiftly and ruthlessly when the situation demands. It all-too-often appears to me that it is solely the bad guys and some of our own gutsy law enforcement, paramilitary and military who have no problem with the "swift" and "ruthless." *Americans need to grow up and toughen up. If we continue to be the kid on the playground who is afraid to play the rough games, the bullies will continue to knock the snot out of us at every opportunity.*

When faced with a situation and the choice of acting or not acting, we should ask ourselves: **if not me, then who?** If I fail to act, who will? What is the worst that can happen if I act? What is the worst that may befall others if I do not? Sometimes these questions must be asked and answered in spilt seconds.

Action can include calling the authorities, making a citizen's arrest, evacuating a room full of people, or demanding that persons in positions of authority do their damn jobs. Action can be showing up at the local school board monthly meeting and asking what the schools are doing about lock-down drills and terror prevention. Action might include mobilizing some moms and dads to keep watch around the perimeter of a church picnic or kid's sporting event.

Sometimes action can mean bending or violating some rules. In 1988, I was in command of British troops, British Army of the Rhine in northern Germany. My mission as commander was to prepare my armor troops for infantry duties as peacekeepers on the "Green Line" in Cyprus.[143] Having only six months to whip tankers into top physical shape as infantrymen, I conducted four-mile runs, five days each week through the German city of Detmold; seventy men carrying sub-machine guns, running through the streets of an unprotected German town.

In the late 1980s, the Irish Republican Army (IRA), at opposition with the British government, conducted many terror attacks against British soldiers and their families stationed in northern Germany. Several occurred in our area. One night I was awakened by a chilling vision: What if, while running my unit through our German town, a van full of IRA terrorists drove up, pointed loaded weapons at my squadron, and demanded that we hand over our eighty machine guns to them. First and foremost,

---

[143] To this day, the Green Line separates the Greek Cypriot soldiers occupying Greek Cyprus on the southern part of the island from the Turkish soldiers that secure Turkish Cyprus on the northern portion of the tiny island.

terrorists would have eighty more machine guns with which to kill British soldiers and their non-combatant family members. Secondly, the embarrassment to the United States Army if an American officer in command was forced to surrender all of those British weapons to IRA terrorists was more bad press than I ever wanted my Army or country to suffer.

The next morning, I asked my sergeant major to come into my office and shut the door. I expressed my concerns to him and asked him if it was legal for my officers and NCOs to carry loaded machine guns during the run, just in case. He replied that that would violate German and British laws and that it was absolutely illegal. I told my sergeant major that I wanted to do it anyway, because I did not want to run the risk of my weapons falling into IRA hands. From that day on, every time we ran through the streets of Detmold, Germany, all of my officers and NCOs carried loaded magazines inserted into their squad machine guns. I took one hell of a chance. Had even one weapon accidentally discharged within the town of Detmold that would have been the end of my command, assignment and military career. I was much more concerned about being able to defend the weapons under my command than I was with my career. I slept well, too, confident that I had my priorities straight.

Action does not require one to be a hero. It simply requires one to care enough to take the extra step that others – for whatever reasons – might not.

NEVER be afraid to act. If millions of Americans are willing to OBSERVE and ACT, the bad guys will experience a much greater degree of difficulty in carrying out their attacks.

Empowerment

Empowerment is all about local and state officials permitting law abiding citizens the leeway to act in the common defense when the situation warrants. It is about tolerance of occasionally well-intentioned citizens who overreact or make mistakes. It is all about fellow citizens understanding how difficult it is to take action, and appreciating the sacrifices of others, as opposed to rushing to criticize or take legal action.

The precedent is set. Our "Good Samaritan" laws are a perfect example. For too many years, persons coming upon the scene of a traffic accident were hesitant to render assistance for fear of being dragged to court if mistakes were made resulting in worse injuries or inadvertent death. Good Samaritan laws empower everyday people to give it their best shot in assisting fellow citizens in need, under protection of immunity from civil liability. So it must be with our fellow Americans who are willing and brave enough to act in the common defense.

At the 1st International Anti-Terror Conference sponsored by Archangel Group in Denver, Colorado, in spring of 2004, a former high ranking Israeli government official and reserve Army Officer who serves at the cabinet level in Israel, told us that for every terror attack in Israel that makes the news headlines in America, there are 20 to 30 incidents that Americans never hear about. Why? Because alert, trained, and empowered citizens take action before the homicide bombers can enter populated establishments and extol mass casualties. We were told that common Israeli citizens, many of whom are armed, often force the terrorists to detonate their homicide bombs in the street before they can enter the restaurants or stores. Israeli citizens are trained to OBSERVE. They are conditioned to ACT. Most importantly, they are EMPOWERED to do so for the common defense.

Americans can learn NOW from the Israeli experiences, or can play catch up ball later after the pain becomes too great. Human nature dictates that we will wait until the pain becomes too great. I wish it were not so.

Legal Protection

In September 2004, terrorists took control of the Beslan Middle School No. 1 in Beslan, Russia, along with more than 1,000 adult and child hostages. Three days later, when the siege concluded, hundreds were dead and injured. The Russian Special Forces (SPETSNAZ) fought more than 40 terrorists holed up in the school. The fighting was fierce. Many children were killed in the exchanges of gunfire. Oftentimes, the only way the Russian soldiers could kill the terrorists who were killing hostages was to shoot through the children whom the terrorists were holding as human shields.

The Russian soldiers did what they knew they had to do to save the majority of the men, women, and children held hostage. Many Russian citizens understood this; they knew that it was a no-win situation, and that some of their children had to die so that many more could survive the ordeal.

Imagine what would happen if a U.S. policeman or soldier accidentally fired at, or intentionally was forced to shoot and kill, a child to put down the terrorists in a school siege scenario. Best case, the officer or GI would be subjected to a lengthy and painful investigation. Worst case, the child's parents would drag the cop or soldier to court in extended litigation, bankrupting the family, and causing years of mental anguish and suffering. Criminal charges might even be filed against him. *We can't ask our first responders to protect and defend us and our children and then crucify them when they attempt to do so. We cannot have it both ways.*

Federal legislation is desperately needed NOW to protect our first responders, federal agents, soldiers, and even fellow citizens who dare to act in good conscience in our common defense. The push should come from prominent chiefs of police and sheriffs, supported by state attorneys general, authorities from the FBI, and the military service chiefs.

In This War On Terror, Individual Citizens Will Be Our Saviors And Heroes

Protecting our critical infrastructure and each other from the threats of terror attacks will very likely continue to be accomplished by common, everyday Americans like you and me.

Ordinary citizens like Eunice Stone, sitting in a Shoney's Restaurant, will become our heroes. In September 2002, while eating at the restaurant, Eunice overheard Middle Eastern-looking and sounding men on the other side of the partition making some allegedly disturbing comments about going to Miami to blow something up. With the tragic events of September 11 fresh in her memory, Eunice mustered the intestinal fortitude to call the authorities. A "Be On The Lookout For" (BOLO) was issued by law enforcement. The cars driven by the men were found and searched. When all was said and done, the men were not charged. Had these three medical students truly been part of a terrorist plot to attack structures in Miami? We will probably never know for sure, but Eunice is still an American hero who quite possibly saved countless innocent lives, infrastructure, portions of the local and national economies and jobs. God bless Eunice Stone. Let's hope there are thousands more out there just like her.

It will also be trusted professionals, such as U.S. Customs inspector Diana Dean, who protect our critical infrastructure; in this case, a major international airport. While screening cars coming into Washington state from Canada in December 1999, Inspector Dean noticed a man driving through her portion of the checkpoint alone in his car. The man looked nervous. Something was not right. Her decade-plus of on-the-job operational experience, coupled with her professionalism and training, caused her to stop this one car, this particular car out of the tens of thousands she simply waved through each year. She asked the gentleman to step out. The man panicked and fled on foot, but he was quickly apprehended.

The man Diana Dean stopped was a 37-year old Algerian terrorist named Ahmed Ressam. Trained in Afghanistan by Al Qaeda, Ressam was transporting nitroglycerin into the United States. He was part of the 1999 Millennium Plot to blow up the Los Angeles International Airport. This one American woman not only saved one of our busiest international airports from disaster, but saved countless innocent lives in the process, not to mention jobs and family livelihoods. God bless Diana Dean. She is also a true American hero. Let's hope there are thousands more out there just like her. Hopefully, we can all be like her if the situation someday demands it: vigilant, aware, and prepared to do what needs to be done.

This War on Terror will undoubtedly produce many more Eunice Stones and Diana Deans. This war will force everyday Americans out of the shadows and into their moments of fame. We cannot fight this war without the vigilance of everyday Americans. We cannot win this war without their guts and determination to prevail. A unique aspect of the War on Terror is that on any given day, one ordinary man or woman – citizen soldiers - can make a considerable contribution towards the defense of our homeland.

The protection of America is all about American vigilance. It is all about public servants doing their jobs to the utmost of their abilities. It is about common people not being afraid to blow the whistle if they suspect that the worst is about to happen.

We can do this. It is time for us to shine. Hundreds of millions of Americans doing their parts is critical to our victory in the War on Terror.

Complacency is not an option, and denial is deadly. So assume the responsibility. Adopt the creed:

If not me, then who? If not now, then when?

BRIEFING # 10

Keeping the Wolves at Bay

Relatively few citizens volunteer to take up arms, swear an oath, and put themselves in harm's way to protect and defend their country. I'm talking about the law enforcement officers and military service members who place their bodies between us and the bad guys, a.k.a the wolves, each and every day.

According to recent statistics, the United States employs approximately 800,000 local, state, and federal law enforcement officers.[144] Our military – active, reserve, National Guard, and auxiliary forces – are comprised of 494,122 Army;[145] 370,445 Navy; 146, 369,523 Air Force[147] personnel; 177,207 Marines;[148] and about 81,000 Coast Guard.[149] Law enforcement and military combined, we have somewhere in the neighborhood of 2,292,297 men and women protecting our total population of around 295,734,134; less than one percent of Americans entrusted to keep all of our predators and enemies at bay.[150]

---

[144] 141 http://www.ojp.usdoj.gov/bjs/lawenf.htm
[145] http://www.pbs.org/now/politics/troopsforiraq.html.
[146] Ibid.
[147] Ibid.
[148] Ibid.
[149] http://www.gocoastguard.com/faq.html.
[150] http://www.cia.gov/cia/publications/factbook/rankorder/2119rank.html.

The Fable of the Sheep, the Sheep Dog, and the Wolf

Lieutenant Colonel Dave Grossman offers an excellent analogy in his books and lectures that is well worth sharing here. Grossman maintains that the vast majority of people, let's say ninety-eight percent of the population, are similar in nature to sheep. They are gentle, harmless creatures. They are non-violent and peace loving. They simply want to live their lives day-to-day with as little worry and hassle as possible. The sheep do not particularly like the sheep dog, because the sheep dog is always bossing them around, telling them when to move and where to go. More often than not, the sheep dog is an annoyance and a nag, and the sheep would rather not have the sheep dog around . . . until the wolf appears.

When the wolf appears on the horizon, begins to scout out the flock and close in for the kill, the sheep immediately look to the sheep dog to stand between them and the wolf. They expect their sheep dog to put his life on the line to protect them, because that's the sheep dog's job. They need that sheep dog, because deep down inside they know that they cannot, or will not, protect themselves. And so it is in life.

While ninety-eight percent of people are sheep, one percent of the population are wolves. The wolves are the murderers, kidnappers, pedophiles, rapists, bank robbers, car thieves, and terrorists. Even though the sheep may not always sense that the wolves are present, they are always there; looking, scouting, stalking, and planning to pounce upon their helpless victims.

Enter the sheep dogs, the remaining one percent. They are the ones who put themselves in harm's way to protect the sheep who cannot protect themselves. They are the cops, the fire fighters, the FBI agents, the drug enforcement officers, the border patrol, the customs officials, the U.S. Marshals, the military service members, and so many more. Without brave men and women willing to confront our enemies, fight our battles, and rescue us from evil, social order simply could not and would not exist. Right, wrong, or indifferent, there can be no law and order without the sheep dogs, able and willing to protect societies by enforcing their rules.

I think that there are many lessons to be gleaned from Grossman's analogy. Here is what I take away from the story:

- There is no shame in being a sheep, unless you are a sheep that does not appreciate the sacrifices of the sheep dog. How can the sheep show their pride, admiration and appreciation for the sheep dogs? They can ensure that their local cops and sheriffs' deputies have the very best body armor, weapons, communications equipment, and training. How about paying them more too? I for one would gladly pay an extra two cents city sales tax on the dollar, if the tax was used to pay police officers and sheriffs' deputies about $30,000 more per year than they are currently making.

- There is certainly no shame in being a sheep dog, provided that the sheep dog never loses respect for the sheep that it protects. Sheep dogs must always keep in mind that they chose to be the ones that protect the flock. They are strong, the flock is weak. There is an inherent responsibility to serve and protect in the relationship between them.

- The wolf is the predator. If the wolf keeps to itself, the sheep dog and the flock have no problem with it: live and let live. But if and when the wolf crosses the line and threatens the sheep dog or the sheep, it must be taken out as ruthlessly and expeditiously as possible. The wolf, like the terrorist, has only one objective: kill and devour.

Respect those who cannot bring themselves to kill, even in a kill or be killed situation, as long as they respect and support those who do the killing for them. Respect those who do the killing, as long as their kills are righteous, and only if they never begin to crave or revel in the killing.

The Greatest Price is Always Paid by Our Military

We have all heard the age-old credo, "freedom isn't free." And it isn't! It never has been, and it never will be. This country's 21st century status as the world's only "super power" was created, matured, and sustained with the employment of military force; the ultimate, violent, and most brutal extension of politics.

Right, wrong, or indifferent, like it or not, this country rose to its greatness, prosperity, and cushy quality of life on the coat tails of wounded, maimed, and deceased servicemen and women. If you doubt my claim for even a second, here is a compilation of all of the armed conflicts that have established and maintained America as the land of the free and the home of the brave.[151] Approximately 1,223,558 of our fellow Americans killed and 1,575,366 wounded from 1775 through present day.[152] I place the lists of our nation's conflicts here in the book's text, and not in an appendix at the end of the book, because I want the reader to realize the magnitude of our American struggles and sacrifices:

Dates of Conflict (U.S. Involvement Only), Type of Conflict, Primary Opponent(s) of the United States

The American Revolution, 1775-1783, Inter-State and Colonial War, Great Britain

The Indian Wars, 1775-1890, Wars of Imperialism, Native (Indian) Tribes and Nations of North America

Shay's Rebellion, 1786-1787, Rebellion, Anti-(state) Government Rebels vs. Massachusetts

---

[151] List extracted from the Web site of the History Guy: United States Military History, at http://www.historyguy.com/american_military_history.html

[152] Figures found at http://www.historyguy.com/american_war_casualties.html.

The Whiskey Rebellion, 1794, Rebellion, Anti-Tax Rebels in Western Pennsylvania

Quasi-War With France, 1798-1800, Inter-State (Naval) War, France

Fries' Rebellion "The Hot Water War", 1799, Rebellion, Anti-Tax Rebels in Pennsylvania

The Barbary Wars, 1800-1815, Inter-State War, The Barbary States (Tripoli, Algiers & Morocco)

The War of 1812, 1812-1815, Inter-State War, Great Britain

Mexican-American War, 1846-1848, Inter-State War, Mexico

U.S. Slave Rebellions, 1800-1865, Slave Rebellions, Various Slave groups

"Bleeding Kansas", 1855-1860, Civil War (state of Kansas), Pro-Slavery vs. Anti-Slavery Kansans

Brown's Raid on Harper's Ferry, 1859, Rebellion, Anti-Slavery Rebels (Led by John Brown)

United States Civil War, 1861-1865, Civil War, United States (The North) vs. the Confederate States (The South)

U.S. Intervention in Hawaiian Revolution, 1893, Internal Rebellion & Foreign Intervention, Hawaiian Government

The Spanish-American War, 1898, Inter-State War, Spain

U.S. Intervention in Samoan Civil War, 1898-1899, Civil War & Foreign Intervention, Samoan Faction

U.S.-Philippine War, 1899-1902, Colonial War, War of Imperialism

The Boxer Rebellion, 1900, Internal Rebellion & Foreign Intervention, Chinese Government & "Boxer" Rebels

The Moro Wars, 1901-1913, Colonial Wars, Philippine Muslim Rebels

U.S. Intervention in Panamanian Revolution, 1903, Secessionist Revolution & Foreign Intervention, Colombia

The Banana Wars, 1909-1933, Civil Wars & Foreign Intervention, Various Rebel Groups In Central America

U.S. Occupation of Vera Cruz, 1914, Inter-State War, Mexico

Pershing's Raid Into Mexico, 1916-1917, Inter-State, Border War, Mexican Government & Mexican Rebels ("Bandits")

World War I, 1917-1918 (American involvement only), Inter-State War, Germany

Allied Intervention in Russian Civil War, 1919-1921, Civil War &
Foreign Intervention, Russian Bolshevik (Soviet) Government

World War II, 1941-1945 (American involvement only), Inter-State
War, Germany, Japan & Italy

The Cold War, 1945-1991, Global Inter-State Cold War, The Soviet
Union & Communist China

The Korean War, 1950-1953, Inter-State War, North Korea & China

The Second Indochina War "Vietnam War", 1956-1975, Civil War,
Inter-State War, North Vietnam & South Vietnamese "Viet Cong"
Rebels

U.S. Intervention in Lebanon, 1958, Civil War & Foreign
Intervention, No real foe for U.S. Troops landed to support
Lebanon Gov.

Dominican Intervention, 1965, Civil War & Foreign Intervention,
Rebels in the Dominican Republic

The Mayaguez Rescue Operation 1975 (May 15), Hostage Rescue
& Inter-State Conflict, Khmer Rouge Guerrillas (the new government
of Cambodia)

**Iranian Hostage Crisis and Rescue Attempt "Desert One" or
"Operation Eagle Claw"**, 1980 (April 25), Hostage Rescue & Inter-
State Conflict, Iran

U.S. Libya Conflict, 1981, 1986, Inter-State War, Libya

U.S. Intervention in Lebanon, 1982-1984, Civil War, Foreign
Intervention

U.S. Invasion of Grenada, 1983, Inter-State War, Marxist Grenadian
Faction & Cuba

The Tanker War "Operation Earnest Will", 1987-1988, Inter-State
War, Iran

U.S. Invasion of Panama, 1989, Inter-State War, Panama

Persian Gulf War "Operation Desert Storm", 1991, Inter-State
War, Iraq

"No-Fly Zone" War, 1991-2003, Inter-State War, Iraq

U.S. Intervention in Somalia, 1992-1994, Civil War & Foreign
Intervention, Various Somali Militias

NATO Intervention in Bosnia (Operation Deliberate Force) 1994-1995, Civil War, Foreign Intervention & Inter-State War, Bosnian Serb Rebels

U.S. Occupation of Haiti, 1994, Foreign Intervention, Haitian Government

U.S. Embassy bombings and strikes on Afghanistan and Sudan (The bin Laden War), August, 1998, Terrorist Conflict, The embassy bombings in August, 1998 by Osama bin Laden caused hundreds of deaths in Kenya and Tanzania. The U.S. retaliated by launching Tomahawk Cruise Missiles at suspected terrorist targets in Afghanistan and Sudan.

"Desert Fox" Campaign (part of U.S.-Iraq Conflict), December, 1998, Inter-State War, Iraq

Kosovo War 1999, Civil War, Foreign Intervention & Inter-State War,

Attack on the USS Cole, October 12, 2000, Terrorist Conflict, Terrorists associated with Osama bin Laden

Attack on the World Trade Center and the Pentagon, September 11, 2001, Terrorist Conflict, Osama bin Laden's Al-Qaeda organization

Afghanistan War (Operation Enduring Freedom) October 7, 2001-Present, War against Terrorism, The Taliban and Osama bin Laden's Al Qaeda organization

Second Persian Gulf War "Operation Iraqi Freedom", March 19, 2003-Present, Inter-State War, Iraq

Intervention in Haiti, March, 2004, Foreign Intervention in a civil conflict, Haiti

Rivers of blood and sweat, oceans of tears, parentless children, widowed spouses, broken mothers and fathers, and memories of fallen comrades will always be the foundation holding up all that we are, all that we have, and everything we cherish. Without our military sheep dogs, we would be ruthlessly devoured.

In order to sustain our global military power and preserve our overall national power, we the people need to insure that we maintain a proper and appropriate balance in the following areas:

- A capable, well-motivated and equipped Armed Forces in sufficient numbers to take care of America's dirty work without being stretched to the breaking point.

- Senior military and civilian leaders who put the genuine needs of the fighting military ahead of politics and personal agendas.

- An American public that supports its men and women in uniform and maintains pressure on the President and Congress to fund, organize, train, equip, and compensate the military appropriately.

- A military of extremely high quality and morale, well led and well cared for by its senior leaders.

- A military respected and revered by coalition partners and feared like hell by all opponents.

- A military that is sent to fight and die only when our civilian leaders possess: (1) achievable strategic goals and military objectives; (2) a doable plan and sufficient numbers on the ground to provide security and stability; and (3) a clear exit strategy.

Our Islamist opponents attempt to drive wedges between all of these. Islamist terror leaders expect that they can erode America's military power. They hope that they can effect this wearing away through sustained, asymmetric terror attacks, many in the form of daily homicides and remotely detonated bombs such as we see in Iraq and London. Attacks abroad and within our homeland over extended periods of time provide the terrorists with the expectations that they will achieve some or all of the following results:

• Make our military appear powerless against the increasing number of asymmetric terrorist attacks in Iraq and points elsewhere.

• Cause Americans to revive the anti-war protests, calling for immediate American withdrawals from Afghanistan and Iraq. Motivate an isolationist or "bring our troops home now" movement in the United States, similar to that which occurred in the 1960s and 1970s in protest to the Vietnam War.

• Significantly reduce the morale of our Armed Forces.

• Cause the American public to blame the failures in this global War on Terror on its political leadership and military.

• Cause Congress and the public to lose confidence in our senior military leaders.

• Adversely affect U.S. military recruiting. Better yet, force Congress to reinstitute the draft to meet all global military commitments.

• Cause average Americans to cease supporting the military efforts in the Global War on Terror (GWOT).

• Push Americans to elect to public office those rep-resentatives who seek peace at any price or who will cut military spending, reduce troop strengths across the board, or worse yet, sit down at the negotiation tables with our Islamist foes.

• Make our fellow Americans blame the men and women of the Armed Forces for the adverse fallout of civilian political decisions, as was the case in the latter years of the Vietnam War.

There is much we can do to help thwart the bad guys' goals and aspirations.

- **Be a Visual Patriot.** Display our national colors on your apartment, house, or place of business. Fly it twenty-four hours each day by illuminating it at night. Stick those magnetic "Support our Troops" ribbons on your cars. Contribute to causes that provide troops abroad with care packages, letters, and cell phones. Be verbal at every public opportunity about what a great job our volunteer men and women are doing. Our mission is two-fold: Make sure the terrorists know that our support for our military will not wane. Just as importantly, ensure that our military knows that we are behind them all the way.

- **Keep Things in Perspective.** We can criticize our government, our politicians, and our senior military leaders. We should not take our frustrations and complaints out on the troops themselves. Soldiers, sailors, airmen, marines, and "coasties" go where they are told to go and do what they are commanded to do. Let us not make the men and women in harm's way suffer for the faults or mistakes of their civilian and military leaders. Always support the troops. Shake their hands. Buy them a beer. Salute them as you pass (I often do so). Make sure that our politicians and senior military leaders are providing them with everything that they need to succeed; from state-of-the-art body armor to the very best chow.

- **Refuse to Support or Accept Cuts in Defense Spending While our Men and Women are Being Shot at Around the World.** This should be a "no brainer" for Americans, including our politicians. Remember that not all of the money in the defense budget goes for buying bullets. It is spent on better vehicles, stronger armor protection, food, medicine and medical care, pay and benefits, logistics support, development, testing, and fielding of better weapons systems and platforms to enable more of our military to survive the rigors and dangers of combat, and for retirement benefits for those of us (like me) who are lucky enough to live to collect it. Consider defense spending cuts ONLY when we are not placing tens of thousands of our fellow Americans in harm's way for years at a clip. *If politicians run on platforms supporting defense cuts, simply do not vote them into, or retain them in, office.*

- **Push for an Increase in Troop Strength.** Ever wonder why we are having such a tough time securing Iraq? We don't have enough soldiers or marines to hold and secure the ground we take. Former Army Chief of Staff, General Shinseki, told the Joint Chiefs and Secretary of Defense Rumsfeld that it was going to take at least 300,000 to 400,000 ground troops to secure Iraq after the formal shooting invasion ended. He made that call before the U.S.-led coalition invaded Iraq, while serving as the Army's top leader. He was allegedly forced into retirement, as happens to four-star generals who have the guts to tell it like it is while they are still on active duty.

The immediate future of war appears to be conflicts such as Operations Enduring and Iraqi Freedom. We have a relatively small standing, active duty military force. Almost half of our nation's divisional troop strength is in Iraq today. Our men and women will be repeatedly sent back into combat again and again because we simply do not have enough "boots on the ground" to draw from in order to give warriors a much earned rest.

The U.S. Army active duty troop strength was around 784,000 at the end of the 1980s during the Cold War. At that time, America was not committing tens of thousands of soldiers to sustained combat. The active Army force today hovers around 480,000. If our politicians are hell bent to keep committing our armed forces to combat, then they must provide us with more military. Let's ramp up. We can always reduce the force when we no longer need it, as we last did during the Clinton Administration following Operation Desert Storm in the early 1990s, and as we have done throughout our nation's history.

- **Know When Your Nation is Bluffing, Because Your Enemies Sure Do.** I throw up my arms each and every time the Bush Administration issues a stern warning to Iran or North Korea. The North Korean and Iranian ruling classes must laugh themselves silly at these idle threats. We cannot invade either nation as long as we are deployed in Afghanistan and Iraq. We are out of boots. The Iranians – much smarter than our politicians make them out to be – know damn well that we would need at least half a million troops on the ground to have a snowball's chance in hell of taking, holding, and SECURING key Iranian urban and rural areas. According to the Central Intelligence Agency's 2005 estimate Iran possesses 15,665,725 men between the ages of 18 and 49 who are fit for military service (many subject to being conscripted).[153] How many of them would take up arms and fight against a U.S.-led invasion is hard to estimate. But even if only 20% decided or were conscripted to do so, that's more than 3 million armed persons fighting for their country against the infidels. Think about it. A war with Iran could get very messy, very quickly.

- **Keep UnAmerican Politicians in Check.** Howard Dean, candidate for the Democratic presidential nomination in 2004, issued statements in December

---

[153] http://www.cia.gov/cia/publications/factbook/geos/ir.html.

2003 saying that we should not prejudge Osama bin Laden.[154] This was after Osama and Al Qaeda took full credit for the 9-11 kills. The statement was unAmerican. It was ignorant. It showed no respect for the thousands who were murdered. It demonstrated a weakness within our national leadership. It no doubt aided terrorist recruiting efforts and motivated potential Al Qaeda supporters by giving terror leaders and recruiters the power to TRUTHFULLY say that a primary American candidate for president did not condemn bin Laden for 9/11. Dean's comment was despicable, unAmerican, and flatly wrong. His Congressional peers did not rebuke him. They share the shame and the blame.

During a time when this nation is at war, and brave men and women are dying for the cause, Howard Dean utters statements like, "Let's remember who the real enemy is. . . George Bush is the enemy."[155] Another anti-American quote to be effectively used to recruit homicide bombers. Thanks, Doctor Dean, for placing partisan politics way above the protection of my country and its citizens. What really upsets me much more than Dean's selfishness and irresponsible ramblings are the millions of my fellow Americans who appear to be just fine with his statements that give comfort, aid, and motivation to terrorists and their recruits. I am at a loss to comprehend Americans' tolerance for men like Dean.

When I say we need to keep politicians from saying ignorant things that aid and abet our enemies, I am talking about the likes of Illinois Senator Dick Durbin, against whom Howard Dean pales in comparison. On June 15, 2005, from the floor of the U.S. Senate, Durbin likened American service men and women to the Nazis and the Soviets. I was shocked by the unmitigated gall of this public servant. The Nazi soldiers exterminated more

---

[154] Re-stated in an interview between Mr. Russert and Dr. Dean on NBC's "Meet the Press, May 22, 2005. Found at http://www.msnbc.msn.com/id/7924139/.
[155] *"Opponents and Enemies."* The National Review Online. July 7, 2005 at http://tks.nationalreview.com/.

than 6 million Jews. The Soviets brutally tortured and killed countless millions in the Gulag under orders to do so. Soldiers of both militaries tortured, maimed, and killed as a matter of accepted political and military course. Though a few U.S. soldiers may go awry from time to time, there is no way that our fighting men and women could or should ever be compared to a nation-state's military that was government-sanctioned to torture and kill thousands or millions of victims.

I maintain that the people of Illinois who let Durbin get away with this verbal assault on our fine military men and women share the blame and the shame.

- Ensure That Our Men and Women DO NOT Suffer and Die in Vain. Our overall troop strength is too low. We are losing the fight in Afghanistan because we chose to invade a second nation-state (Iraq) before the job was finished in Afghanistan. Our nation is not providing its military the strength in numbers it needs to succeed. In doing so, we dishonor our fighting men and women.

- Show an Enlisted GI[156] and Others Around That You Appreciate the Hell Out of What They Are Sacrificing For You. I travel quite a bit. I regularly perform a gesture in airports and restaurants to show my support for enlisted GIs. If I see a soldier, sailor, airman, marine, or "coastie" in uniform getting a bite to eat or enjoying an adult beverage, I pick up the tab. Usually, it doesn't cost much: five dollars for a GI's beer or ten bucks for lunch. Sometimes, when I can afford to do so, I pay for a soldier in uniform dining with his wife and kids. I make a habit of shaking their hands, thanking them for their service and asking them if they would permit me the honor of picking up the tab as a demonstration of my appreciation for

---

[156] Officers make enough money. They can pay for their own meals. But the enlisted don't make nearly what they are worth. I pay for them.

their brave contribution in time of war. It makes them feel appreciated. It makes me feel great.

While flying home from meetings at the Pentagon, I had a two hour layover in Cincinnati. I went into a bar to grab a sandwich and a drink. An Army sergeant was sitting at the bar, in his desert BDUs,[157] enjoying a beer and a burger. I got up from my table, thanked him for his service, and told the bartender to put the GI's food and drink on my tab. I was still eating when the sergeant finished his lunch, got up and walked over to me, thanked me once again, and departed for his flight. The bartender came over to me and, with a tear in his eye, told me since the war in Iraq began, hardly a GI in uniform at his bar had to pay for anything. He said that someone like me always picked up their tabs. This made me proud to be an American, and brought a tear to my eye too.

When we do little things like this for our soldiers, it not only shows them that we are behind them all the way, but demonstrates to any terrorist or terror sympathizer who may be watching or listening that Americans are behind their military men and women.

Buy a GI lunch; let a GI go ahead of you in the checkout line. If you see a uniformed marine with his or her significant other at a movie theater, buy their tickets for them. You'll feel so wonderful for having done so. I guarantee that GI will be telling his buddies the story for weeks. You will be supporting the war and boosting morale at the same time. As they say at Nike, "JUST DO IT!"

Complacency is not an option, and denial is deadly. So assume the responsibility. Adopt the creed:

If not me, then who? If not now, then when?

---

[157] Battle Dress Uniform.

Sustaining Our National Economic Power

The Economy: It's Where The Bad Guys Can Really Hurt Us

We must preserve and protect our economic power. Repeated terror attacks of the magnitude of those perpetrated on 9/11 could very well produce detrimental and long-term economic affects on our nation. These attacks do not need to be back-to-back. They can be few and spread out over time, and still exact a cumulative, devastating toll.

The outcome of each terror attack on the home front will be destruction, injury and death. Each attack will inflict and exacerbate existing psychological and physiological trauma upon society at large. Should our steadfastness and tenacity ever fall victim to apathy, social correctness and partisan politics, the terrorists may eventually even force us to sit at their bargaining table.[158] They did so in the Vietnam era during President Nixon's administration. We must never permit them to do so again.

---

[158] For those of you that think that the U.S. does not negotiate with terrorists: WRONG. As previously stated American Presidents have hosted and negotiated with the Palestinian Authority (PA) leader Yasser Arafat on several occasions. So the next time you hear one of our government spokes-persons say that "we do not negotiate with terrorists," you know that they are either liars or ignorant of recent American history.

Terror attacks of even worse magnitude than those of 9-11 could seriously chip away at our economy. Osama bin Laden stated publicly that our economy is a primary target of Al Qaeda, and will remain so throughout this fight to the death.

We Americans can deal adequately with terror day in and day out as long as it does not seriously affect our quality of life. We like our SUVs, steaks on the grill, air conditioning on hot summer days, micro-brewed beer, and two-dollar cups of gourmet coffee. We work long and hard for what we are able to put away in our savings accounts, investments, 401Ks, college and vacation funds. We will all survive the hard times, even gas at $3.50 per gallon, as long as our American economy remains strong.

Our American economy is strong: valued in the trillions of dollars. Yet it is amazing how frail and vulnerable it remains at the hands of the likes of Al Qaeda. The aggregate, economic damage to the United States from the 9-11 New York City carnage alone is both sobering and stunning.

New York City Comptroller William C. Thompson released a report on the fiscal impact of 9/11 on the City of New York.[159] At the time this report was published, Thompson estimated that the economic cost of 9-11 could total as much as $95 billion. Thirteen and a half million square feet of office space was lost, "equal to the entire office space inventory in the central business districts of Atlanta or Miami."[160] Here are more staggering 9-11 facts:

- Number killed in the World Trade Center (WTC): 2,823.[161]

---

[159] Thompson, William C. "One Year Later, the Fiscal Impact of 9/11 on New York City" September 4, 2002. at http://www.comptroller.nyc.gov/press/2002_releases/02-09-054.shtm.
[160] Ibid.
[161] "9/11 in numbers." Tom Templeton and Tom Lumley. The Observer. August 18, 2002. at http://observer.guardian.co.uk/waronterrorism/story/0,1373,776451,00.html.

- Number employed inside WTC: 50,000 daily averages.[162]

- Average number of daily visitors to WTC: 140,000.[163]

- The estimated costs of attacks based upon property losses and insurance costs are $21 billion.[164]

- The estimated total losses to the world insurance market are as high as $75 billion.[165]

- The amount that U.S. commercial insurance premiums rose to cover the potential future cost of terror attacks was 50% between 2002 and 2004.[166]

- The Dow Jones Industrial Average suffered its biggest one day fall, 685 points, On September 17, 2001, the first day the market opened after the week of 9-11. It dropped a total of 1,370 points within two weeks of September 11.[167]

- The number of jobs lost in lower Manhattan was around 100,000. The calculated number of jobs lost in the U.S. by the end of 2002 as a result of 9/11 was 1.8 million.

Here's the one fact that should scare the "you know what" out of us: all of the losses our nation suffered from the twin tower attacks including physical, emotional, psychological, financial, and economic, were inflicted by only nine terrorists.[168] Less

---

[162] Ibid
[163] Ibid
[164] Ibid.
[165] Ibid.
[166] Ibid.
[167] "Chart of the Dow Jones Industrial Averages Since 1974."
http://www.the-privateer.com/chart/dow-long.html, page 2 of 2.
[168] Five terrorists took down American Flight 11 that struck the north tower and four on United Flight 175 that flew into the south tower.

than a dozen warriors, who carried no guns, brought one of our nation's biggest cities to a grinding standstill. Nine committed men willing to fight for the cause of Al Qaeda and to die for Allah. If nine murderers can inflict this much pain and damage, what can twenty mete out? What about fifty? Remember, there are an estimated 20,000 Islamist jihadists in the world today, most of whom were trained by Al Qaeda and its branch affiliates.

Our government tells us that the economy is and will remain strong and resilient. I hope so. I am not an economist, investment expert, or genius with numbers. Yet by simply applying a little history, logic, and worst case planning, what I deduce concerns me greatly.

Many more American cities and their landmark buildings might have suffered devastation at the hands of other Al Qaeda 9/11 homicide pilots had the federal authorities not grounded all planes over U.S. air space within hours of the World Trade Center attacks. Perhaps the Sears Building in Chicago would have been destroyed or the Seattle Space Needle, a Disney or Six Flags park, downtown Hollywood, the Hoover Damn, or Caesar's Palace. The speculation is endless.

Terror attacks the likes of 9/11 produce an economic domino affect. Planes are grounded. When planes are grounded, airports close. Supplies and services are put on hold. Businessmen stop purchasing air travel tickets through their company travel agent. Hotels and restaurants that cater to the traveling public lose patrons. People make less money, and therefore spend less, especially on luxury items. It all rolls down hill.

Our economy is robust, but it is not bulletproof. Take all of the economic disaster associated with the downing of the Twin Towers and multiply that by Chicago, Los Angeles, Boston, Miami, Baltimore, New Orleans, Dallas, Kansas City, Detroit, Dallas/Fort Worth, and Atlanta. How much would the Dow

Jones industrial average plummet? How many more tens of millions of Americans would cease receiving paychecks? How many more hundreds of billions or even trillions of dollars would be required to recover, reconstitute, and rebuild? What would be the toll upon information systems, critical infrastructure, and surrounding communities? I shudder to think.

What if a terror pilot flies a Cessna full of explosives packed with expended, radioactive fuel rods,[169] such as the ones that have somehow come up missing from two U.S. nuclear power plants[170] into a major Chrysler, Ford, or General Motors automobile manufacturing plant? What if the levels of radioactivity after the crash make the plant uninhabitable for many lifetimes? A closed auto plant results in thousands of lay offs. Companies that supply the auto plant with everything from headlights to tires to food are forced to cut back production and terminate employees. Area vendors do not sell the same volumes of commodities. Sudden and dramatic boosts in the numbers of unemployed in big cities are unhealthy for the urban environment. Crime rates rise. Neighborhoods fall into disarray. The economic domino affect takes root.

"It Can Never Happen to Us" Syndrome

When the bright sun and blue skies appeared over New York City on the morning of September 11 it was business as usual for the 430 companies that called the World Trade Center home. Not one of the 50,000 employees ever imagined that within a few hours of the beginning of that business day, their offices, co-workers, records, files, communications systems, clients and so much more would be vaporized. The Sandler O'Neill investment firm was located on the 104th floor of World Trade Center Two.

---

[169] Often referred to as an "RDD" or radiological dispersion device.
[170] CBS news reported on April 22, 2004 that "Two pieces of a highly radioactive fuel rod are missing from a Vermont nuclear plant." And that "In 2002 a Connecticut nuclear plant was fined $288,000 after a similar loss. That fuel was never accounted for." Details at
http://www.cbsnews.com /stories/2004/04/22/national/main613090.shtml.

Eighty-three employees showed up for work on September 11. Only seventeen went home that night. Treasured co-workers gone forever, and with them, all of the institutional knowledge, business savvy and corporate contacts that made Sandler O'Neill the successful firm it was at eight o'clock that morning.

I felt the enormity of the human losses on 9/11 when I first read the list of the dead and missing but presumed dead days after the attack. I realized the magnitude of the economic losses only after I viewed a complete list of all of the corporations and government entities whose offices were incinerated. I share the list within the text of the book to insure that my readers, at a minimum, scan to appreciate the magnitude of the losses themselves:

All Companies Lost, With Floor Number and Tower:

A I G Aviation Brokerage Insurance 53 North Tower

Abad, Castilla and Mallonga Attorneys 18 South Tower

ABN-AMRO Mortgage Brokers 35 South Tower

Adecco SA Employment Agency 21 South Tower

Agricor Commodities Corp. Investments 80 North Tower

Airport Access Program Banks/Financial 63 North Tower

Alan Anthony Consultants NA North Tower

Alliance Consulting Consultants 18 South Tower

Allstate Insurance Co. Insurance 24 South Tower

American Bureau of Shipping Engineers 91 North Tower

American Lota Intl. NA 45 North Tower

American TCC Intl. Group Investments 47,90 North Tower

Amerson Group Co. Organizations 8 North Tower

Ann Taylor Loft Retail Concourse North Tower

Anne Pope, Law Offices of Attorneys 35 North Tower

Antal Intl. Employment Agency 22 South Tower

AON Corporation Insurance 92,99,100 South Tower

Asahi Bank Banks/Financial 60 North Tower

ASTDC Organizations 46 North Tower

AT&T Corporation Telecommunication 51 North Tower

Atlantic Bank of New York Financial Institute 106 South Tower

Auto Imperial Co. Wholesalers 46 North Tower

Avenir Computer Services 78 North Tower

Avesta Computer Services Data Processing 21 North Tower

Avis Car Rental Lobby North Tower

Baltic Oil Corporation Corporate 78 North Tower

Banco LatinoAmericano de Exportacione Banks/Financial 32 North Tower

Bank of America Banks/Financial 9-11,81 North Tower

Bank of Taiwan Banks/Financial 53 North Tower

Barcley Dwyer NA 89 North Tower

bepaid.com NA 84 South Tower

Berel & Mullen Attorneys 33 North Tower

Big A Travel Agency Travel 28 South Tower

Blue Sky Technologies Computer Services 46 North Tower

Bramax Manufacturing (USA) Corp. Wholesalers 52 North Tower

Bright China Capital Investments 84 North Tower

Broad USA Wholesalers 89 North Tower

Brown & Wood, L.L.P. Attorneys 54,56-59 North Tower

C & P Press Business Services 51 North Tower

California Bank & Trust Banks/Financial 16 North Tower

Can-Achieve Consultants 46 North Tower

Candia Shipping Wholesalers 15 South Tower

Cantor Fitzgerald Securities Investments 101-105 North Tower

Career Engine Research 21 South Tower

Caserta & Co. NA 18 South Tower

Cedar Capital Management Associates Banks/Financial 78 North Tower

Channel 2 (WCBS) Television 110 North Tower

Channel 31 (WBIS) Television 110 North Tower

Channel 4 (NBC) Television 104 North Tower

Channel 47 (WNJU) Television 110 North Tower

Channel 5 (WNYW) Television 110 North Tower

Charna Chemicals Manufacturing 14 South Tower

Charoen Pokphand USA Transport/Utility 21 South Tower

Chen, Lin, Li, & Jiang LLP Investments 18 South Tower

Cheng Cheng Enterprises Holding Inc. Retailers 78 North Tower

Cheng Xiang Trading USA Computer Services 22 North Tower

Chicago Options Exchange Corp. Investments 22 North Tower

China Chamber of Commerce Organizations 24 South Tower

China Construction America Construction 45 North Tower

China Daily Distribution Corp. Business Services 33 North Tower

China Patent & Trademark USA Attorneys 29 North Tower

China Resource Products USA Ltd. NA 53 North Tower

CIIC Group (USA) Investments 89 North Tower

CNN Television 110 North Tower

Colortek Kodak Imaging Center Business Services 1 South Tower

Commerzbank Capital Markets Investments 32 South Tower

Commodity Futures Trading Commission Investments 37 North Tower

Consolidated Steelex Corp. Manufacturing 46 North Tower

Continental Insurance Co. Insurance NA South Tower

Continental Logistics Business Services 21 North Tower

Corporation Service Co. NA 87 South Tower

Cultural Institutions Retirement Systems Trusts39 North Tower

Daehan Intl. Investments 89 North Tower

Dahao USA Corp Wholesalers 46 North Tower

Dai-Ichi Kangyo Trust Co. Trusts 48-50 North Tower

Data Transmission Network Corp. NA 33 North Tower

David Peterson Attorneys 84 North Tower

Daynard & Van Thunen Co. Insurance 79 North Tower

December First Productions LLCNA 24 South Tower

Delta Airlines Airline Lobby North Tower

Dongwon Securities Co. Ltd. Investments 21 North Tower

Dow Jones & Co. Printers/Publisher 57,58 South Tower

Dr. Tadasu Tokumaru, M.D. Doctors 21 North Tower

Drinker Biddle & Reath Attorneys 89 North Tower

Dun & Bradstreet Research 14 North Tower

Dunavant Commodity Corp. Investments 45 North Tower

eMeritus Communications Telecommunication 83 North Tower

Empire Health Choice Insurance 17,19,20,23,24 North Tower

Employee Merit Employment Agency 45 North Tower

EuroBrokers Investments 12 South Tower

Fertitta Enterprises NA 45 North Tower

Fiduciary Trust Co. Intl. Financial Institute 90,94,95,96,97 South Tower

Fireman's Fund Insurance Co. Insurance 48 South Tower

First Commercial Bank Financial Institute 78 South Tower

First Liberty Investment Group Investments 79 North Tower

Fred Alger Management Investments 93 North Tower

Frenkel & Co. Insurance 35,36 South Tower

Friends Ivory & Sime Investments 21 North Tower

Friends Villas Fischer Trust Investments 21 North Tower

Fuji Bank Financial Institute 79-82 South Tower

G. Z. Stephens Employment Agency 47 North Tower

G.C. Services Collection Agency 22 North Tower

Garban Intercapital NA 55 South Tower

Garban-Intercapital Investments 25-26 North Tower

Gayer Shyu & Wiesel Investments 52 North Tower

Gayer, Shyu & Wiesel Accountants 5 North Tower

Geiger & Geiger Attorneys 78 North Tower

General Telecommunications Telecommunication 83 North Tower

Gibbs & Hill Engineers 91 South Tower

Global Crossings Holdings Ltd. Computer Services 83 North Tower

Globe Tour & Travel Travel 24 South Tower

Gold Sky Manufacturing 22 North Tower

Golden King (USA) Limited NA 33 North Tower

Government of Thailand Government 37 North Tower

Greatest Bar on Earth Bar 107 North Tower

Guy Carpenter Insurance 47-54 South Tower

Hal Roth Agency Insurance 77 North Tower

Harris Beach & Wilcox LLP Attorneys 85 South Tower

Hartford Steam Boiler Insurance 30 South Tower

Hill Betts & Nash LLP Attorneys 52 North Tower

Howly (US) Corporation NA 52 North Tower

Hu Tong Intl. (USA) Co. Wholesalers 33 North Tower

Hua Nan Commercial Bank Ltd. Financial Institute 28 South Tower

Hyundai Securities Co. Investments 78 North Tower

Infotech NA 21 North Tower

Instinet Investments 13,14 North Tower

Intera Group Employment Agency 18 South Tower

Intl. Office Centers Corporation Business Services 79 North Tower

Intl. Trade Center Public Relations 78 North Tower

Intrust Investment Realty Real Estate 80 North Tower

J & X Tans Intl. NA 46 North Tower

James T. Ratner, Law Office of Attorneys 15 South Tower

John J. McMullen Associates Engineers 15 South Tower

John W. Loofbourrow Associates Investments 15 South Tower

Johnston & Murphy NA Concourse South Tower

Julien J. Studley Real Estate 86 North Tower

Jun He Law Office, LLC Attorneys 77 North Tower

Kaiser Overseas Manufacturing 22 North Tower

Kanebo Information Systems Corp. Computer Services 46 North Tower

Karoon Capital Management Investments 22 North Tower

Keefe, Bruyette & Woods Investments 85,88,89 South Tower

Keenan Powers & Andrews Attorneys 53 North Tower

Kemper Insurance Companies Insurance 35,36 North Tower

Kidder Peabody & Co. Banks/Financial 101 North Tower

KITC Investments 84 North Tower

Korea Local Auth. Foundation for Intl Government/Schools 78 North Tower

Koudis Intl. NA 33 North Tower

Landmark Education Corporation Government/Schools 15 North Tower

Lava Trading, LLC NA 83 North Tower

Law Office of Joseph Bellard Attorneys 28 South Tower

Law Offices of Roman V. Popik Attorneys 21 North Tower

Leeds & Morrelli Attorneys 52 North Tower

Lehman Brothers Investment c 38-40 North Tower

LG Insurance Co. Insurance NA North Tower

LG Securities America Investments 84 North Tower

Lief Intl. USA Manufacturing 21 North Tower

LoCurto & Funk Investments 53 North Tower

M.A. Katz, CPA Accountants 45 North Tower

MANAA Trading Group Investments 33 North Tower

Mancini Duffy Architects 15,21,22 South Tower

Marsh USA Insurance 93-100 North Tower

Martin Progressive LLC Computer Services 77 North Tower

May Davis Group Investments 87 North Tower

Mechanical Floor NA 41-43 North Tower

Meganet Management Consultants Computer Services 46 North Tower

Meridian Ventures Holding Financial 78 North Tower

Metropolitan Life Insurance Co. Insurance 89 North Tower

MIS Service Co. NA 33 North Tower

MLU Investment Investment 22 North Tower

Morgan Stanley Investments 43-46,56,59-74 South Tower

Mutual Intl. Forwarding NA 89 North Tower

N.Y. Institute of Finance Consultants 17 South Tower

N.Y. Society of Security Analysts Government/Schools 44 North Tower

National Development & Research Inst. Research16 South Tower

Natural Nydegger Transport Corp. NA 53 North Tower

Network Plus Telecommunication 81 North Tower

New Continental Enterprises NA 81 North Tower

New York Stock Exchange Financial 28-30 South Tower

New-ey Intl. Corp. Business Services 77 North Tower

NFA/GGG NA 47 North Tower

Nichols Foundation Government/Schools Ground South Tower

Nikko Securities Banks/Financial 79 North Tower

Noga Commodities Overseas Investments 80 North Tower

Northern Trust Intl. Banking Corp. Banks/Financial NA North Tower

NY Coffee Station Food Retail Concourse North Tower

NY Dept. of Taxation & Finance Government 86,87 South Tower

NY Metro Transportation Council Government/Schools 82 North Tower

NY Shipping Association Transportation 19,20 South Tower

Okasan Intl. (American) Investments 52 North Tower

Okato Shoji Co. Computer Services 79 North Tower

Olympia Airport Express NA Lobby North Tower

Oppenheimer Funds Investments 31-34 South Tower

Orient Intl. NA 15 South Tower

Overseas Union Bank Banks/Financial 39 North Tower

P. Wolfe Consultants Consultants 22 North Tower

Pace University Government/Schools 55 North Tower

Pacific American Co. Wholesalers 47 North Tower

Pacrim Trading & Shipping NA 53,78 North Tower

Paging Network of New York Telecommunication 14 South Tower

Patinka Intl. (USA) Business Services 14 South Tower

Phink Path Employment Agency 78 North Tower

Pines Investment Investment 18 South Tower

Porcella Vicini & Co. NA 11 North Tower

Port Authority of NY & New Jersey Government 3,14,19,24,28,31 North Tower

Primarch Decision Economics Consultants 11 North Tower

Professional Assistance & Consulting Consultants 18 South Tower

Prospect Intl. NA 46 North Tower

Pure Energy Corp. Wholesalers 45,53 North Tower

Quint Amasis, L.L.C. Business Services 47 North Tower

R.H. Wrightson & Associates Investments 25 North Tower

Rachel & Associates Manufacturing 33 North Tower

Raytheon Co. Manufacturing 91 South Tower

Regional Alliance Small Contractors Construction 38 North Tower

Regus Business Centres Employment Agency 93 South Tower

RGL Gallagher PC Accountants 52 North Tower

Richard A. Zimmerman, Esq. Attorneys 52 North Tower

RLI Insurance Co. Insurance 80 North Tower

Rohde & LiesenfeldNA 32 North Tower

Royal Thai Embassy Office Government NA North Tower

Sandler O'Neill & Partners Investments 104 South Tower

San-In Godo Bank Ltd. Banks/Financial 84 North Tower

Sassoons NA 45 North Tower

SCOR U.S. Corporation Insurance 23,24 South Tower

Seabury & Smith Insurance 49 South Tower

Securant Technologies Computer Services 79 North Tower
Security Traders Association Organizations 45 North Tower
Serko & Simon Attorneys 33 North Tower
Shizuoka Bank Ltd. Banks/Financial 80 North Tower
Showtime Pictures Business Services 18,107 South Tower
Sinochem American Holdings Investments 22 South Tower
Sinolion NA 24 South Tower
Sinopec USA Wholesalers 46 North Tower
Sitailong Intl. USANA 40 South Tower
SMW Trading Corp. Investments 85 North Tower
SRA NA 45 North Tower
Strategic Communications Telecommunication 89 North Tower
Strawberry Retailers Concourse North Tower
Streamline Capital, LLCNA 45 North Tower
Suggested Open Systems Computer Services 46 North Tower
Sun Microsystems Computer Services 25,26 South Tower
Suntendy America Wholesalers 46 North Tower
T&T Enterprises Intl. Inc Miscellaneous 46 North Tower
Tai Fook Securities Investments 22,39 North Tower
Taipei Bank Banks/Financial 83 North Tower
TD Waterhouse Group Investments 24 South Tower
Temenos USA Wholesalers 52,84 North Tower
Tes USA Investments NA North Tower
Thacher, Proffitt & Wood Attorneys 20,38-40 South Tower
Thai Farmers Bank Banks/Financial 7 North Tower
The Beast.Comm Computer Services 80 North Tower
The Chugoku Bank Banks/Financial 90 North Tower
The Co. Store Retailers 45 North Tower
The Nishi-Nippon Bank Banks/Financial 102 North Tower
The SCPIE Companies NA 22 North Tower
The Williams Capital Group NA 52 North Tower
Thermo Electron NA 85 North Tower

Tower Computer Service Retailers 21 North Tower

Traders Access Center Investments 78 North Tower

Turner Construction Co. Construction 38 North Tower

Unicom Capital Advisors LLP Investments 22,84 North Tower

Union Bank of California Intl. Financial Institute 14 South Tower

Unistrat Corporation of America Consultants 23 South Tower

United Hercules Travel NA North Tower

United Seamen's Service AMMLA Social Services 21 North Tower

Verizon Communications Telecommunication 9-12 South Tower

W.J. Export-Import Wholesalers 47 North Tower

Wai Gao Qiao USA Consultants 89 North Tower

Wall Street Planning Assoc. NA 89 North Tower

Washington Mutual NA 22 South Tower

Waterfront Commission of NY Harbor Government 19 South Tower

Weatherly Securities Corp. Investments 29 South Tower

Weiland Intl. Investments 18 South Tower

Windows on the World Retailers 106 North Tower

World Trade Centers Association Organizations 77 North Tower

World Trade Club NA 107 North Tower

World Trade Institute NA 55 North Tower

World Travel Travel 29 North Tower

Xcel Federal Credit Union Banks/Financial 39 North Tower

Xerox Document Co. Manufacturing Basement South Tower

Yong Ren America NA 46 North Tower

Zim-American Israeli Shipping Co. NA 16,17 North Tower

(List extracted from http://www.startabroad.com/wtc_ companies.htm.)

In this age of infinite information systems and business at the speed of light, both the government and private sectors must be able to recover, reconstitute, and keep the wheels of employment turning following any catastrophic loss. After the devastation of

911, "it can never happen to us" is the ultimate expression of denial. It reflects a distorted view of reality and a lack of resolve to support our nation and its employees during these difficult times. Why would any company worth its salt not plan to keep its revenue flowing after a hurricane, flood, tornado, fire, chlorine gas leak, or terror attack? I cannot think of a sound business reason for not planning for the worst-case scenario.

Sustaining Our Economic Power in an Age of Terror: Business Continuity & Disaster Recovery Planning

"If the Twin Towers nightmare taught us anything, it's the need to resist complacency and prepare for the worst."[171]

Greater than ninety-five percent of the critical infrastructure upon which the United States economy depends is designed, financed, built, and sustained by our private sector corporations. Our satellite systems, the Internet, information systems, fiber optic networks, and telecommunications, just to name a few, are brought to you by America's capitalist movers and shakers. Even our government, including our military forces, relies upon the commercial sector's infrastructure and conduits for more than ninety-five percent of all global command, control, communications, and computer interface (C4).

Who's responsibility is it to ensure that plans are in place to keep our private sector companies operating if and when a disaster befalls them? It is the private companies that are responsible. Federal and state governments can advise, recommend, and provide tax breaks and incentives for private sector cooperation and compliance. Within this great democracy though, federal, state, and local governments cannot dictate to commercial companies what they must do and how much money they must spend

---

[171] *Corporate Security: Business Continuity and Disaster Recovery Post 9/11*. Lucent Technologies White Paper, excerpted from "The Black Book on Corporate Security" by Dr. Jim Kennedy. Larstan Publishing. 2005, cover page.

to effect all-hazards business continuity and disaster recovery planning. Recommendations can only be offered in hopes of receiving the private sector's teamwork and cooperation.

We must rely upon the private sector to perform its own risk analyses and commit to business continuity and disaster recovery planning (BC & DR).[172] Fortune 500, multi-billion dollar corporations institute the very best BC and DR planning, as they can both financially afford it and ill afford not to at the same time.

Business continuity and disaster recovery planning is all about the ability to earn money and keep folks employed for another day. It's all about being prepared to be at our very best during the very worst of times. The 9-11 tragedy carries with it many stories of how BC and DR planning paid big dividends for those companies who were smart enough to invest some time and money to circumvent worst case scenarios. But for all too many others on that tragic day, a hard lesson was brutally driven home.

Economic security and stability means different things to different people. For the majority of working stiffs, economic security is sustaining a paycheck in order to pay all of our bills each month, including the interest charges on our credit card debt. To others, it is being able to save enough to send kids to college. Still others strive to invest enough to live a lavish retirement. For the financial elite, economic stability may be all about keeping the house in the Hamptons, the vacation condo in the Caribbean, and the race horses, without having to lay off the chauffeur or the gardener.

Sustaining and maintaining our global economic power is all about keeping people employed, paychecks flowing, and profits edging upwards, all of which remain at great risk given under constant threats from global terror.

---

[172] Many different terms are used throughout industry, to include business continuity of operations, continuity of business operations, all-hazards planning, and business continuity solutions.

This book is primarily for everyday working stiffs such as me. So let's talk about what we can do in the BC and DR arena to hold up our nation's economic power at the "building block" level: the individual job. Business continuity planning does not have to be expensive or complicated to achieve the objective of keeping our fellow citizens employed. Much of it is simply requires a little time, creativity, and common sense.

For example, consider that you are the owner of a popular, national restaurant franchise, and that your retail food store is located in downtown Atlanta, Georgia. Knowing that terrorists go for the big American targets, you feel that your restaurant is more at risk from collateral damage of a downtown terror attack than many of your competitors' restaurants in the suburbs. Out of your 30 employees, 25 are damn good workers who give you their best efforts. If anything ever happened to your restaurant, fire, flood, terror attack collateral damage, and the franchise was forced to close indefinitely, many good people and their loved ones would suffer economically. You ask yourself what could be done to keep paychecks flowing for your food service employees should a terror attack force you to discontinue employing them.

You get a great idea in one of your more creative and coherent moments. You coordinate with the local chamber of commerce to host a meeting of all restaurant franchise owners in and around the Atlanta metro area. You propose the following. In case any one or more of the city's franchise restaurants is forced to close due to a natural or man made disaster, the others still in operation agree to take in one of the more sterling employees from the downed franchise, until that restaurant can get back up on its feet. Memoranda of agreement are signed. It works to everyone's collective advantage. It assists in keeping the local economy running. It provides job security for dedicated employees. It enables business owners and operators to defeat the desired, end result of the terror attacks— more American misery and economic loss. Well done, you! Quite often, such as in the case of a sole proprietorship, individuals are responsible to make sure they keep themselves employed. Let's take a mom and pop consignment shop, for example. An elderly couple is living on a fixed retirement income, except from the significant extra they take in monthly running the consignments. What if a fire in the small strip mall inflicts smoke and water damage that makes their little corner of it uninhabitable? What do they do for extra cash during the six months that it takes to handle investigations, pay insurance claims, and rebuild? An alternate location for their consignment shop should be scouted and secured now, just in case, while business is up and running. Maybe business insurance is an option.

Employers who can do something to keep the economy up and running in the face of post 9-11 terror threats are obligated to do so. Some contributions will be huge. Some will be so small as to go virtually unnoticed. No matter. All are important. If every American does his or her part to plan for the worst, our economy will be the stronger and the better for it, and the terrorists will not stand a chance of achieving their objectives.

Excellent references, white papers, historical and background information pertaining to BC and DR planning, what it is and how to go about doing it, can be found at the following wesites:

http://www.lucent.com/knowledge/download/docreg. html?/livelink/0900940380095c5b_White_paper.pdf

http://www.drj.com/newzdr/gov-rep-kelley.doc

http://www.continuitycentral.com/bcpd.htm

Complacency is not an option, and denial is deadly. So assume the responsibility. Adopt the creed:

If not me, then who? If not now, then when?

BRIEFING # 12

Communities Taking Charge

I ask average, civilian citizens to seek the answers to two questions. "What does my country want me to do to help fight and win this War on Terror? What guidance has my state, city or community provided to help me be more aware and prepared to deal with terror in my lifetime?" Chances are pretty fair that you will have a difficult time answering either of them.

Not enough is being promulgated at the national or even state levels to keep our citizens-at-large aware, informed, and energized in this War on Terror. I have never seen a full-page anti-terror ad in my hometown newspaper. I cannot recall seeing even one anti-terror public service announcement on the television. If there are anti-terror awareness billboards lining our highways and byways, I seem to have missed them all. No community or state volunteer has ever dropped a terror awareness, prevention, and response pamphlet at my doorstep.

Americans need to be reminded regularly that ours is a nation at war. We must remain alert and vigilant. Human beings exhibit a natural tendency to slide into complacency fairly quickly, even with respect to important things such as their personal safety. We all need those occasional reminders to keep us pumped.

Terrorists are not unlike common criminals in that they will attack where they perceive us to be weakest. Would a criminal prefer to break into a house that he knows is locked or unlocked each night? Would a criminal prefer to break into a house where he knows the owner keeps a loaded gun, or one where the owner is an anti-gun fanatic? I'd break into the anti-gun fanatic's residence, because the risk is much lower. So it is with terrorists. If given a clear choice, they prefer to target a community whose law enforcement, schools, businesses, and citizenry-at-large are uninformed, unaware, and ill-prepared. It makes good operational sense to do so.

Don't Wait for Federal or State Government to Lead You by the Hand

Communities do not have to wait for the feds or their state homeland defense officials to issue guidance and direction before moving out smartly with their own brand of anti-terror awareness campaign. Every town, municipality and city should initiate its own OPERATION TERROR AWARE AND PREPARED (OPTAP) program. Ideally, the state governments can assist by providing needed resources such as subject matter experts, public information support, and money. If not, remember the good old adage: "Where there's a will, there's a way."

All OPTAP programs need not be similar. The innovative techniques and venues used to train and educate the local public may vary greatly. That's OK. To my way of thinking, it is only the main OPTAP objectives that should be embraced across the board:

- Get all of the local movers and shakers on board and rendering their support. This includes but is certainly not limited to:

» Mayors and city council members
» Law Enforcement Activities (police and sheriff's departments, local FBI field office, etc.)
» Medical first responders
» Hospitals, clinics, other medical facilities
» Newspapers, TV and radio stations
» Chambers of Commerce & their members
» School Superintendents and Boards
» Middle and high school principals
» Local college and university chancellors
» Shopping mall and movie theater authorities
» Local kids sports organizers
» Sporting arena authorities
» Public transportation workers (school bus, public bus, and taxi drivers)

• Provide anti-terror awareness and preparedness training to all of the movers and shakers listed above. Training should include but not necessarily be limited to:

» Terror tactics, techniques, and procedures
» Terror attack lessons learned from Israeli and Russian experiences
» Suspicious persons and actions: what to look for and what to do
» Law enforcement tactics, weapons, and equipment necessary to combat terrorists during a hostage siege situation
» How they can help with a public awareness campaign
» Table top and field training exercises among local, state, and federal law enforcement and military

- Conduct town hall meetings sponsored by city and/or private business entities to educate the general public about such topics as:

  » Terror tactics, techniques, and procedures
  » Suspicious persons and actions: what to look for and what to do
  » Lessons learned in Israeli and Russian terror attack experiences
  » The worst that could happen in our city
  » Measures that the city council, school boards, and law enforcement are taking to be more prepared
  » What the average citizen can do to help

- Educate the children in middle and high schools as to how they can assist with vigilance and preparedness. Conduct terror lock down drills and safer evacuation techniques in schools.

- Energize our youth to go door-to-door in their neighborhoods distributing OPERATION TERROR AWARE AND PREPARED information and action leaflets or pamphlets. The kids can receive community service hours while doing their parts in the War on Terror.

- Get local TV, radio, and newspapers to run regular anti-terror awareness ads.

- Get local billboard companies to donate billboards that advertise anti-terror public awareness messages.

- Work to obtain national media coverage for your community's efforts. Let the terrorists know that you are aware and prepared. If the bad guys think your community is extremely vigilant and ready, they might just go somewhere else to attack, in which case, MISSION ACCOMPLISHED FOR YOUR HOME TOWN.

Public Awareness Campaigns (PACs)

They are called by many names: public information campaigns, media campaigns, media blitzes and advertising campaigns. I call them public awareness campaigns, or "PACs." We need PACs to keep Americans squarely in the anti-terror fight.

Public awareness campaigns really do work. Twentieth-century America can boast several extremely successful PACs. I went to the National Ad Council's website (www.adcouncil.org/campaigns) to extract examples of some of the most winning and well-known PACs of the 20th Century:

- United Negro College Fund: 1972 – Present
"A Mind is a Terrible Thing to Waste."
This campaign raised more than $2.2 billion and has helped to graduate more than 350,000 minority students from colleges and graduate schools. "A Mind is a Terrible Thing to Waste" has not only survived the test of time, more than three decades, but has become part of the American vernacular.

- Lance and Vance the Crash Test Dummies: 1985-1999
"You Could Learn A Lot From a Dummy!"
Since Lance and Vance, the Crash Test Dummies, were introduced to the American public in 1985, safety belt usage has increased from fourteen percent to seventy-nine percent, saving an estimated 85,000 lives, and $3.2 billion in costs to society.

- McGruff the Crime Dog: 1979 – Present
"Take a Bite Out of Crime!"
Today, ninety-three percent of children recognize the icon that provides safety tips for adults and kids. Over the years, the Crime Prevention campaign has helped teach kids, teens, and adults about violence and drugs, and the public service announcements inspired all citizens to get involved in building safer, more caring communities.

- Drunk Driving Prevention: 1983 – Present
"Friends Don't Let Friends Drive Drunk."
Since launching this campaign in 1983, more than sixty-eight percent of Americans exposed to the advertising have tried to prevent someone from driving drunk.

- Women in War Jobs: 1942 -1945
"Rosy the Riveter"
Still the most successful advertising recruitment campaign in American history, this powerful symbol recruited two million women into the workforce to support the war economy. The underlying theme was that the social change required to bring women into the workforce was a patriotic responsibility for women and employers. Those ads made a tremendous change in the relationship between women and the workplace. Employment outside of the home became socially acceptable and even desirable.

Convinced that PACs do work? I hope so.

Public information campaigns can do two things for us collectively in the fight against terror in our homeland. First and foremost, they help keep us aware, informed, alert, and engaged. Second, they send a message to our enemies, telling the bad guys that American's citizens are in the fight too, and for the long haul.

I firmly believe that sound, effective planning and training on the parts of law enforcement, firefighters, medical responders, schools, businesses, and city officials, coupled with PACs that publicize how alert and prepared a city truly is, can cause the terrorists to think twice about perpetrating an attack there.

Terrorists seek the paths of least resistance. They prefer to attack weak targets, not strong ones. They endeavor to select targets, times, and places that will afford them the greatest success and the biggest bang for their bucks. If they deem the risk too high, they may develop alternative plans or abort all together. Can terrorist operations be diverted by an alert and prepared citizenry? You bet. Here's an example.

Some years ago, while still on active duty as an Army lieutenant colonel, I was having lunch with an old colleague of mine who worked for the Central Intelligence Agency. We ran across each other at a classified meeting at the Pentagon. We inevitably talked shop when we met, and that day was no exception. The discussion turned to disrupting terrorist plans and operations. My associate related a very interesting story.

The CIA recently raided a terrorist safe house in one of the European NATO countries. Several terrorists were taken into custody along with their plans to kidnap prominent European businessmen and hold them for ransom. One of the European business elite had been scratched off of the hit list. When asked why during interrogation, the terror cell leader said that this man posed too much of a risk to a successful kidnapping operation. What raised the risk to a high enough level that the terror cell aborted the kidnapping? Simply this: the terrorist reconnaissance cell observed that every morning the target would exit his townhouse, stand on his porch and light a cigarette. He would smoke the entire cigarette while constantly glancing up and down the street and in all directions. When he finished his smoke, he would crush it out on the cement and then walk to his car to begin his day. The terrorists assessed that this gentleman's operational awareness was too keen. This man, they reckoned, would have recognized anything out of place the day of the kidnapping; such as a strange car, persons walking near his house, etc. His early morning "porch reconnaissance" made any kidnapping operation too risky. Sometimes all that it takes is awareness, vigilance, and attention to detail to stop them dead in their tracks.

States and communities can easily institute solid public awareness campaigns. Radio stations could air anti-terror public service announcements. Newspapers could run full-page weekend ads. Billboards could display a variety of bold tags such as:

"THIS IS A TERROR AWARE AND PREPARED STATE. NO TERROR ON OUR WATCH!"

"TERROR PREVENTION IS EVERYONE'S RESPONSIBILITY: LOOK! LISTEN! REPORT!"

"THE WAR ON TERROR: WE CAN'T WIN WITHOUT YOUR HELP!"

"ONE CITIZEN CAN SAVE COUNTLESS OTHERS! LOOK! LISTEN! OBSERVE! REPORT!"

"FIGHTING TERROR IN OUR STATE: MILLIONS OF EYES WIDE OPEN!"

Public awareness campaigns can be developed by school districts, sports associations, churches, communities, town councils, colleges and universities, shopping malls, and businesses. They can be developed by virtually any group of persons or any organizations that desire to make a difference.

Schools can hang posters in their hallways; malls can hang banners; businesses can send canned awareness emails to their employees. Churches can train their greeters as to what to look for and how to respond. Police departments can place citizen cooperation messages on billboards and in local papers. Students doing community service can go door-to-door with leaflets and pamphlets. Collectively, we are limited only by time, imagination, and budget. What nation in history is more creative, imaginative, and productive than the good old U. S. of A? Not one. That is a fact.

Complacency is not an option, and denial is deadly. So assume the responsibility. Adopt the creed:

If not me, then who? If not now, then when?

BRIEFING # 13

Prepare for the Worst
Pray & Hope for the Best

It's A Question of Balance

The majority of Americans will never become direct victims of terror attacks. They will not be physically wounded, maimed, or killed. Ours is a big country. It is more likely that the many of us will suffer from psychological and physiological affects of terror attacks that we witness or learn about from the media.

Millions of Americans were affected in varying degrees by the September 11 carnage. The films of the collapsing towers repeated day after day on the news made it quite difficult for many to control their emotions. Some of us experienced difficulty sleeping at night, especially children, spouses, and relatives of family members who continued to work in high-visibility skyscrapers, on airplanes, or as firefighters and cops.

Worst case planning for the most vile scenarios that terrorists can inflict upon us is not indicative of paranoia, but of good sense. As responsible adults, we prepare for worst-case scenarios throughout our lives, although we may not always realize that we do so. Let's discuss some examples.

Purchasing homeowner's insurance most advantageously means planning worst case, for our houses to be completely destroyed by flood, tornado, hurricane, fire, or earthquake. I submit that the most astute of us would never insure our homes for merely one third of their market value, even if the banks and mortgage companies permitted us to do so. We insure them for total destruction. We do this because we do want to be responsible for mortgage payments on a home that is no longer habitable. We also purchase sufficient insurance because it keeps us within our comfort zone. When we place our heads on pillows at night, we can think to ourselves, "Well, as bad as things are this month, if everything goes to hell, at least we will always have a roof over our heads."

Let's consider a forty year-old woman who is a well compensated senior account executive for a Fortune 500 company, as well as the single wage earner for her family of four; her disabled war veteran husband and their two children. How much life insurance should this woman purchase? Planning prudently and for the worst case, she asks herself the tough question, "If I die tomorrow, how much money will my family need to pay off the mortgage on our $450,000 home, settle all credit card and purchase debts, put the two kids through a reasonable college, and keep my disabled husband comfortable for the remainder of his natural life. She decides that whatever that number turns out to be will be the minimum amount of life insurance she secures. Not to plan worst case for the survival of her family would be irresponsible.

Sometimes the risks associated with terror attack are not immediately obvious to the potential victims. A hypothetical case in point is a prosperous dairy and wheat farmer in rural Texas. Let us say that this farmer and his family gross a comfortable half million dollars each year from their agrarian trade. Their farm is 90 miles from the nearest big city. They live and work in the middle of "nowhere." They assess that the chance of their livelihood being affected by a terrorist attack upon the great state of Texas is virtually nil. But what they fail to consider is the nuclear power plant situated 60 miles to the northwest of their farm, with prevailing winds that normally blow in their direction. Should a terror attack destroy the reactor's nuclear core, causing it to spew radioactive elements into the air, what would be the affect on their farm 60 miles downwind? If they are not sure, they should seek expert counsel, consider the recommendations, and then plan accordingly.

Every organization, business, church, school, amusement park, movie theater, airport, football stadium, government office complex, and shopping mall should conduct a risk assessment to determine what anti-terror preparedness measures are mandatory, which are prudent, and which fall into the "nice to have if we can afford it" category. Each assessment should be catered to the culture, modus operandi, and distinctive needs of the entity being assessed. **This assessment should be guided by vigilance and standards of due care and diligence, not by fear and paranoia.**

Different organizations are subject to varying risk factors. A hub of federal office buildings in one central location, such as Crystal City complex in Washington, D.C., will require a more thorough and detailed assessment than will a small strip mall in Park Ridge, New Jersey. Logic dictates that the federal buildings in Washington D.C. are more at risk from a terror attack or collateral damage than the side-by-side suburban stores in rural New Jersey. Continuing along this same line of thought, the "Mall of the Americas" is probably a more lucrative terror target than is the 45-plus year old Prince Georges County Mall in Maryland. The Mall of the Americas, like Disney World or Six Flags, is an American family icon known throughout the world. It represents freedom, the affluent American lifestyle, and a safe and secure place to visit for family fun and quality time. The psychological affect of a large body count at the Mall of the Americas would be devastating to millions of Americans. Attendance at similar venues and theme parks would plummet. Local and state economies would take a hit. A terror attack against the Mall of the Americas would also generate extended media coverage and hype ideally suited to the terrorists' propaganda and recruiting goals.

Individual and Family Anti-Terror Needs Assessments

Individual citizens without any formal security or risk analysis training are quite capable of making fairly sound risk assessments for themselves and their loves ones. They can do it by employing common sense, logic, and situational awareness that involves keeping up with current events and reading the occasional book like this one. Consider the following examples.

If you are a professional woman who works at the Sears Building in Chicago, a waitress in the Seattle Space Needle busting her butt with the hungry lunch crowd, or a flight attendant on a new Airbus jet that seats over 500 passengers, then you are probably more at risk of being a terror attack victim than a woman who is assistant manager at the local 7-11.

If you are a businessman who makes a six figure salary slaving on Wall Street, an agent at FBI headquarters, or a clerk on Capitol Hill, you are most assuredly more at risk than a man who services automobiles at the local Toyota dealership in Topeka, Kansas. Can I prove this quantitatively with hard scientific data? No. Should I need to do so? I think not. It is just plain common sense.

Every man and woman should perform his or her own "Self Assessment For Emergencies" (SAFE). How does one conduct a "SAFE?"

A SAFE can be as simple or complicated as one desires it to be. I prefer the more simple approach. To perform your own SAFE, simply ask yourself and your significant other(s) the following questions and determine whether or not you are comfortable with your answers. If you are not, then make the changes in your life necessary for you and the ones closest to you to get those "warm and fuzzy" feelings where there were "cold and prickly" thoughts before:

- Got risk?
- Got communications?
- Got a family emergency plan?
- Got a rallying point?
- Got records?
- Got survival supplies?
- Got protection?
- Got a will?
- Got a living will?
- Got power of attorney?
- Got life insurance?
- Got a Final Goodbye?

Let's briefly quantify each point listed above for the SAFE.

Got Risk?

Where do you work or what do you do for a living? As discussed previously, if you work at a nuclear power plant or as a fire fighter in New York City, you may decide that you are more at risk of becoming a victim of the War on Terror than you are comfortable being. How much at risk one determines himself to be will determine how many of the following SAFE concerns one takes into account.

Got Communications?

It is most important for us to be able to immediately assess our loved ones' health and welfare when tragedy occurs. The first thing human beings need to know when an incident occurs at or near locations where their loved ones live, learn, work, or play is, "Is he all right?" "Is she all right?" "Are they safe?"

Cell phone communications are probably the quickest way of assessing the status of loved ones. But during a catastrophic take down like the one with the Twin Towers, the cell phone infrastructure can become overloaded by an extremely high volume of calls or rendered inoperable by the destruction of one or more relay stations. In these cases, landline telephone calls are the more reliable means. As part of the family plan, discussed in more detail further in this chapter, each member should know that if ever a terror event occurs within reasonable proximity to where they are, those in the fray IMMEDIATELY call loved ones to let them know that they are safe or injured. If they are too injured to make the call, but are still conscious, they need to know to ask someone to make the call for them, such as an emergency medical responder, police officer, or passerby.

In case there are no family cell phone or computer communications (emails), always ensure that loved ones carry a "just in case" pre-paid phone card so that the nearest landline can be accessed. Remember that in a crisis situation, cell phone service may not be available, as services may be limited by controlling service providers in order to insure that emergency communications for responding authorities are up and running. Also remember that in some instances, it may be easier to make a long distance call than a call across town. If the across town call does not go through, try calling a friend or relative long-distance and ask them to notify your loved ones locally.

Got a Family Plan?

A family plan does not have to be put into writing. It simply has to be known and understood by all parties concerned. A family plan can even be spur of the moment. Family plans should take into account potential emergency situations under two circumstances: (1) the family is together in its entirety when the incident occurs; and (2) some members of the family are physically separated from the others when the bad stuff goes down. Let's look at a few examples.

You and your family are visiting the Mall of the Americas. You plan to spend an entire day inside this wonderful facility. Your two teenagers will most probably take off together to check out the stores and ride the rides. As the family enters the mall, mom or dad might just say something like, "OK, if there is an emergency or we get separated for some reason, let's all agree to meet over there in front of the Bed, Bath, and Beyond store. If that's not possible, we'll all meet at the McDonalds in the food court." This is a spur of the moment family plan to ensure that a headcount can be taken if, God forbid, something should happen during this family's visit to this huge mall.

What if mom and dad are at work and their middle school child comes home after a two-block walk from his school at 3:30 in the afternoon, and something bad happens near the house. A middle school or high school-aged child needs a neighbor to go to. The child probably needs more than just one neighbor he can rely on just in case the primary contact isn't home. The child needs to know to phone the "on call" neighborhood guardian, get the guardian's guidance, such as "You come right over here now!" Once safe with the guardian, the child or guardian needs to know to CALL a parent to say that everyone is accounted for and safe. Bottom line is that any child who is regularly home alone for several hours each day should have a neighbor to go to in an emergency. It must be a neighbor that the both the adults and children trust implicitly.

Some family plans can be more like military SOPs (Standing Operating Procedures). They are written down and placed at a location in the house where they remain easily accessible by family members. A family plan for natural disasters, such as tornados, may tell children step-by-step: (1) grab a cell phone and the charger and go to the corner of the basement with the bathroom;(2) get the hand crank radio from the emergency box and tune to AM 1260 for emergency information; (3) sit in the bathtub for safety; and (4) call mom or dad on the cell phone and we will tell you where we are, when we will be home, and what you should do next.

The government maintains a website that provides the basics for emergency family planning. The site is called "READY America" and can be computer accessed at website www.ready.gov. Since one hundred percent of Americans cannot, or do not as yet, access the World Wide Web, I have extracted some of the planning basics from the government website and included them here. These are simply general guidelines or questions individual family leaders should be able to answer when the time comes:

- Whether at home, work, school, or elsewhere, in some situations it may be best to evacuate, but in others it might be prudent to stay where you are. Hopefully emergency assistance on TV and radio will guide you. Having a radio and/or TV that will work if the local power is interrupted or goes out altogether is a must for every family. Small crank radios or even battery powered ones are very inexpensive and could save your life.

- In case of airborne threats such as chlorine gas from an overturned rail car or other chemical or radiological dispersions in your area, you may be instructed by local authorities to "shelter in place and seal the room." To be able to shelter in place, you need to have some supplies on hand. The basic steps for sheltering in place are:

  » Lock doors, close all windows, air vents, and fireplace dampers.

» Turn off all air conditioning, heating, and fans.
» Unless it is contaminated, take your emergency supply kit with you.
» Go to an interior room – one with the least number of windows or no windows at all.
» Seal all windows, doors, and vents with plastic sheeting and duct tape. Listen to local emergency radio or watch TV news for instructions.

Families also need an evacuation plan in case the authorities advise or direct leaving the neighborhood. An evacuation plan should contain a couple of essentials:

• Plan where your family will rendezvous if they are separated when the evacuation order is given. Further, plan what to do in the event that the family cannot reunite before evacuating.

• If you have a car or truck, always try to keep a full tank of fuel in it. A military habit ingrained in me from day one in the armor corps was to fill my tank completely and as many times as I had the opportunity to do so each day, because there may come a time when little or no fuel is available. It's been 30 years since I was a new second lieutenant, however to this day, I fill my car's tank to the brim each and every time I gas up. In an emergency situation, when hundreds of cars are stacked up to get what little gas remains in the local pumps, I'll be good for at least a 300-mile head start.

• Have several alternate routes, including back roads, in case the primary one is not usable.

• Do not forget to take your emergency supply kit with you.

• Do not forget to lock all doors when you leave your house.

• As local, state, and federal laws permit, take a firearm and ammunition for personal protection. This is not on the government's website, but is my recommendation. Under stress, normal people can do dangerous things, and criminals can take advantage of situations.

• Make sure you call or email your out-of-state emergency contacts as to what is going on, how you can be contacted, or when they may expect to hear from you again.

• If there is damage to your home before you depart, or if you were instructed by emergency services to do so, turn off water, gas, and electricity before leaving.

• If you have room, it might be nice to see if a neighbor, especially an elderly or impaired one, needs a ride out of town.

• Make sure you bring a few days' food and water for all travelers. Remember that water is much more important, in the short, term than food. A human can go weeks without food, but not very long without hydration. Along with the water, my family plans to bring several twelve packs of Seven-Up. This soda possesses many of the sugars, salts, and other good things one needs to maintain a fairly sound chemical balance when dehydration from such afflictions as diarrhea occurs.

• Remember that your pets may not be permitted inside emergency shelters. You may have to keep your pets in your car, so plan for the basic comforts for your animal: food, water, and proper body temperature.

Got a Rallying Point?

A "rallying point" (RP) is an old army term. Before combat troops proceed with a mission, or in case they are caught in an ambush, their leaders pre-designate rallying points. These rallying points are terrain features or man-made features on the ground that every soldier knows he must get to when everything goes to hell. At the rallying point, leaders can take a head count of those OK, wounded in action, missing, or presumed dead. Once the situation is under control, the leader can plan and execute the next move.

In the earlier "Mall of the Americas" example, two rallying points were selected for the family members: Bed Bath & Beyond and McDonalds. An RP can be agreed upon anywhere to support most every contingency situation. A lot of parents establish RPs for their young children without specifically designating them as "rallying points." When a mom says to her seven year old, "Now, if you get separated from Mommy or you get lost for a moment, you walk right to that candy stand over there, and I'll go there too and meet you," she has established an RP for herself and the young child. In a crowded sports stadium, an RP can be a souvenir stand, a snack shack, or a ticket booth. The possibilities are endless. The one RP rule to follow in a combat situation is to make the RP far enough from where the bad stuff goes down to where everyone is safely away from immediate danger.

Got Records?

When a disaster is imminent and the family is hunkered down in the basement waiting for a possible tornado touchdown, it would be nice to have transported important documents into the family safe place. If a tornado or hurricane inflicts catastrophic damage to a home in Kansas, the owner would not want his family's birth certificates, marriage licenses, and insurance policies to get blown clear to West Virginia. A small, fireproof metal case the size of a large briefcase is fairly inexpensive. Get one. Put only the documents and records you cannot live without inside of it, and put it with your emergency supply kit.

Got Survival Supplies?

Portable, compact, and properly stored survival supplies are always good to have on hand. Make your own emergency supplies kit. You can make one for the office, home, family vacations, or whatever makes you the most comfortable.

What should be set aside for family emergencies? READY America recommends the following:

• One gallon of water per person per day for drinking and minimum sanitation (children, nursing mothers, and sick persons may need more hydration; in warmer climates more water will definitely be needed).

• Store water in containers that can be tightly sealed and will keep the water fresh, such as plastic containers.

• Keep at least three days' supply of water per person.

• A method of storing water in the home, not mentioned in READY America, is to fill all of the bathtubs in the house full of water before the disaster strikes. This is only a good idea if the water will not become contaminated from the disaster itself, like chemical or biological agents. For example, if a hurricane is blowing through and there's a chance that the city water might become contaminated or turned off for a few days, a bathtub filled with water will come in handy while you are waiting for your city or private utilities to restore service.

• Select foods that require no refrigeration and that will remain edible in extreme heat or cold. Make sure the food does not require cooking. Today's market is filled with high fat, high protein, and high-energy food under wrap. They don't take up a lot of room and consuming a few each day can sustain a person for many days with no problem. Sports energy bars provide a lot of sustaining nutrients while taking up very little space.

• Pack a manual can opener and eating utensils.

• Explosions and high winds can send very small particles into the air we breathe. Terror attacks could send tiny microscopic "junk" into the air. Nose and mouth protection, especially for those suffering from respiratory ailments, is always a good thing. Facemasks such as the types worn by medical personnel or dense weave cotton material which snuggly covers the nose and mouth might come in handy.

• In case really bad stuff is in the air floating towards your domicile, heavyweight plastic garbage bags or plastic sheeting, duct tape, and scissors to "shelter in place" should be included in the emergency supplies.

• READY America suggests purchasing HEPA (High Efficiency Particulate Air Filtration) fans. These fans circulate the air in your living space. They filter out contaminates that can get into your body and make you ill, such as dust, mold, smoke, and even some biological agents. They WILL NOT stop chemical gases. A portable air purifier with a HEPA filter is the recommended way to go.

• It is prudent to build a family first aid kit containing:

» Pairs of sterile gloves
» Sterile dressings to stop bleeding
» Cleansing agent or antibacterial wipes to disinfect
» Antibiotic ointment
» Burn ointment

- » Adhesive bandages
- » Eye wash solution
- » Thermometer
- » Prescription medications
- » Any prescribed medical supplies such as glucose, blood pressure monitoring equipment, etc.
- » Scissors, medical tape, tweezers, lubricant (petroleum jelly)
- » Aspirin or non-aspirin pain reliever
- » Anti-diarrhea medication
- » Antacid for stomach upset
- » Laxative
- » First aid manual

- Other items to consider:

- » First aid manual
- » Feminine hygiene supplies
- » Battery-powered or hand crank radio (extra batteries)
- » Whistle (to signal)
- » Flashlight (Extra batteries)
- » Wrench and pliers (to turn off utilities)
- » Baby formula/diapers
- » Toilet paper, garbage bags, and plastic ties for sanitation
- » Wet weather gear
- » Waterproof matches
- » Fire Extinguisher
- » Disinfectant & household bleach
- » Signal flare
- » Writing materials
- » Denture needs
- » Eyeglasses, contact lenses and supplies
- » Additional needs for seniors or infirmed/disabled

Got Protection?

I mean firearms. First, the disclaimer. Only trained and qualified persons should own and handle firearms. The National Rifle
Association certifies top-notch instructors who train citizens in
every state. Every law-abiding citizen must comply with federal,
state and local firearms ordinances, laws, and restrictions. Gun
safety in the home is first and foremost.

I firmly believe in a citizen's constitutional right to provide for
the defense of his loved ones, neighbors, persons in distress, or
the common defense in general. One of the reasons I reside in
the State of Colorado is that our state recognizes and provides
for our rights to bear arms.

Even normally decent, law abiding people may come a little
unglued in times of public stress and crisis. Bad guys run ram-
pant during blackouts, evacuations, and other panic situations.
Providing that all of the legal, training, and safety requirements
to own a firearm are complied with, what does it hurt to have
one with you just in case? There's an old, well-known adage:
"Never bring a knife to a gunfight."

I firmly believe that in this day and age, responsible, of-age
family members should have a healthy respect for firearms. Most
importantly, they should not be afraid to use one if their lives
or the lives of their loved ones depend upon it. My family is
comfortable firing 9mm and .45 automatic pistols, .44 magnum
revolvers, and Western-style single-action Colts. At 50 yards my
seventeen-year-old son shoots a World War I Springfield rifle
with more accuracy than I can muster.

Mine IS NOT a family of gun nuts. I keep the guns in my house
under lock and key except when needed. We simply remain prepared to defend ourselves against bad people who have done
bad things to others at gunpoint. These are dangerous times.
Enough said. It is your choice.

Got a Will?

It never ceases to amaze me how many people die without a will or one that is invalid for whatever reasons. Now, if you ain't got nothin' and you ain't got no one, then you don't need a will. Remember that a will insures that those things of value for which you worked so hard all of your life remain with those whom you want to have them after you are gone. A will also dictates such things as who will be the legal guardian and caretaker for your minor children. The best possible quality of life for them after you are gone may be more important in the short term than any amount of money in their trust fund. It's a family's call.

Got a Living Will?

Do you want to be kept alive by machine indefinitely, or do you want quick closure for you and your loved ones? It is an individual, legal choice, but one I recommend be made. Before a decision is made either way, we should most certainly discuss our feelings and choices with those who will survive us, those that will have to live with our decision to live or die.

Got a Power of Attorney?

In the event that you are injured to the extent that you cannot communicate or function normally for a given period of time, your significant other may have to pay the mortgage, put food on the table, clothes on the kids, etc. Talk it over with the people who have to exist if you involuntarily "step out" for a while.

Got Life Insurance? Got Enough of It?

Life insurance is a funny thing. Those of us who buy life insurance, the premium payers, are betting that we are going to fall victim to early and untimely deaths. The insurance companies take our money, betting that we will not.

Some family breadwinners carry little or no life insurance. Some have too much. Precisely how much life insurance a person should buy is an individual judgment call. I think that the rationale for determining a dollar amount is not that difficult. Ask yourself these questions:

- How many things do I need to provide for and for how many years? In answering this, consider mortgage, car payments, credit card debt, car payments, monthly expenses, child education through college, a comfortable nest egg for your spouse or significant other, etc.

- How much life insurance can I afford annually?

Got a Final Goodbye?

A final farewell letter may be the way to go for a soldier going off to war, a fire fighter or cop who faces death every day on the job, or a person who simply wants to reassure the ones left behind how he or she felt about them. Write as many copies of however many letters are appropriate, and leave them in different locations with friends or family under strict instructions not to deliver the letters to the recipients until death is confirmed.

These letters can be short and simple. "I always loved you - every minute of every moment we were together." "I was always so proud of you. Keep doing what you do. You're the greatest!" "Remember when you view me at my wake that you still owe me fifty bucks, you bastard!"

Complacency is not an option, and denial is deadly. So assume the responsibility. Adopt the creed:

If not me, then who? If not now, then when?

Conclusion

Free nations are only as strong as the will of the majority of their citizens. Democratic governments remain no more honorable, effective or responsible than their voters, taxpayers, and partisan financial supporters bind them to be. So it is with our great republic, the United States of America, the single most phenomenal and successful experiment in freedom the world has ever known. WE THE PEOPLE founded this nation, and WE THE PEOPLE are solely responsible to nourish, guide, protect and sustain it. More than any other time in our brief yet glorious history, common citizens must stand and fight, guide and protect, and perpetuate our heritage for future generations.

These can be disheartening and confusing times for Americans. We search for answers. We seek solutions. Individually and collectively, we explore our minds and hearts and turn to each other for direction and strength. As we do so, let us also embrace the wisdom and guidance of our Founding Fathers, for their vision was profound, their sacrifices countless, and their charge to each American, abundantly clear. You and I, the common citizens, are responsible for all that our nation does and all that it fails to do.

Our government as an institution is not the heart and soul of America; WE THE PEOPLE are. Our greatest duty and responsibility as Americans in this War on Terror is to protect ourselves, our families, our fellow citizens, and our communities, and thus, preserve our freedoms and our great republic. Thomas Jefferson summed it up nicely in 1810 when he wrote, *"A strict observance of the written laws is doubtless one of the highest duties of a good citizen, but it is not the highest. The laws of necessity, of self-preservation, of saving our country when in danger, are of higher obligation."*[173] With these words, Mr. Jefferson charged WE THE PEOPLE to protect ourselves and preserve our nation, whatever it takes, for as long as it takes, whenever required to do so.

We discussed much in this book, from the sources of hatred and discontent that fuel Islamist extremism to our government's shortfalls and apparent inability to date to "get it right." It is our responsibility as a nation to defeat the hate before it contaminates future generations. It is also our obligation to remove from public office those men and women who, for whatever reason, refuse to execute their duties and responsibilities in our best interests. Our Founding Fathers warned us to guard against and exercise control over those in power. Once again their collective wisdom is there to guide us, keep us focused, and add credibility to our efforts to hold our public servants accountable. James Madison was confident that the will of citizens and their communities would ultimately triumph over the whims of our leaders: *"As the cool and deliberate sense of community ought in all governments, and actually will in all free governments, ultimately prevail over the views of its rulers."*[174] Abraham Lincoln reminded us of our responsibility to remove from office those who do not serve the public good when he stated, *"We, the people, are the rightful masters of both Congress and the courts – not to overthrow the Constitution, but to overthrow the men who pervert the Constitution."*[175] I ask my readers that which I ask myself: If not me, then who? If not now, then when?

---

[173] http://etext.virginia.edu/jefferson/quotations/jeff5.htm. Quotes compiled by Eyler Robert Coates, Sr. Permission granted to quote single excerpts separately.
[174] Ibid.

In this book, we examined the psyche of terror leaders such as Osama bin Laden and their promise to bring to our homeland the terrors that they have perpetrated to date against countless innocent men, women, and children in so many other countries. Most frightening of all, we acknowledge, if we did not do so before, that the terrorists will come for our children, in their schools, in our communities. Shall we wait, suffer harsh consequences, and react, or shall we act, preempt, and keep the wolves at bay? I implore my readers to ask themselves: If not me, then who? If not now, then when?

There is much we as individuals and communities can do now to educate, prepare for, and even prevent terror attacks in our communities. We have discussed solutions in this book. We are Americans: the most innovative and capable breed on the planet. We are limited only by imagination, resources, and lack of will. We are all citizen soldiers. Each one of us has a role to execute. Some contributions will be huge. Others will go unnoticed. But each role, no matter how big or small, is critically important and contributes immeasurably to the whole of the effort to fight, win, and persevere. George Washington reminded us that, *"Every post is honorable in which a man can serve his country."*[176] Let us never forget that in this war one person – one average citizen - can make an immense difference. One mayor, a single police chief, a resolute city councilman, or a dedicated school district superintendent, can start the ball of awareness, preparedness, and prevention rolling in their community. One individual American, vigilant and unafraid, can save countless others from the ravages of raw terror. Before we look to others to take up our fight, let us look to ourselves and summon up the warrior within. President John Fitzgerald Kennedy's now famous inaugural address words are more relevant today than they were in his time: *"Ask not what your country can do for you, ask what you can do for your country."*

---

[175] Ibid.
[176] Ibid.

There is an old adage: "United we stand; divided, we fall." It is a truism. We must not allow our country to backslide to the Vietnam era, when we spent more time fighting each other than we did an adversary that ultimately defeated us.

Our unique freedoms are worth all of the trials and tribulations, and ultimate sacrifices, which we as Americans may be called upon to endure. Free men willing to fight for their self-determination are always an immeasurable cut above any mentally or physically enslaved opponent on this Earth. Each of us has a responsibility to do whatever we can to safeguard our families, co-workers, communities, and economy from the threat of global terror.

Americans remain the envy of the world. The truest, most genuine individual freedoms on the planet reside within the United States of America. We can and must preserve what we have become, and what the rest of the world aspires to be. I believe Thomas Paine was correct when he said that, *"The cause of America is in a great measure the cause of all mankind."*[177]

We are Americans. We are capable of being the purest of heart, the most genuine of spirit, the most kind and charitable people on the face of this Earth. We will persevere. We will win this War on Terror. We will remain the land of the free and the home of the brave. We must, for we remain the shining example of what can be achieved when men and women are willing to sacrifice all that they are, all that they have, and all that they dream, not simply for themselves, but for the generations to follow.

The Founding Fathers who created this great experiment in freedom - the United States of America - are among the greatest of men. Those who fight to preserve it for posterity are the greatest of men and women, for ...

IF NOT ME, THEN WHO? IF NOT NOW, THEN WHEN?

---

[177] Ibid.

BIBLIOGRAPHY

BOOKS

Anonymous. Imperial Hubris Why the West is Losing the War on Terror: Washington, D.C.: Brassey's, Inc., 2004.

Anonymous. Through Our Enemies' Eyes. Washington, D.C.: Brassey's, Inc., 2002.

Baer, Robert. See No Evil. New York, New York: Three Rivers Press, 2002.

Baer, Robert. Sleeping With the Devil. New York, New York: Crown Publishers, 2003.

Barber, Benjamin R. Jihad vs. Mc World. New York, New York: Ballantine Books, 2001.

Barnett, Thomas P.M. The Pentagon's New Map. New York, New York: G.P. Putnam's Sons, 2004.

Cragin, Kim and Gerwehr, Scott. Dissuading Terror: Strategic Influence and the Struggle Against Terrorism. Santa Monica, CA: the Rand Corporation, 2005.

Davis, Jayna. The Third Terrorist: The Middle East Connection to the Oklahoma City Bombing. Nashville, Tennessee. Nelson Current, 2004.

Dorn, Michael & Chris. Innocent Targets: When Terrorism Comes to Schools. Canada. Safe Havens International, 2005.

El Fadl, Khaled Abou. Islam and the Challenge of Democracy. New York, New York: Princeton Press, 2004.

Emerson, Steven. American Jihad. New York, New York: The Free Press, 2002.

Gertz, Bill. Breakdown. Washington, D.C.: Plume Books, 2003.

Giduck, John. Terror at Beslan. United States. Archangel Group, Inc., 2005.

Gold, Dore. Hatred's Kingdom. Washington, D.C.: Regnery Publishing, Inc., 2003.

Grossman, Dave. On Killing: The Psychological Cost of Learning to Kill in War and Society. New York. Little, Brown & Company, 1995, 1996.

Grossman, Dave. On Combat: The Psychology and Physiology of Deadly Conflict in War and Peace. United States. PPCT Research Publications, 2004.

Gunaratna, Rohan. Inside Al Qaeda: Global Network of Terror. New York. A Berkley Book. 2002-2003.

Iskandar, Mohammed El-Nawawy Adel. Al-Jazeera. Cambridge, Massachussetts: Wetsview Press, 2003.

Kepel, Gilles. Jihad The Trail of Political Islam. Cambridge, Massachussetts: The Belknap Press of Harvard University Press, 2002.

Kessler, Ronald. The CIA at War. New York, New York: St. Martin's Press, 2003.

Rashid, Ahmed Jihad the Rise of Militant Islam in Central Asia. New York, New York: Penguin Books, 2002.

Ressa, Maria A. Seeds of Terror. New York, New York: Free Press, 2003.

Sardar, Ziauddin and Davies, Merryl Wyn. Why Do People Hate America? New York, New York: The Disinformation Company Limited, 2002.

Sifaoui, Mohamed. Inside Al Qaeda. New York, New York: Thunder's Mouth Press, 2003.

Thatcher, Margaret. Statecraft. New York, New York: HarperCollinsPublishers, 2002.

Timmerman, Kenneth R.. Preachers of Hate. New York, New York: Crown Forum. 2003.

Tzu, Sun. The Art of War. New York, New York. Barnes & Nobles Classics. 2003.

Verton, Dan. Black Ice. New York, New York: McGraw-Hill/Osborne, 2003.

Weaver, Mary Anne. Pakistan in the Shadow of Jihad and Afghanistan. New York, New York: Farrar, Straus, and Giroux, 2002.

CD-ROMs

"A Pretext for War." James Bamford. CD-ROM. New York, New York: Random House Audio, 2004.
"An End to Evil." David Frum and Richard Perle. CD-ROM. U.S.A.: Random House, 2004.

"Art of War." Sun Tzu. Translated by Ralph D. Sawyer. CD-ROM. New York, New York: Recorded Books, LLC, 2001.

"Naked in Baghdad." Ann Garrels. CD-ROM. New York, New York: Audio Renaissance Audiobook, 2003.

"Plan of Attack." Bob Woodward. CD-ROM. New York, New York: Simon and Shuster Audio, 2004.

NEWSPAPER ARTICLES

"200 Arrested in Ahvaz Skirmishes." MehrNews.com. Tehran, iran. April 18, 2005.

"22 Killed as Pre-Election Violence Deepens." MSNBC. Baghdad, Iraq. January 17, 2005.

"Abdullah Warns Arabs of Falling Further Behind." New Straits Times. Dubai, UAE. December 17, 2004.

"Agencies Scramble for Good Intel Analysts." The Associated Press. Washington, D.C. December 28, 2004.

"Agencies Still at Odds Over Fingerprinting." The Associated Press. December 29, 2004.

"Al Qaeda Controls Young Operatives by Torture Threats." Arab News. Jeddah, Saudi Arabia. September 23, 2004.

"AON SRT Terrorism Report: Terrorist Incidents & Threats – 1 May 2003.

"Arab Media Coverage of Pope's Death Infuriates Islamists." AFP. April 3, 2005.

"Arabiya TV Says Threatened Over Syria Broadcast." World-Reuters. February 27, 2005.

"Army Says It's Spending $ 4 Billion on Armor." The Associated Press. Washington, D.C. December 15, 2004.

"Bush Signs Vaccine Stockpile Legislation." The Associated Press. Washington, D.C. July 21, 2004.

"Changes in the Kingdom – on Our Timetable." The Washington Post. Washington, D.C. February 27, 2005.

"China 'Smothering' Islam to Control Uighurs – Report." Reuters. Beijing, China. April 11, 2005.

"Fatwa Warns Dutch Muslims to Shun Violence." FBIS. Rottewrdam, Amsterdam. December 13, 2004

"FBI Alerts Boston About Four Suspects." MSNBC News. Boston, Massachusetts. January 20, 2005.

"FBI Computer Overhaul Hits Another Snag." The Associated Press. Washington, D.C. January 13, 2005.

"FBI Holds Huge Cache of Traveler Data." The Associated Press. Washington, D.C. January 14, 2005.

"Group Vows More Attacks After Qatar Bombing." Reuters. Doha, Qatar. March 22, 2005.

"Iran: U.S. Tops List for Threatening World Peace." Reuters. Tehran. January 26, 2005.

"Lebanon's Top Shiite Muslim Cleric Criticizes Iraq's Elections Under U.S. Occupation." The Associated Press. Beirut, Lebanon. January 17, 2005.

"Malaysian TV Runs Anti-Terror Campaign Aimed at Muslims." AFP. Kuala Lumpur. January 26, 2005.

"Middle East Gets First Superheroes." BBC News. March 7, 2005.

"More Muslim Brotherhood Supporters Held." Arab News. Cairo, Egypt. March 29, 2005.

"Nightly Vigil Demands 'Syria Out!'." The Daily Star. Beirut, Lebanon. February 21, 2005.

"Opinion Polls Taken in Saudi Arabia." Reuters. Mecca, Saudi Arabia. March 8, 2005.

"Palestinian Forces Told to Curb Militant Attacks." The Associated Press. Gaza. January 17, 2005.

"Pentagon Spy Branch Kept Secret for Two Years." The Washington Post. Washington, D.C. January 23, 2005.

"Report: White House Fought Interrogation." Reuters. January 13, 2005.

"Representative of Top Shiite Cleric in Iraq." The Associated Press. Baghdad, Iraq. January 13, 2005.

"Rice Talks Tough on Iranian Nukes." The Associated Press. Brussels, Belgium. February 9, 2005.

"Saudi Cleric Faults Islamic Militants." The Associated Press. Mount Arafat, Saudi Arabia. January 20, 2005.

"Saudi Dads Condemn Militant Sons on TV." Straits Times International (Singapore). Dubai, UAE. December 6, 2004.

"Saudi Scholars Back Anti-U.S. Jihad in Iraq." Reuters. Riyadh, Saudi Arabia. November 8, 2004.

"Saudi TV: Cleric Denounces Anti-Islam Campaigns in Hajj Sermon." Foreign Broadcast Information Service (FBIS), CIA. January 19, 2005.

"Sharing Germ Information Outweighs Risks." The Associated Press. September 9, 2004.

"Spanish Clerics Issue Osama Fatwa." The Associated Press. Madrid, Spain. March 11, 2005.

"Spending of Port Security Grants Faulted." The Associated Press. Washington, D.C. December 28, 2004.

"Syria Activists Call for Pullout From Lebanon." The Daily Star. February 21, 2005.

"Tantawi Condemns Violence Against Iraqis." Reuters. Riyadh, Saudi Arabia. January 15, 2005.

"Terrorism on Agenda as Indonesia Plans Asian Religious Summit." AFP. Jakarta. November 11, 2004.

"Terrorists 'Recalibrating' Rumsfeld Says." The Associated Press. Washington, D.C. February 16, 2005.

"The Growth of Radical Islam in Central Asia." Asia Times. March 31, 2004.

"U.S. Charges 18 After Arms Smuggling Sting." The Associated Press. New York. March 15, 2005.

"U.S. Faces Crossroads in Ties With Islamic World." Agence France Presse. Washington, D.C. March 8, 2005.

"U.S. Slams Some Muslims for Paltry Tsunami Aid." Straits Times International. February 12, 2005.

"U.S. Faces Crossroads in Ties With Islamic World." Agence France Press, Washington, D.C. March 8, 2005.

"U.S. Funds Imams Training in Bangladesh." IslamOnline.net. Cairo, Egypt. April 17, 2005.

"Western-Educated Fundamentalists." Straits Times International (Singapore). Karachi. October 6, 2004.;

Afghan, Mirwais. Taliban returns to Afghanistan's Airwaves." Reuters. April 18, 2005.

Ambah, Faiza Saleh. "The Case the Saudis can't make. The Washington Post. March 27, 2005. B01.

Baker, Luke. "Anti-Rebel Hotline Gives U.S. Troops Boost in Iraq." Reuters. April 1, 2005.

Barstow, David & Stein, Robin. "Under Bush, a New Age of Pre-Packaged TV News." The New York Times. March 13, 2005.

Bartlett, Lawrence. "Aid Not Enough to Win Muslim Hearts, U.S. Told." Agence France Presse. January 28, 2005.

Berkowitz, Peter & McFaul, Michael. "Studying Islam, Strengthening the Nation." The Washington Post. April 12, 2005. A21.

Bonner, Raymond and Greenlees, Donald. "U.S. Losing Favor With Australia." International Herald Tribune, The New York Times. March 29, 2005.

Braude, Joseph. "On Message." The New Republic Online. February 11, 2005.

Brinkley, Joel. "Saudis Blame U.S. and Its Role in Iraq for Rise of Terror. The New York Times. October 13, 2004.

Brooks, David. "The Art of Intelligence." The New York Times. April 2, 2005.

Cadano, Edgar C. "Filipinbo Expats Slam Manila's Racist Move." Saudi Gazette English Daily. April 3, 2005.

Caldwell, Christopher. "Daughter of Enlightenment." The New York Times. April 3, 2005.

Castaneda, Antonio. "Sunni Clerics Tell Iraqis to Join Security Forces." The Associated Press. April 1, 2005.

Chanda, Nayan. "Crouching Tiger, Swimming Dragon." The New York Times. April 11, 2005.

Clark, Matthew. "U.S. Covert Military Operations in Iran?" Christian Science Monitor. January 19, 2005.

Coll, Steve. "What Bin Laden Sees in Hiroshima." The Washington Post. February 6, 2005. B01.

Cragin, Kim & Gerwehr, Scott. "Dissuading Terror: Strategic Influence and the Struggle Against Terrorism." Rand Corporation. 2005.

Dapfner, Mathias. "Europe – They Name is Cowardice." Die Welt. March 31, 2005.

De Borchgrave, Arnaud. "2002: Yearend: Whither Radical Islam?" United Press International. December 8, 2002.

Deeb, Sarah El. "Groups Use Internet to Scare Iraqi Voters." The Associated Press. January 29, 2005.

Diehl, Jackson. "Chavez's Censorship: Where Disrespect Can Land You in Jail." The Washington Post. March 28, 2005.

Diehl, Jackson. "Democracy From the Inside Out." The Washington Post. March 14, 2005.

Eckert, Paul. "China's 'Nationalist Fire' Seen as a U.S. Worry. Reuters. April 14, 2005.

El-Magd, Nadia Abou. "Among Muslims and Arabs, Suspicion Meets America's Aid to Tsunami Victims." The Associated Press. January 5, 2005.

Evans, Dominic. "Saudi Says Web Campaign Wins Over Militant Backers." Reuters. February 6, 2005.

Evans, Dominic. "Saudi Says Web Campaign Wins Over Militant Backers." Reuters. February 6, 2005.

Fakhreddine, Jihad N. "Iraqis Broke Their Democratic Fast; Indigestion Follows." The Daily Star. February 5, 2005.

Faramarzi, Scheherezade. "Fundamentalist Islamic Leaders in Saudi Arabia are Telling . . ." The The Associated Press. January 1, 2005.

Friedman, Thomas L. "A Day to Remember." The New York Times. February 3, 2005.

Friedman, Thomas L. "A Political Arabesque." The New York Times. December 19, 2004.

Friedman, Thomas L. "Arabs Lift Their Voices." The New York Times. April 7, 2005.

Friedman, Thomas L. "Brave, Young and Muslim." The New York Times. March 3, 2005.

Friedman, Thomas L. "New Signs on the Arab Street." The New York Times. March 13, 2005.

Friedman, Thomas L. "The Other Intelligence Failure." The New York Times. October 10, 2004.

Georgy, Michael. "Iraq Wages Propaganda War With TV Interrogations." Reuters. February 21, 2005.

Ghosh, Nirmal. "Thai South Hit By First Case of Car Bombing." Straits Times International. February 19, 2005.

Goodenough, Patrick. "No Comment From Bin Laden on Tsunami Distaster." CNS News. January 26, 2005.

Gossett, Sherrie. "Islam in America: part 1 WND Goes Inside 'Mainstream' Muslim Conference." WorldNet Daily. January 3, 2004.

Gossett, Sherrie. "WND Goes Inside 'Mainstream' Muslim Conference." WorldNetDaily. January 3, 2004.

Hamzawy, Amr. "The Real 'Arab Street'." The Washington Post. February 6, 2005.

Harris, Edward. "Indonesia Muslims Warn Against Evangelism." The Associated Press. January 14, 2005.

Hauser, Christine. "Iraqis Turn Tables on Insurgents With Confession Videos." The New York Times News Service. February 9, 2005.
Hoagland, Jim. "From Terrorism to Tolerance." The Washington Post. October 6, 2004. A27.

Hong, Carolyn. "Muslim Group Calls For Religious Law Review: Sisters in Islam Pushing for Suspension of Islamic Laws Treating 'Sins' as a Crime." STI. February 4, 2005.

Ibrahim, Youssef M. "'Kifaya' is the Bud of a New Movement on Arab Streets." Gulf News Daily & Al Itihad Daily. March 8, 2005.

Ibrahim, Youssef M. "Apathy and Opposition Parties do no Good to Arab Nations." Gulf News Daily. January 18, 2005.

Ibrahim, Youssef M. "New Kind of Awe in Mideast." USA Today. February 1, 2005.

Jaffe, Greg & Cloud, Davis S. "Pentagon's New War Planning to Stress Postconflict Stability." The Wall Street Journal. October 25, 2004. A2.

Jewell, Mark. MIT Designs Laptop for the World's Poor." The Associated Press. April 5, 2005.

Kaplan, David E. "Hearts, Minds, Dollars." U.S. News.com. April 16, 2005.

Kaplan, Robert D. "Non-Stop Turbulence." The Wall Street Journal. March 14, 2005. A16.

Kelley, Jack. "Terror Groups Hide Behind Web Encryption." USA Today. February 5, 2001.

Kahn, Joseph. "China Pushing and Scripting Anti-Japanese Protects." The New York Times. April 15, 2005.

Krane, Jim. "On Terrorist Use of the Web, and Counters." The Associated Press. February 3, 2005

Kristof, Nicholas D. "Martyrs, Virgins and Grapes." The New York Times. August 4, 2004.

Kurtz, Howard. "Osama Who? When No News is 'Bad News'." The Washington Post. January 24, 2005.

Lasker, John. "U.S. Military's Elite Hacker Crew." Wired.com. April 18, 2005.

Linzer, Dafna. "Nuclear Capabilities May Elude Terrorists, Experts Say." The Washington Post. December 28, 2004.

Lobe,Jim. "Pentagon Uncovers Propaganda Failures." Asia Times. December 1, 2004.

Lovell, Jeremy. "Amnesty: Iraqi Women No Better Off Post-Saddam." Reuters. February 21, 2005.

Low, Eugene. "Anti-US Sentiment in Indonesia Improving Survey Finds Tsunami Aid Efforts Bring Stunning Turnaround in War Against Terror." Straits Times International. March 7, 2005.

MacFarquhar, Neil. "Anti-Western and Extremist Views Pervade Saudi Schools." The New York Times. October 19, 2001.

Mann, William C. "U.S.-Owned TV Station Cancels Syria Series." The Associated Press. April 21, 2005.

Majid, Sa'ad Abdul & Delwani, Tareq. "Iraqis Abroad Show Scant Interest in Elections." IslamOnline. Amman, Jordan. January 25, 2005.

Margasak, Larry. "Bin Laden, Al-Zarqawi Benefit in Alliance." The Associated Press. December 28, 2004.

McCarthy, Rory. "Babylon Wrecked by War." The Guardian. January 15, 2005.

McDonald, Joe. "China rejects Demand for Apology." The Associated Press. April 17, 2005.

Meixler, Louis. "Turkish Best-Seller Describes War Against America, Exposing Turkish Fears of Eroding Relationship." The Associated Press. February 28, 2005.

Min, Neo Hui. "Muslim Schools Urged to Widen Curriculum." Straits Times International. January 19, 2005.

Mintz, John. "Bioterror War Game Shows Lack of Readiness." The Washington Post. January 14, 2005.

Moore, Charles. "It is the Muslims Who Have the Most to Fear From Islamists." London Daily Telegraph. December 18, 2004.
Morgan, David. "Al-Hurra Coming to Europe Soon." Reuters. Washington, D.C. February 27, 2005.

Murphy, Brian. "Islamic Group Offers Aid, Courts Support." Seattle Post- Intelligencer. January 18, 2005.

Myers, Lisa & the NBC Investigative Unit. "FBI Monitors Islamic Group for Terror Ties: Secret Memo Suggests U.S. Group Could Recruit Terrorists." MSNBC News. January 18, 2005.

Nakhoul, Samia. "Sunni Neighbors Dread Spectre of Shi'ite Iraq." Reuters. January 19, 2005.

Nasrawi, Salah of the The Associated Press. "Syria Insists on Lebanon Troops Presence." London, England. The Guardian. March 3, 2005

Ottaway, David B. "Islamic Group Banned by Many is not on U.S. Terrorist List." The Washington Post. December 27, 2005.

Ottaway, Marina. "Listen to Arab Voices." The Washington Post. April 5, 2005. A23.

Ottaway, Marina. "Tyranny's Full Tank." The New York Times. March 31, 2005.
Rohde, David. "A World of Ways to Say 'Islamic Law'." The New York Times. March 13, 2005.

Oweis, Khaled Yacoub. "Iraq Cleric Inspires Arab Democrats From His Grave." Reuters. December 7, 2004.

Ricks, Thomas E. "Army Contests Rumsfeld Bid on Occupation." The Washington Post. January 16, 2005.

Ricks, Thomas E. "Images of Fighting in Fallujah Compel at Different Levels." The Washington Post. December 5, 2004.

Roy, Olivier. "Al-Qaida Brand Name Ready for Franchise." Le Monde Diplomatique. September 1, 2004.

Sands, Chris. "Media Must Not Succumb to Pressure." Gulf News. January 10, 2005.

Schuster, Henry. "Studios of Terror: Al Qaeda's Media Strategy." CNN. February 15, 2005.
Schuster, Henry. "Experts: Tsunami Disaster Might Ease Terrorism." CNN. January 5, 2005.

Sedarat, Firouz. "Al Qaeda Uses Internet to Defy Saudi Manhunt." Reuters. November 16, 2004.

Sennott, Charles M. "Saudi Schools Fuel Anti-U.S. Anger." The Boston Globe. March 4, 2002.

Shuster, David. "Conflict Within the Pentagon: Disagreements About War Planning Then and Now." MSNBC News. January 12, 2005.

Smeltz, Dina & Wallach, Michael. Office of Research, Opinion Analysis, U.S. Department of State. "Independent Survey of Arab Publics Shows Bad U.S. Image Based Primarily on U.S. Regional Policy." March 23, 2005.

The Associated Press. "Terrorists 'Recalibrating,' Rumsfeld Says." MSNBC News. Washington, D.C. February 16, 2005.

Van Natta, Jr., Don and Bergman, Lowell. "Militant Imams Under Scrutiny Across Europe." New York Times. January 25, 2005.

Weisman, Steven R. "Under Pressure, Qatar May Sell Jazeera Station." January 30, 2005.

Whitaker, Brian. "Saudi Textbooks 'Demonize West'." *The Guardian.* July 14, 2004.

Williams, Daniel. "Egyptian Diplomat Rebuts Bush's Views on Mideast." Washington Post Foreign Service. March 10, 2005. A12.

Williams, Daniel & Cooperman, Alan. Vatican is Rethinking Relations With islam." The Washington Post. April 15, 2005.

Wilson, Scott. "For Arab Writers, New Lines in the Sand." The Washington Post. March 16, 2005.

Windrem, Robert. "CIA is Looking for a Few Good Doctors." NBC News. December 29, 2004.

Wright, Robin & Kamen Al. "U.S. Outreach to Islamic World gets Slow Start, Minus leaders." The Washington Post. April 18, 2005.

Youssef, Maamoun. "Egypt's Mubarak Orders Election Amendment." The Associated Press. February 26, 2005.

PERSON/EXPERT INTERVIEW

Connable, Major Ben, USMC. "Marines are From Mars, Iraqis are From Venus." Expert Opinion. 2004.

Krohn, Charles A. on Psychological Operations and Public Affairs. Expert Opinion. April 2005.

McRoy, Anthony. "There Can Be No End to Jihad." Personal Interview With Sheikh Omar Bakri Muhammad. February 1, 2005.

Muhammad, Sheikh Omar Bakri. Islamic Leader in the United Kingdom, Christianity Today Personal Interview. February 1, 2005.

Rubin, Barry. "Counsel From a Terrorist." Expert Opinion. November 2, 2004.

Ryan, Don. Air Intelligence Agency, US Air Force. "Historical Perspective on Geneva Conventions." Expert Opinion. January 6, 2005.

Stalinsky, Steven. "Preliminary Overview – Saudi Arabia's Education System: Curriculum, Spreading Saudi Education to the World and the Official Saudi Position on Education Policy." Expert Opinion. 2003.

Tang, Yong. "I Don't Think U.S. Should be the Leader of the World." Personal Interview with Washington Post Managing Editor Philip Bennett. 2005.

Thompson, Loren B. "Remarks to the SAIC Leadership Council." Expert Opinion. November 11, 2004.

Turecek, Diana. Analyst with CIA's Global Information and Influence Team. Expert Opinion. March 31, 2005.

Weymouth, Lally. "Changes in the Kingdom – on 'Our Timetable'." Personal Interview with Prince Saud Faisal, Saudi Arabia's Foreign Minister. The Washington Post. London, England. February 27, 2005.

MAGAZINE ARTICLES

"Advisory group rates pentagon 'poor' in Open Source Intelligence." Geostrategy-Direct. April 26, 2005.

Brooks, David. "Kicking the Secularist Habit." The Atlantic Monthly. March 2003.

Brownfield, A. "The Future of the War on Terrorism." Jane's Terrorism & Security Monitor. November 1, 2004.

Cook, Steven A. "The Right Way to Promote Arab Reform." Foreign Affairs. March/April 2005.

Dowd-Gailey, Jonathan. "Islamism's Campus Club: The Muslim Students' Association." The Middle East Quarterly. Spring 2004.

Dreher, Rod. "Trouble in My 'Hood: The Muslim Question in Brooklyn." National Review. April 7, 2003.

Fakhreddine, Jihad N. "Mirror on the Wall: Who is the best Communicator of Them all – Al Jazeera or Al Hurra?" Global Media Journal. Volume 4, Issue 6, Spring 2005.

Fallows, James. "Success Without Victory." The Atlantic Monthly. January/February 2005.

Hersh, Seymour M. "The Coming Wars." The New Yorker. Issue of 2005-01-24 and 31.

Hirsh, Michael & Barry, John. "'The Salvador Option:' The Pentagon May Put Special Forces-Led Assassination or Kidnapping Teams in Iraq." Newsweek. January 8, 2005.

Isikoff, Michael & Hosenball, Mark. "Virtual Jihad." Newsweek. February 9, 2005.

Murdock, Deroy. "Terror and the English Language: Making Use of a Chief Weapon." National Review. March 2, 2005.

Pipes, Daniel. "The Islamic States of America?" FrontPageMagazine.com. September 23, 2004.

Rauch, Jonathan. "Cheer Up, Karen Hughes. Your Job is Not Quite Impossible." Jewish World Review. March 29, 2005.

Seib, Philip. "The News Media and the 'Clash of Civilizations'." Parameters. Winter 2004-05. 71-85.

WORLD WIDE WEB

44% of Americnas Back Limits on Muslim Rights." (Online) Available: http://www.islamonline.net/English/News/2004-12/18/article03.shtml. December 18, 2004.

"Bush: 'Historic Day' for Palestinians." (Online) Available: http://www.cnn.com/2005/WORLD/meast/01/09/bush.palestinians.reut/index.html

"China Filters Strong, Subtle." (Online) Available: http://www.wired.com/news/privacy/0,1848,67221,00.html April 14, 2005.

"Current Entities." (Online) Available: http://www.trackingthethreat.com. February 22, 2005.

"France Backs China Anti-Secession Law, Vows to Push for End to Arms Embargo." (Online) Available: http://www.channelnewsasia.com/stories/afp_asiapacific/view/143762/1/.html. April 21, 2005.

"Iraq Occupation Watch: Continuing Crisis." (Online) Available: http://www.occupationwatch.org/index.php. Undated.

"Mahathir Rebuked for Thai Comments." (Online) Available: http://straitstimes.asia1.com.sg/sub/storyprintfriendly/0,5578,282470,00.html? November 1, 2004.

"New Islamist Radical Web Sites." (Online) Available: http://www.e-prism.org/pages/1/index.htm. Undated.

"Palestinian Moderate Abbas Claims Victory." (Online) Available: http://www.cnn.com/2005/WORLD/meast/01/09/palestinian.elections/index.html. January 9, 2005.

"Report: More Gay Linguists Discharged Than First Thought." The Associated Press. (Online) Available: http://www.msnbc.msn.com/id/6824206. January 13, 2005.

"Saudi Government Daily Accuses U.S. Army of Harvesting Organs of Iraqis." MEMRI. (Online) Available: http://memri.org/bin/opener_latest.cgi?ID=SD83404. December 24, 2004.

"Terror Attacks on Americans, 1979-1988." (Online) Available: http://www.pbs.org/wgbh/pages/frontline/shows/target/etc/cron.html. Undated.

"Terrorism on the Web: Militants Play Cat and Mouse to Post Killings on the Web." (Online) Available: http://www.cnn.com/2005/TECH/internet/03/30/al.qaeda.sites.reut/index.html?section=cnn_latest. March 30, 2005.

"The Evolution of Islamic Terrorism: An Overview." (Online) Available: http://www.pbs.org/wgbh/pages/frontline/shows/target/etc/modern.html. Undated.

"The Evolution of Terrorism." (Online) Available: http://www.pbs.org/wgbh/pages/frontline/shows/target/etc/modern.html

"The Growth of Radical Islam in Central Asia." (Online) Available: http://www.atimes.com/atimes/Central_Asia/FC31Ag02.html. January 30, 2005.

"Understanding Islam: Middle East/North African Report No 37." (Online) Available: http://www.crisisgroup.org/home/index.cfm?id=3301&l=1. March 2, 2005.

BBC News World Edition. "Middle East gets First Superheroes." (Online) Available: http://news.bbc.co.uk/2/hi/middle_east/43125447.stm. March 7, 2005.

Braude, Joseph. "On Message." (Online) Available: TNR Online. February 11, 2005.

Cole, Juan. "Bin Laden Votes in Iraq and Shoots Himself in the Foot." (Online) Available: http://www.juancole.com. December 28, 2004.

Deeb, Sarah. "Groups Use Internet to Scare Iraqi Voters." (Online) Available: http://www.guardian.co.uk/worldlatest/story/0,1280,-4764205,00.html. January 29, 2005.

Haeri Safa. "Iran Confirms Building Secret Nuclear Tunnels." (Online) Available: http://www.iran-press-service.com/ips/articles-2005/frbuary/iran_nuke_25205.shtml. February 25, 2005.

Isikoff, Michael and Hosenball, Mark. "Virtual Jihad." (Online) Available: http://www.msnbc.msn.com/id/6940849/site/newsweek. February 9, 2005.

Loconte, Joseph. "CS Lewis on Osama bin Laden." (Online) Available: http://www.heritage.org. April 1, 2005.

Lovell, Jeremy. "Amnesty: Iraqi Women No better Off Post-Saddam." (Online) Available: http://www.washingtonpost.com. February 21, 2005

LTC Ryan, Tim. "Aiding and Abetting the Enemy: the Media in Iraq." (Online) Available: http://www.blackfive.net/main/2005/01/aiding_and_abbe.html. January 17, 2005.

Moore, John. "The Evolution of Islamic Terrorism: An Overview." (Online) Available: http://www.pbs.org/wgbh/pages/frontlione/shows/target/etc/modern.html. Undated.

Raman, B. "South Asia: Spies, Terrorists, and Pakistan." (Online) Available: http://atimes.com/atimes/Souht_Asia/FL10Df05.html. Undated.

Report of the National Intelligence Council's 2020 Project. "Mapping the Global Future." (Online) Available: http://www.globalsecurity.orgt/intell/library/reports/2005/nic_globaltrends2020_es.htm

Romano, Carlin. What Islam Says of Democracy: Scholar Shows Terrorists' Perversion." (Online) Available: http://www.bostonreview.net/BR28.2/abou.html. March 7, 2005.

Rubin, Barry. "After Hariri." (Online) Available: http://gloria.idc.ac.il/columes/2005/02_22.html. February 22, 2005.

Rubin, Barry. "Free for All, for Now." (Online) Available: http://gloria.idc.ac.il/columns/2005/02_01.html. February 12005.

Rubin, Barry. "Reform of the Arab World: The Last Great Battle?")Online) Available: http://gloria.idc.ac.il/columns/2004/12_28.html. December 28, 2004.

Schuster, Henry. "Studios of Terror." (Online) Available: http://www.cnn.com. February 15, 2005.

Shapiro, Samantha M. "The War Inside the Arab News Room." (Online) Available: http://www.nytimes.com/2005/01/02/magazine/02ARAB.html?pagewanted=print &position. January 2, 2005.

The Project for Research of Islamist Movements (PRISM). "New Islamist Radical Web Sites." (Online) Available: http://www.e-prism.org/pages/1/index.htm. Undated. The The Associated Press. "Rice Talks Tough on Iranian Nukes." (Online) Available: http://www.msnbc.msn.com/id/6911810. February 9, 2005.

The The Associated Press. "U.S. Charges 18 After Smuggling Sting." (Online) Available: http://www.msnbc.msn.com/id/7188615. March 15, 2005.

Toameh, Khaled Abu. "Koran Scholar: U.S. Will Cease to Exist in 2007." (Online) Available: http://www.jpost.com/servlet/Satellite?pagename=Jpost/JPArticle/Printer &cid=1111980180248&p=1101615860782. April 1, 2005.

Yong Tang. "I Don't think the U.S. Should be the leader of the World." (Online) Available: http://english.people.com.cn. March, 2005.

E-MAILs

Leventhal, Todd. "State Launches a Web Collection on identifying Misinformation." (Online) Available email: leventhalta@state.gov. Washington, D.C. March 9, 2005.

Leventhal, Todd. "Disinformation Alert: U.S. Forces Did Not Use Mustard Gas in Fallujah." (Online) Available email: leventhalta@state.gov. Washington, D.C. March 9, 2005.

Guirard, Jim. "War of Words Advisory to DoD from TrueSpeak Institute." (Online) Available email: justcauses@aol.com. Alexandria, Virginia. February 9, 2005.

Greg D. Rowe. "Iraqis Turn Tables on Insurgents with Confessions Videos." (Online) Available email: rowe@icpp.info. Washington, D.C. February 9, 2005.

"Association of Former Intelligence Officers (AFIO) Weekly Notes for 11 April 2005."

Greg D. Rowe. "Public Diplomacy Council Calls for Transformation." (Online) Available email: rowe@icpp.info. Washington, D.C. January 24, 2005.

Guirard, Jim. "Muslim Clerics' Fatwa Condeming Bin Laden as Apostate and Infidel." Available email: Justcauses@aol.com. Washington, D.C. March 14, 2005.

Greg D. Rowe. "Election Day Update 2." Available email: rowe@icpp.info, Washington, D.C. January 31, 2005.

Guirard, Jim. "War of Words Advisory to DoD From TrueSpeak." Available email: Justcauses@aol.com. Washington, D.C. February 9, 2005.

Leventhal, Todd. "Disinformation Alert: U.S. Forces Did Not Use Mustard Gas in Fallujah." Available email: leventhalta@state.gov. March 7, 2005.

McCallister, William. "Mess Tent Attacks: What is the Best Response?" Available email: William.mccakkister@us.army.mil. January 4, 2005.

TELEVISION SHOWs

"A Terror Breeding Ground?" 60 Minutes. CBS Television. February 27, 2005.

ABOUT THE AUTHOR

Joe Ruffini was born in Washington, D.C. He attended the University of Virginia on an Army ROTC scholarship and was commissioned upon graduation in 1974. His diverse military experience includes command of armor and armored cavalry units in both the U.S. and British Armies and anti-terror operations in Germany and Cyprus.

Throughout his career Joe' wide experience falls across the full spectrum of security disciplines, from operations and communications security, to computer, information, and physical security. One of the first Information Warfare and Information Operations Officers in DOD, Joe studied world threats to the United States Government and private enterprises on a wide scale – from the overseas theft of American intellectual property to the impending 9/11-type terrorist attacks, which he predicted as early as 1993.

Since retiring from the U.S. Army, Joe has pursued a diverse range of commercial initiatives, from entrepreneurial training projects in the Middle East to enterprise security consulting for Fortune 1000 companies. Joe is President and Founder of JPR & Associates, LLC, based in Colorado Springs, Colorado (www.jpr-online.com).

A featured national presenter for numerous security societies and associations, Joe's no nonsense approach to personal, corporate, and national security educates and entertains audiences from coast to coast. Joe is represented by Keppler Speakers.

To enquire about speaking engagements for Joe Ruffini contact:

Keppler Speakers
4350 North Fairfax Drive, Arlington, Virginia 22203
www.kepplerspeakers.com
703.516.4000

Or via: JPR & Associates, LLC
jprallc@jpr-online.com 719.930.4776